Gendered Risks

The shift toward 'government by risk' and the fore-fronting of 'risk consciousness' has not had the same impact on men and women alike. Complex and multiple understandings of femininity and masculinity inform risk thinking, as well as institutional and individual responses to various risks. This unique collection of international and interdisciplinary papers analyses what we currently know about gendered risks. It also identifies some of the new directions and challenges for research and theory that emerge out of thinking risk as a governmental technique, as a form of consciousness and action, and as a political issue, that shapes, and is shaped by, gender in contemporary society.

Kelly Hannah-Moffat is Associate Professor in the Department of Sociology at the University of Toronto.

Pat O'Malley is a Professor at Sydney Law School.

Gendered Risks

Edited by Kelly Hannah-Moffat
and Pat O'Malley

Routledge·Cavendish
Taylor & Francis Group

a GlassHouse book

First published 2007
by Routledge-Cavendish
2 Park Square, Milton Park, Abingdon, Oxon, OX14 4RN

Simultaneously published in the USA and Canada
by Routledge-Cavendish
270 Madison Ave, New York NY 10016

*Routledge-Cavendish is an imprint of the Taylor & Francis Group, an
informa business*

Transferred to Digital Printing 2009

© 2007 Kelly Hannah-Moffat and Pat O'Malley

Typeset in Times by
RefineCatch Limited, Bungay, Suffolk

British Library Cataloguing in Publication Data
A catalogue record for this book is available from the British Library

Library of Congress Cataloging-in-Publication Data
Gendered risks / edited by Kelly Hannah-Moffat and Pat O'Malley.
  p. cm.
  ISBN 978-1-904385-78-3 (hardback : alk. paper)
1. Risk management. 2. Sex discrimination against women.
1. Hannah-Moffat, Kelly, 1967– II. O'Malley, Pat.
  HD61.G46 2007
  305.42–dc22
                                                    2007003792

ISBN10: 1-904385-78-8 (hbk)
ISBN10: 0-415-57444-7 (pbk)
ISBN10: 0-203-94055-5 (ebk)

ISBN13: 978-1-904385-78-3 (hbk)
ISBN13: 978-0-415-57444-0 (pbk)
ISBN13: 978-0-203-94055-6 (ebk)

Contents

Acknowledgements

In 2002, we began a series of conversations about the absence of gender in what was then an emerging area of risk scholarship. These discussions led to a small interdisciplinary workshop funded by the Centre of Criminology, University of Toronto on risk and gender. Many of the conference participants have contributed chapters to this book. We are grateful to all the participants at the conference for their lively and frank contributions. Special thanks are due to Mariana Valverde who encouraged us to pursue this project and provided comments.

We would like to offer thanks to those who read and commented on various drafts of the manuscript, in particular Linn Clark, Richard Ericson, Mike Graydon, Paula Maurutto, Sarah Turnbull and the gender reading group. We are especially grateful for the organizational skills of Ashley Butts, who assisted with the preparation of the manuscript for publication. Many thanks are also due to Colin Perrin for his support and for the production assistance of Madeleine Langford.

Lastly we would like to thank Margret Foddy, Paul Moffat, Alexandra Moffat and Samantha Moffat for their ongoing support and encouragement.

Chapter I

Gendered risks

An introduction

Kelly Hannah-Moffat* and Pat O'Malley†

INTRODUCTION

Risk saturates everyday life. Our diets are shaped by our own knowledge of the risks associated with certain food and drinks, and our consumption choices are made from those already vetted by prior scientific risk assessments. If our children misbehave at school, they may be subjected to tests in case their behaviour aligns with risk profiles for pre-delinquency, cognitive abnormality or worse. Corporations, governments and institutions cannot be without a risk management plan, a matter often required by law. The environment has become something that is both a source of risk and 'at risk' from the effects of population and industrial growth. In many ways we are intruded upon and disciplined by risk regimes meant to protect us from future harms, and if we fail to buy in, we must suffer the consequences. If, for example, we fail to take precautions against 'crime risks' we may be labelled victims of our own carelessness; if we smoke and develop lung cancer, blame is clear because the risks are known. We often participate willingly in these regimes of risk because they promise, and often deliver, greater safety and security. Yet we buy in at a cost: we allow much of our daily lives to be delimited by considerations of risk that take into account futures that are unlikely to happen to the average person. Still, this defensive and negative side is only one aspect of the development of risk. An array of 'positive' and 'productive' risks has been made salient and available. Pension plans may now be linked with share market portfolios so that we can select the 'level of risk' that suits us; gambling has become a 'leisure industry' valued for the employment it creates and the tax revenues it generates; and extreme sports are becoming a popularized form of recreation through which we can fulfil ourselves rather than merely demonstrate foolhardiness.

Perhaps what is new today is not simply the salience of risk, but also the

* Department of Sociology, University of Toronto Mississauga
† Sydney Law School, University of Sydney

sense that ordinary people should exhibit some level of responsibility for, and even expertise in managing, risk. It is assumed that the average person understands the basic idea of statistical probability and is able to apply such abstractions as templates to set against our own lives. Social theorists argue that our lives are now governed by the knowledge and techniques of risk. For example, there is considerable analysis of how neoliberal governments have sought to create 'responsibilized' subjects – subjects who are expected to take over personal responsibility for the government of many of life's familiar risks to health, employment, wealth and personal safety (e.g. O'Malley 1992; Garland 1996). Until now, most research and theory on risk has focused on the official creation of abstract universal and gender-neutral subjects such as 'members of health-risk categories' and 'potential crime victims' who must take preventative steps to protect themselves against disease and predation. Feminist scholars, however, have gone beyond such gender-neutral analyses to examine how risk policies and practices are gendered. Both Sandra Walklate (1997) and Elizabeth Stanko (1990; 1997), for example, have pointed to the ways in which women were made responsible for avoiding criminal victimization in gender specific ways, notably through instructions to organize their lifestyles in ways that avoid 'high risk situations'. In this sense, risk techniques envisaged the production of a certain kind of woman whose life was to be structured by risk in ways that differed significantly from those said to affect men.[1]

Related to this, Kelly Hannah-Moffat's (2004a; 2004b) work illustrates how particular gendered understandings of risk produce new responsibilities and patterns of action, as well as new strategies for the definition, control and neutralization of risk. She argues that although female offenders have not traditionally been considered dangerous, increasingly within correctional practice their histories, needs and experiences (such as self-injury, victimization and mental health concerns) are being reframed as problematic through the imposition of new risk-based decision-making templates that evoke particular masculine normative standards, stereotyped constructions of femininity and offending (Hannah-Moffat 1999; 2004b). Of particular concern is how current penal understandings of risk are linked to a narrow understanding of women's 'needs' – for risk needs are only those that reduce crime risks. Linked to this, welfarist concerns about women's needs, such as those associated with poverty and children's welfare, have shifted and merged with a concern about risk[2] (Parton 1996; Kemshall 2003; Maurutto and

---

1 As Stanko (1997) stressed, of course, much such instruction was not only politically objectionable, but also superfluous as precaution was 'normal' for women confronting gendered risks that mold their public lives from infancy (see also Walklate 2002).

2 Within risk-based penality, 'needs' are narrowly defined as either criminogenic or not; they are conceived of in terms of risk reduction. Criminogenic needs are dynamic attributes of an offender that, when changed, are associated with shifts in the probability of recidivism (risk of

Hannah-Moffat 2005). Hannah-Moffat (2004a; 2004b) argues that this new configuration of need/risk results in broader gender-structured relations being either ignored or constructed as individual failures or inadequacies.[3]

In a different institutional context, Lealle Ruhl's (1999) work on pregnancy risks also highlights the contemporary process of risk-responsibilization and its attempt to form risk-conscious women. Where pregnancy once was treated as an illness or disability, with an emphasis on the care of the pregnant woman, risk techniques have played a key role in shifting attention to the foetus and to the responsibility of the mother in becoming knowledgeable and competent regarding risks to her baby. Diet, exercise, alcohol and caffeine consumption and smoking are all factors that have become cast as risks to the foetus, not so much to the woman. Additionally, the pregnant woman (especially if over 35 years) is expected to actively participate in gendered practices of risk detection and regulation, including scrutiny of family histories with respect to genetically related risk factors. In a sense, the subjectivity and the responsibilities of pregnant women are being reformulated by risk. As Rapp (1995: 180) has indicated, while previous generations of women might have been aware of some of these risks, it is only the present generation of 'statistically graded pregnant women' that has been given specific risk figures and thus been led to identify 'generic pregnancy anxieties with their particular characteristics and behaviours'. Many aspects of pregnancy, prenatal care and childbirth are defined and interpreted through risk (Weir 2006). Governed by risk, the pregnant woman re-emerges as a revised subject of gender: a 'risky subjectivity'.

Comparable concerns are identified in Dawn Moore and Tara Lyons' chapter on Ottawa's drug courts. This analysis reveals that within drug courts pregnancy, motherhood and involvement in the sex trade become gendered fields of risk management that differentially affect the legal regulation of drug addicts. For example, courts place considerable emphasis on women's relationships with their families. Frequently, their parental relations become a

---

continued offending). Non-criminogenic needs, though also dynamic and 'changeable', are not clearly associated with the probability of recidivism. Significant variables that are not related to recidivism, and yet require intervention, are deemed non-criminogenic (e.g., poverty, health) and considered a low priority in terms of intervention, except for 'humane' consideration.

3 Contrary to many feminist understandings of 'need', when needs are conflated with risk they are no longer an individual's self-perceived need, but rather a characteristic someone shares with a population that has been shown to be statistically correlated with recidivism. In this context, needs are defined not only through the availability of resources and structural arrangements that allow for intervention and possible amelioration, but also through statistical knowledge of need as a variable that is predictive of an undesirable and preventable outcome – in this case recidivism. Under such conditions some 'needs' become risks. This assemblage of risk and need is conceptually different from the framing of women's need in most feminist literatures.

resource for the courts' assessments of risk, and though men's continued and renewed contact with their children was often viewed as positive, women's was viewed both as placing the children 'at risk' and as jeopardizing their own treatment by having to divide attention between parenting and recovery. Moore and Lyons argue that women deploy their own forms of counter-risk management to assist them in navigating the criminal justice involvement.

Risk has become formative of gendered subjectivities, but this should by no means conflate gender with women. Linneman's (2000) work, which explores how diverse gay masculinities are formed in relation to risk, emphasizes some of the intricacies of risk and gender. Where the risk of exposure to HIV/AIDS appears as a threat to men who seek sex with men but do not identify as gay, risk avoidance becomes central to the formation and maintenance of their preferred masculinity (see also Humphreys 1970). For others, this same risk may appear as integral to an aggressively gay identity, and a certain persona forms around this. For still others, the riskiness of certain practices becomes valued in itself (Linneman 2000: 92–94). As Kane Race shows in this volume, 'serosorting' (selecting partners of the same HIV status) may appear as a risk-minimizing strategy and/or a way in which gay men may literally brand themselves – becoming a formative aspect of their gendered identity, and in significant ways setting themselves apart from other gay men. The risk of HIV/AIDS influences diverse cultural representations of heterosexual and gay masculinities and how individuals govern or even ignore this risk in their everyday lives. As indicated earlier, these practices are tied into recursive systems of meaning.

Catherine Waldby (1996) has examined the ways that sexualized identities interact with regulatory categorisations in this respect, so that self-identification becomes a critical component of official risk management with respect to HIV. If individuals 'serosort' as a matter of choice, this links with official discourses of testing for the presence of HIV that require them to 'know themselves as sexual identities and make themselves available for sexual identification' (Waldby 1996: 113). In turn, since risk hierarchies are variously gendered, sorting does not only occur within masculinities. By extension, it occurs in terms that associate heterosexuality as being 'at risk' or vulnerable and under threat, and conversely, male homosexuality appears as threatening or risk-creating. Thus 'risk rationalities' may be understood not only to 'responsibilise: or create self-regulating individuals in regard to health risks, but also to define and call into being so called "risky" or "high risk" groups, that is, a hierarchy of risk identities' (Adkins 2002: 34).

That this may occur in a far more formal and pervasive, but less visible, fashion is made clear by Jonathan Simon's (1988) pioneering research that drew attention to how insurance companies' actuarial calculation of women's lifespans led to women paying higher premiums than men. Insurance companies justified differentials in premiums on the 'actuarial' grounds that given their greater longevity, women would be beneficiaries for longer.

The US Supreme Courts' *Manhart* decision,[4] however, found there to be discrimination on the basis of gender. To the insurers, their practices merely reflected scientific reality, a neutral statistical correlation of fact, and thus their policy constituted 'fair discrimination'. Simon argues that in the process of 'fair discrimination' insurance 'makes' and 'unmakes' people. People are fragmented by insurance imagination into actuarial categories according to criteria and logics that do not correspond with those of everyday life and experience. Women, in this example, appear as a category united by a common risk factor. However, in terms of some other risk factors, the category of 'woman' is fragmented or obliterated. Thus, within the domain of risk, gender can be constituted, reconstituted or erased.

Taking this further, some theorists have argued that risk has shifted 'gender' as a category so that it has become defined in important ways by shared, gender-specific or gender-characteristic, risks (Beck 1992). This is partly because of the numerous ways that women have, differently than men, been affected by risk-based government. Women have had their material living conditions affected, their social duties and responsibilities restructured and expanded, and their image in popular culture reframed and re-moralized because of risk governance. The representation of pregnancy, noted above as a condition defined extensively by risks to the foetus, places new responsibilities on women and subjects them to new lines of evaluation. The changing organization of the market place has created a new domain of 'high risk' work into which women have disproportionately been channelled. At the same time (especially working-class) women are often acutely affected by the erosion of certain institutions, such as the patriarchal family and the welfare state, that have traditionally acted to manage risks (Beck and Beck-Gernsheim 2002). The same is true with respect to other gender subjectivities and categories. We have already noted how risks associated with HIV/AIDS, for example, have played a role in forming certain gay identities and have been issues around which political organization and social networks have formed to produce gay 'communities' (Slavin *et al* 1998).

Much of this discussion points to ways in which gender is being affected by risk. But the reverse is equally true – gender and risk are mutually constitutive. Gendered knowledges, norms and hierarchies are linked with understandings of what constitutes a risk; the tolerance level of risk; the extent to which risk consciousness will be accepted or denied in public discourse or self-image; and whether risks are to be avoided and feared, regarded as just one of the costs of a certain lifestyle, or even valued as an experience and valorised as an opportunity for displays of courage and strength. Women's fear of crime, for example, is often regarded as exaggerated; yet it is linked to routine experiences of sexual harassment and related 'quasi crimes' that

4 *City of Los Angeles Department of Power v Manhart* (435 US 702) [1978].

shape their interpretations of risky situations, though usually fall beneath the gaze of law (Holgate 1989; Campbell 2005). It is in this light that Elizabeth Stanko has remarked that 'risk is not about modernity and the ontological insecurity people experience; for women it is about misogyny and the continued perpetuation of women's oppression through fear of crime and blame for their situation' (1997: 492). Sandra Walklate (1997) similarly notes that though, statistically, young men have the highest risk of violent victimization, they are among the least likely to report fear of violence, while the reverse is true for elderly women. Rather than seeing this as 'irrational' on the part of both gender categories, she suggests that sociological analyses must explain how risks are experienced and interpreted in different and gendered ways. In fields such as workplace safety, recent evidence (Breslin *et al.* 2007) indicates that rates of complaints regarding injuries were influenced by gendered understandings of 'complaining'. The study showed that such understandings were associated with under-reporting, particularly by young men, and that young women felt that their complaints were discounted by management. As Breslin and colleagues (2007: 790) suggest, these patterns were linked, because 'young workers' depictions of complaining as a largely female preoccupation informed and reinforced the understanding that complaints made by women need not be taken seriously'.

Despite the apparent obviousness of risk/gender nexus, research on risk has often proceeded as if it can be understood without clear reference to gender. For example, Steven Lyng's (1990) early work on 'edgework' analysed risk taking as related to universal modern experiences of alienation. Yet as feminist criticisms immediately made clear (Miller 1991), and as Lyng explores further in this volume, such analysis could not be sustained without exploring the possibility that this is an archetypal male approach to risk. It is clear that there are gendered differences in preferences for risk taking and kinds of risk-taking activities as well as in exposure to risks of different kinds (whether chosen or not). Consequently, there are gendered variations in familiarity with the challenges posed by, and techniques to deal with, risks (Miller 1991; Lois 2005).

As this suggests, the risk/gender nexus is capable of considerable complexity and variability. However, as others have noted (Gustafson 1998), the majority of research relating risk to gender is concerned only with risk factors associated with a male-female binary, is most often simply statistical in nature and most frequently explores risk factors limited to health. Typical studies are medical and public health analyses of the relationships between gender-linked patterns and pathological conditions, such as risks associated with breast cancer, heart disease or mental illness. We are by no means suggesting that this work is unimportant. Rather, we contend that the possibilities for theory development and theoretically informed empirical studies of risk and gender are limited in such work. This work is, in fact, the subject matter of the kind of research and theory that are the focus of this book – both because of the assumptions that it often makes about gender, and because of its implications for shaping gendered identities and relations. For example, frequently, such research effectively reduces 'gay' or 'homosexual' to a synonym for anal sex, since that appears as the 'relevant' risk factor (Waldby 1996: 112–5). We agree that sexuality is linked closely with gender and that anal sex is linked to HIV transmission, but like most social theorists we argue that gender cannot be reduced either to biology or to sexual activity. Rather, gender is irreducibly social and resides in complex meanings, practices and relationships. From this point of view, as Kane Race points out in this volume, the 'objective' act of correlating 'anal sex', 'gay' and 'HIV/AIDS' is itself a gendered act with gendered implications. On the one hand, by reducing 'gay' to 'anal sex', violence is done to the complexity and variability of relationships (even just the sexual relationships) between gay men. On the other hand, this creates a set of gendered meanings and practices that impact on gay men and their relationships in varied and often reflexive fashion. Among other things, it may be associated with the now familiar idea that gay men engage in unprotected anal sex because the HIV risk is an added thrill (Ridge 2004, Slavin *et al* 1998). But that idea, gradually entering the realms of gendered stereotypes, has its own second order effects. Such assumptions become part of medical and public health knowledge and begin to inform subsequent policy calculations – even though as Race (in this volume) indicates, such 'risky' thrill-seeking motives are rare. It is precisely towards analysis of this kind of complex nexus between gender and risk that future research and theory needs to be oriented.

Given the importance of risk in everyday life and policy and its prominence in social theory and research, combined with the substantial body of research and theory on gender amassed over the last 30 years, we would expect the risk/gender nexus to have a high profile in social theory and research. Yet to the best of our knowledge this is the first edited collection that has taken this nexus as its sole focus. Gender studies – and especially feminist theory and research – tend to underestimate and underanalyse the implications of risk's contemporary centrality. Analogously, risk theory tends either to ignore gender or to deal with it in terms of highly abstract generalizations that have little foundation in empirical research.

The hallmark of the papers in this collection is that they are theoretically-guided examinations of how gender and risk are interlinked and often mutually constitutive. Each takes a specific issue or area of risk as its focus and analyses how risk bears on the formation, transformation or expression of gendered subjectivities and experiences. In this introduction we outline some of the main developments in risk theory and research and how they have – or have not – taken gender into account. We will also examine some of the contributions and shortcomings of existing attempts to bring risk and gender together. In so doing, rather than attempting to develop a new theorization of risk and gender, we hope to provide the groundwork from which more nuanced and mutually constitutive analyses of risk and gender can advance.

However, some caution is required in this exercise. Postmodern feminist critiques of the analytic category of 'woman' (and 'man') emphasize that these are fluid categories that are multiply organized across variable axes of difference. As Sandra Harding's (1991: 179) critique of universal categories aptly notes 'there are no gender relations per se, but only gender relations as constructed by and between classes, races and cultures'. The fractured nature of female and male subjectivity necessitates that we also consider the import-ance of other forms of inequality and their relationship to the risk/gender nexus. Feminist scholarship[5] has devoted considerable attention to under-standing the complexity and interconnectedness of race, gender and class. The breadth and nuances of this scholarship cannot be covered here; how-ever, we wish to reinforce a critical contribution of this work – that gender is integrally linked to race, class and other inequalities. Conceptually, the notion of simultaneous and interconnected inequalities is important to understand-ings of risk gender nexuses. Risk is shaped by, interacts with and (re)produces various configurations of inequality.

In this collection, the work of Gaynor Bramhall and Barbara Hudson on risk and Asian masculinities in the British criminal justice system, for example, shows how conceptualizations of male Asian-ness and dominant cultural views of family life influence the interpretation of risk. For white males, strong family ties are regarded as a risk-reducing factor, fostering possibilities for social reintegration and the reduction of recidivism. But for Asian males in the prison system, family ties shift from being a resource to being a risk factor. Risk profiles become a site in which stereotypes associated with the 'otherness' of being Asian are translated into a new objective reality: for these men's risk profiles, tightly knit families come to be associated with deviousness, misguided loyalties and secrecy. The interconnected nature of inequalities, gender and risk are also illustrated in Kelly Hannah-Moffat's chapter, which demonstrates how gendered as well as heteronormative, white, middle-class understandings of parenting are used to define women's marital and family relationships as risky and thus legitimate targets of correctional programming. She shows how aboriginal understandings of family and community necessitate different but equally problematic characterizations of motherhood and forms of intervention.

Clearly, the gender/risk nexus is multifaceted and in need of greater theor-etical and empirical analysis. The following sections provide a broader theoretical context for the subsequent chapters. We will show how dominant theories of risk have grappled with gender and inequality more broadly, and

---

5 Multiracial, queer theory and poststructural theorizations of difference locate gender within a broader matrix of inequality.

we demonstrate how gender and feminist scholars have worked to advance the theorization of gender and to empirically document various dimensions of the risk/gender nexus.

GENDERING THEORIES OF RISK

Risk is understood in the various social science literatures in the following ways: as a real characteristic of events; as a category of experience; and/or as a technique for thinking about and managing problems. Though it is not the case that these three approaches to risk are mutually exclusive, each way of thinking about risk has its own set of implications for the nexus between risk and gender, and each is associated with specific ways of theorizing risk. For 'governmentality' analyses – while not denying that risk is experienced, or that events do inflict harms and injuries – the focus is neither on the reality of risks, nor on how they are experienced. Instead, the focus is on the ways that such events are considered to be risks rather than some other kind of phenomenon. Cultural and feminist theorizing of risk focuses more on the experience of risks and their impact on everyday life. In the 'risk society' approach, all three meanings of risk are valorized although, arguably, much greater stress is placed on the reality of risks as an emerging feature of 'reflexive modernity'. Any understanding of the risk/gender nexus must therefore pay attention to the differences among these principle sociological approaches.

Gender and the risk society thesis

For Ulrich Beck (1992; 1994), major changes in gender politics and con-sciousness can be traced to changes in the structure of risks in contemporary society. His primary concerns are with the 'modernization risks' created by the runaway expansion of science and technology, especially as driven by the demands of capitalism. Exemplified by global warming, nuclear contamin-ation and the globalization of the economy, modernization risks are central to understanding the emergence of the 'risk society' or 'reflexive modernity'. In this new context, traditional modernist ideas of progress have been chal-lenged by the emergence of risks that threaten life itself. Such risks have a double status: as real threats (global warming is not dependent on our social apprehension of it); and as constructs through which they are to be governed (these threats may appear as statistical risks because experts constitute them that way). In the world of modernization risks, Beck argues, traditional forms of expertise begin to break down because statistical prediction cannot work with events that have never occurred before or whose existence is unknown until they are no longer just probabilities. Rather than being governed by risk-based techniques, these modernization risks must be governed by tech-niques of 'uncertainty' – speculative estimations that can locate only future possibilities rather than probabilities.[6] A key result is that experts often fundamentally disagree and their predictions often prove wrong – hence expertise itself is opened up to challenge.

As many have pointed out (e.g. Wynne 1996), Beck unintentionally privileges expertise by suggesting that it is only when modernization risks defeat experts' predictive capacities that the hegemony of risk and science is questioned. However, as Deborah Lupton (1999a: 76) has urged, women have long drawn on many other sources of knowledge about risks, such as experiences and feelings of health and well-being, and do not solely rely on expertise. In their contribution to this volume, Jessica Polzer and Ann Robertson argue at length that 'the *production of knowledge* about genetic risk for breast cancer is a gendered activity which necessarily requires and harnesses the energies of women who, through their will to know the truth of their susceptibility to breast cancer, labour to gather information about disease in their families'. Such knowledge is vital to the governance of breast cancer but is not in any sense 'expert' knowledge – or more precisely it is knowledge that calls into question the privileging of that knowledge described as 'expert'. Likewise, with respect to the governance of risks associated with 'midlife', Eileen Green and her co-researchers (2002) have found that expert advice is rarely the sole determinant of health decisions and practices. For both 'lay' women *and* health professionals, this advice reflects a complex mixture of expert knowledge and advice and embodied cultural experience. And as Lorna Weir (1996: 385–6) has indicated, current concerns to govern the pregnant woman through her participation and enlistment in risk-based regimes 'has as its dialogic partner, feminism'. That is, the responsibilization of the pregnant woman does not merely reflect an autonomous change in medical thought and practice, nor can it be regarded simply as an effect of neoliberal ideas about active citizenship – although both of these play a part (Ruhle 1999). Rather, feminist resistance to such subordination, especially in the form of demands that women be extensively consulted and participate actively in the governance of their own pregnancies, has played a major role in this shift. Risk regimes may thus be multi-vocal rather than simply an expression of expertise.

Given that the reach of modernization risks is global, and their development escapes detection until their effects are registered in catastrophic ways, Beck contends that contemporary society is pathologically insecure. The discovery of, and intervention against, risks leads to the search for more risks, but each new discovery only makes clearer that our security was illusory: life

---

6 Beck is a little unclear on this. While he stresses statistical versus non-statistical prediction, it is also clear throughout his text that he is critiquing scientific prediction more generally. This is not surprising since the key issue for him is predictability and the limits of scientific knowledge, not statistics per se.

is endless risk. Awareness of risks and thinking in terms of risks ('risk consciousnesses') increasingly permeates contemporary life, and it is argued that this is registered in many ways in gender relations. In the class society said to be in place until about the 1970s, *need* was the organizing principal, and equality of opportunity was the normative project of progressive politics. However, in reflexive modernity since then, *anxiety and insecurity* become the central principles and safety becomes the normative project of progressives (Beck 1992: 49). In this view, solidarity arising out of anxiety becomes the central theme of politics, and the principal solidarities – including gender – become communities of anxiety. Thus, while gender relations do not disappear, nor become less important, they are focused more on inequalities of safety than inequalities of need (Beck 1992: 49–84). This effect is heightened by the process of individualization. Individualization refers to the increased responsibility of individuals for managing the risks that once were covered by the institutions of class society – the patriarchal family, welfare states, trade unions and so on – as such institutions become unable to deal with the risks of safety rather than need. Such changes in risk's governance are held especially to have affected women, who escape the patriarchal family only to be exposed to increased insecurities, for example, on the margins of the workforce (Beck and Beck-Gernsheim 2002: 55–100). Thus, Beck (1992: 98–100) considers that individualization does not actually remove inequality of gender, class or race – a common misinterpretation of his position. Rather, he stresses that such inequalities

> become redefined in terms of an *individualization of social risks*. The result is that social problems are increasingly perceived in terms of psychological dispositions: as personal inadequacies, guilt feelings, anxieties, conflicts and neuroses. There emerges, paradoxically, *a new immediacy of individual and society, a direct relation between crises and sickness.* Social crises appear as individual crises which are no longer (or are only very indirectly) perceived in terms of their rootedness in the social realm.

Of course, many feminist scholars would dispute his idea that inequality of need is being displaced either in experience or as an organizing principle. They might also challenge the assertion that inequalities of safety and insecurity are novel issues for gendered solidarity. Certainly Beck produces little or no evidence that risk consciousness *is* now becoming the primary shaper of gender relations: he tends to assume that consciousness simply reflects changes in the world order as he depicts them. More than this, as others have noted (Tulloch and Lupton 2003), there is no sense in such work that the subjects themselves respond to the new risk environment in gendered ways. There is no consideration, for example, that men and women perceive environmental or technological risks differently. Yet as Cutter *et al*

(1992) found in relation to the kinds of technological risks with which Beck is concerned, while men *do* tend to be less concerned about risks than women, the conclusion drawn by psychological studies that women are more risk conscious and have lower thresholds of risk tolerance is misleading. Cutter's research, to the contrary, suggests that such studies consistently measure women's responses to risks that reflect primarily male experience and knowledge, and with respect to which women are less familiar and have less confidence in managing. This conforms to the findings of Schubert and her colleagues (Schubert *et al* 2000) that while all individuals are more comfortable with ambiguity and risk in familiar situations, this translates into specifically gendered patterns. In particular, women demonstrate much higher levels of risk aversion with respect to investment decisions in finance markets because the masculine nature of the domain means that women opt for risk avoidance since 'women themselves do not feel competent in investment decisions and therefore cannot take credit for winning but just take blame for losing' (2000: 6).

In short, the totalizing assumptions of risk society and risk consciousness conflict with analyses sympathetic to gendered diversity of interpretation and action. Perhaps such problems explain why comparatively few feminist writers, or scholars concerned with issues of gender more generally, have engaged with risk through this otherwise influential 'risk society' literature. There are exceptions within this literature, however, and studies do exist in which trouble has been taken to uncover what form risk-based experiences take, and the degree to which gender is a constitutive element in this process. But in our view these tell more of the limitations of Beck's approach rather than its strengths.

In a substantial empirical example of risk society research concerned with gender, Tulloch and Lupton's (2003) analysis is concerned with the experience of risk, and assumes in good measure that the salience of risk among their respondents is an effect of the rise of risk society. However, as they stress, their analysis indicates that interviewees' responses to risk were strongly shaped by such factors as gender, age, occupation, nationality and sexual identity (2003: 132). Rather than simply reading off universal risk-experience from this starting point, they highlight cultural facets influencing risk assessment and responses to it that concern non-work time and lifestyle issues. These, in turn, lead to the formation of identities that are multidimensional in thought and action, changing and adaptive, so that

> Beck's notion of risk in everyday life needs to be expanded to embrace all these shifting states and performativities . . . Identity is constantly built and re-built through social contact and the appropriation and consumption of cultural artifacts such as technology, the media, mass-produced commodities and expert knowledges.
>
> (Tulloch and Lupton 2003: 133)

In this respect, a difficulty with the risk society thesis is perhaps the obverse side of its strength. Pitched at a very high level of abstraction, it may encompass and provide an account that can make sense of many changes associated with risk in contemporary life. But as such it suffers because its remoteness from specific developments leaves much of the explanatory work – and most of the gendered understanding – to be done through other approaches altogether, as Tulloch and Lupton illustrate.

Perhaps another manifestation of this kind of problem is associated with two marked tendencies of the risk society thesis. First, 'gender' gets collapsed into 'women'. In defence of Beck, he does stress that the primary site of gendered changes related to risk society has been that of women – by implication suggesting that he is aware of other sites. It would not be difficult, for example, to read the impact of HIV/AIDS in terms of the risk society thesis, for its catastrophic status and spread can be linked to globalizing forces. Also, it could be argued that in such ways the rise of the risk society has fostered risk consciousness and thus the formation of gay identities, groupings and categories around risk consciousness. Again, however, any or all of these changes could be assigned to some other explanation – perhaps being gay *always was* a risk identity in a homophobic world, and HIV/AIDS has just provided another specific and more publicly visible focus for this.

The second problem parallels this, but concerns the collapsing of risk into a monolithic entity; for the risk society thesis, risk's diversity of forms is of no great importance, and not a salient subject of theorizing within the approach. Yet we have argued that this diversity appears critical to an understanding of risk and gender. We would not assume, for example, that the governance of gay men under risk-minimizing HIV/AIDS transmission programmes shares much of consequence in common with that of women subjected to risk-needs assessments in prisons, or with the discriminatory regulation of women under the guise of insurance actuarialism. The forms of risk are diverse, as is the nature of the respective implications for gender issues. This is particularly salient when considering the effects of risk on gender and vice-versa, the diversity and specificity of the ways in which risk is deployed is what really matters; yet the thesis of the risk society does not provide an account that allows this to be understood. Consideration of such issues is probably best carried out through governmental analysis – or 'governmentality' – to which we now turn.

Gender, governmentality and risk

Governmentality concerns itself with analysis of the ways that 'government' (i.e. not just state programmes but any systematic practice attempting to direct the conduct of others) envisions the world. This emphasis on the ways in which government 'imagines' the world should not be taken to imply that this refers merely to philosophical discourses. Unlike political philosophies, to paraphrase Marx, government's aim is to change the world. Therefore governmental visions are linked to techniques of action intended to effect remedies or improvements in any identified problem. Risk, in this approach, appears as a particular way of envisioning problems and forming the techniques of governance to deal with them. As we have seen, both Weir (1996) and Ruhl (1999) working with this approach suggest that the re-imagining of pregnancy in terms of risks subjects women to new regimes that interrogate their bodies and their backgrounds in new ways. Monica Greco (1993) has examined how neoliberalism has re-imagined psychosomatics in such a way that there has emerged a 'duty to be well' – something that applies to pregnancy as well as to other aspects of health. If illness can be predicted and forestalled by risk techniques, for example through knowledge of the nexus between smoking and lung cancer or between heart disease and obesity, then to fall prey to sickness is to be culpable. Without making any of Beck's assumptions about whether the world is becoming more risky, governmental analysis examines the ways government uses risk as a way of changing the world, and analyses what the implications of these changes might be. This 'irrealist' or agnostic position toward the reality of risks is easily misinterpreted, and the question of the reality of risks is sufficiently important to explore in the context of this approach.

As noted by Elizabeth Stanko (1990, 1997) with respect to government crime prevention research, official research assumed that 'objectively' it had unearthed sexed and gender-related risks, to which it tied policy advice concerning women avoiding certain public spaces, especially at night. This official risk calculation revealed a reality of gendered risk: women were at risk from male assault under certain conditions. Alternatively Stanko argues that there is another level of 'reality' that lurks below this apparent objectivity. She reveals that official calculations of gendered risk are themselves gendered – because they focus on risks to women in public places thus ignoring the (greater) risks of sexual violence to women in domestic settings. Although official statistical calculations of risk are thereby shown to be problematic, even a distortion, the critical approach adopted by Stanko challenges the primacy accorded to stranger-danger. The risk that appears in official discourse is shown to be itself a gendered construction that conceals another, and more salient, 'real' gendered risk to women.

This critical realist approach to risk is characteristic of a considerable body of other feminist research and theory. For example, Mary Condon in this volume and elsewhere (2001; 2002) has analysed the gendered impact of changes to Canadian pension policies under neoliberal government and the politics that have emerged around these. On the face of things, a key change was gender-neutral: a decentring of the Canada Pension Plan (CPP) in welfare policies. The CPP is a socialized contributory pension fund, but neoliberal governments planned for an increased role in welfare provision to be given to market-based retirement savings plans. Such a shift increased women's financial risks because previously the CPP had begun to take account of some of the financial disadvantages faced by women, such as their role in providing unpaid family support and their high rates of fractional employment. In the new arrangement, women's benefits would be tied to the ability to invest in a private pension plan out of their discretionary income, which would average less than that for men. In addition, women are less likely to be employed by large companies that offer pension plans as part of the employment package. An apparently gender-neutral shift in the provision of risk management thus worked at another level to place women at an increased level of real or material risk.[7] In such analyses, then, there is an assumption that risk is *both* an objective statistical construct deployed by government and a real, underlying and gendered risk. But, to return to Stanko's point that the risk of domestic violence is not simply experiential, it is also objectively demonstrable through statistical risk techniques. It is, politically speaking, only because of this fact that the experiential level could no longer be discredited as 'irrational'. In Stanko and Condon's approach, recognition of the reality of these underlying gendered risks is essential to certain feminist political struggles over the material condition of women.

Against this kind of realist analysis, the governmentality school regards risk as a particular way of comprehending problems and generating responses to them. This assumption is most clearly expressed by Ewald (1991: 199) who argues that 'nothing is a risk in itself; there is no risk in reality. But on the other hand anything *can* be a risk; it all depends on how one analyses the danger, considers the event . . . rather than with the notions of danger or peril, the notion of risk goes together with those of chance, hazard, probability, eventuality or randomness . . .'. Thus, while some critics of governmentality (e.g. Chan and Rigakos 2002) assume that the approach naively denies the 'ontologically real' underlying levels of risk, the point that governmentality makes is not that harms and threats don't exist or can be ignored, but that these events do not become *risks* until interpreted in a very specific way. In other words, governmentality is interested in how government *codes* these fears, threats, hazards and menaces as 'risks', with very specific governmental consequences. Ruhl and Weir's 1990s work on pregnancy, for example, uses governmentality to this end, indicating the gendered implications of the framework of risk and the use of risk technologies. In this specific light Lorna Weir deploys governmentality to refine feminist thought. After noting the tendency in feminist research on pregnancy to focus on specific technological developments such as sex selection and prenatal testing, she suggests that:

---

7 Echoing debates examined by Simon (1988) and discussed above, Condon points to subsequent neoliberal critiques of the CPP on the basis that 'under the CPP women who live longer collect more in total benefits but do not pay higher premiums. This is, simply put, inequitable . . . You're subsidizing the women's pensions with the contributions of men . . .' (quoted by Condon 2000:94).

From a feminist perspective, the keying of investigation to government rather than to technologies in the narrow sense moves the beginning point of inquiry away from critical and reactive commentaries on technical innovations to a very thick description of the administrative and discursive construction of pregnancy. The analysis of the production of the foetus in writing extends previous feminist work on the production of the foetus as a (site). Recent work in the governance literature . . . provides a resource for a close description and organizational analysis of population-based risk assessment and screening of pregnancy; it opens up for feminist theory the complexity and heterogeneity of risk as a category.

(1996: 389)

Weir thus uses governmentality's strength to good effect within an explicitly gendered theoretical project. Nevertheless, a tendency for governmentality to remain at the level of the 'blueprints' for governance may be the source of significant problems. Focusing on the 'ideal knowledges' (Miller and Rose 1990) of planners is a deliberate tactic that reflects intent to avoid the morass of sociological empiricism that rapidly emerges when we examine implementation. The aim of this analytical manoeuvre is to diagnose the implications of governmental programmes, such as the kinds of subjects they intend to make of their targets, rather than to explore the particular ways they are put into effect (Barry *et al* 1993). Governmentality, in this sense, diagnoses in terms of the reality imagined by the programme – the governmental programme's own vision of the problem.

While many gender scholars would have no problem with this as far as it goes, most would want to push the analysis forward to examine the effects of programmes in practice. This is precisely what has happened in many cases where governmentality is deployed for limited purposes only. Thus, for example, much of Kelly Hannah-Moffat's (1999; 2001) analyses of the 'feminisation' of the Canadian women's prison system focuses on the ways in which the translation of feminist-inspired programming produced a repressive penal regime. While a 'self change model' was introduced in order to give increased autonomy and self-direction for inmates, the result for the woman prisoner was not as might be imagined from reading the blueprints. Instead, the prisoner

is expected to constantly monitor herself and to control her own risk-generating behaviour. When she fails, more coercive disciplinary techniques of government are mobilized. For example, a positive urine test for drugs or visible signs of drug or alcohol use can lead to institutional charges, segregation, revocation of privileges . . . However, it is also evident that these new techniques do not so much replace traditional measures as embed them in a far more comprehensive web of monitoring and intervention . . . In some respects, models of self-help and responsibility ultimately re-legitimate the prison and the continued reliance on discipline.

(Hannah-Moffat 1999: 174)

In practice, recent work on governmentality (Rose *et al* 2006) regards it as one analytical tool among many that even fosters such articulation with research on the implementation for government programmes. In short, governmentality is not seen as a theory and does not set out as its project the explanation of risk in the same way that is attempted by the risk society thesis. While the latter can be criticized on the basis of not dealing with the gendered *experience* of risk, this criticism is irrelevant to a rather more modest approach that focuses only on governmental rationalities of risk and makes no claims about how (or even whether) people confront and interpret threats as risks.

Objectivity and statistical determinations of risk

Many scholars in the governmentality literature argue that the concept of statistical probability is central to the definition of risk and justify this claim, in part, by pointing to the increased use of actuarial techniques in the determination of risk and to how the prevalence of such techniques has changed dramatically in the last 30 years or so. Uses of statistical profiling to identify potential criminals and crime sites or to pinpoint probable victims of genetically related diseases are two such risk-based practices that have attracted much attention in recent years. By contrast, it is suggested that prior to the 1970s prediction emphasized various forms of professional knowledge, experience or rules of thumb to a much greater extent. While these means of prediction are still widespread, statistical prediction, it is argued, has come to be regarded as the ideal basis for governmental decisions – to be preferred whenever available and to be developed where it is not available. Techniques of statistical prediction are regarded as one of the central characteristics of neoliberal governance, and as such they figure prominently in many theorizations of risk. Of particular interest is how the wider use of statistical probability is associated with the reported shift of prediction practices from a contestable matter of opinion to an apparently 'objective' fact, and with broadening the scope of governmental intervention from particular individuals to entire categories of persons sharing 'risk factors' (Castel 1991; Ewald 1991; Simon 1987). The apparent objectivity and certainty of statistical representations of risk plays a critical ideological role (Beck 1992; 1999). By appearing objective and precise, statistical pronouncements about 'significant risks', 'acceptable risks' or 'remote probabilities' operate as a form of ideological impression management giving authority to the assertions of scientists and states. In turn, this elevates the role and importance of certain types of 'expertise' while discrediting other forms of knowledge.

The association of risk assessment with technical computation and objectivity is often institutionally perceived as a means of minimizing discrimination, as statistical procedures are thought to reduce bias inherent in opinion and judgement. Research attentive to the risk/gender nexus and to the interpretive politics of risk, however, has highlighted the inequalities that these statistical risk practices obscure and perpetuate (Hannah-Moffat 2004b). Empirical analysis of such tools have shown that the criteria for establishing levels of risk typically and routinely pay little attention to gender, racial or ethnic differences or to the differing social, economic and political contexts in which these tools are deployed (Maurutto and Hannah-Moffat 2005; Hannah-Moffat and Shaw 2000). Technical calculations of risk use categories that assume universal hetero-normative and masculine values. For instance, the vast majority of tools used in the criminal justice system to make decisions about the 'risk' posed by a particular offender or to a particular victim are developed and validated on white, adult, male offender populations. These analyses document how calculative risk scores obscure a range of gendered moral and subjective judgments about an offenders' past, character and relationships. For example, women's histories of self injury, victimization and intimate relationships are considered a central risk factor for managing women on parole – factors rarely considered or comparably prioritized in men's parole applications. Such decisions and judgements form the basis on which statistical scores are then computed so that apparently neutral statistical conceptualizations of risk reinforce and reproduce hegemonic gender norms.

An insistence on viewing risk as a neutral statistical technique limits our understanding of how 'gender' constitutes what we define as risk and the categories used to identify and assess levels of risk. By design, statistical actuarial techniques cannot address a multiplicity and complexity of differences between, and among, groups of men and women primarily because they operate at the level of the aggregate. For example, risk instruments do not account for the gendered contexts and qualitative and quantitative differences between male and female offending. Gender is abstracted and made invisible by risk assessments that govern individuals as members of statistical distributions rather than as unique cases. There is a general failure to capture the complex interplay between risk and gender. For example, in most statistically informed risk instruments, gender is reduced to a set of psychological/ social traits or, as in the case of the tools used in criminal justice, gender is conceptualized as a unitary variable in a statistical analysis of recidivism risk. Embedding essentialist interpretations of sex difference in risk assessment tools obscures empirical differences among women, institutionalizes narrow, deterministic characterizations of criminalized women (and men) and leaves the effects of gendered risk governance unarticulated and marginalized. This process and the conceptualization of risky subjectivity that results have important practical implications (cf. Castel 1991). In the penal context, for instance, risk tools are intended to determine programming needs, to determine access to programmes and to aid in institutional placement and parole decisions. Extending this logic further, some argue that statistical calculations of risk are a particular masculine form of control-oriented calculative rationality (e.g. Walklate 1997). Of concern is how 'certain masculine norms' inform the very concept of risk. In sum, we should always question how so-called 'objective' statistical risk categories are defined, interpreted and used to govern. More specifically, critical attention should be given to the gendered character or effects of the data on which risk calculations are based, the conclusions drawn from these calculations, and the programmes of government based upon them.

While it has to be agreed that statistical calculation of risk has become much more widespread of late, some have argued that to restrict risk to statistical techniques is to miss the true extent to which government through risk has spread and how we are made responsible for risk management to a much greater extent than before (Haggerty 2003). As this may suggest, a significant characteristic of risk, whether or not it is statistical in form, is its capacity to extend the reach of governance, for it requires only the licence of prediction in order to act. As Mariana Valverde (1999) has pointed out, the extension of government through risk occurs to an even greater extent where statistics are never at issue. Reviewing Canadian cases on the 'risk of harms' generated by pornography, she notes that while it would be tempting to argue that Canadian law was becoming actuarial, in practice probability calculations of such risks were not introduced into the court even though they were known to exist. Rather, she suggests, the court was not interested in actuarial aspects of risk, but in risk's capacity to extend judicial reach: while 'actual harm' requires empirical proof, virtually anything can be considered under the category of 'risk'. She concludes that 'risk of harm' is a useful phrase not so much because it uses actuarial language to conceal moral argument, 'but precisely because it is so capacious' (Valverde 1999: 190–91).

We do not need to pronounce on the issue of whether risk should conform to statistical or broader definitions of risk-based government. As in the literature generally, the contributors to this volume adopt a variety of positions within this range. The critical matter in our view is recognition of the fact that in various guises and forms, statistical and otherwise, 'risk' has become a central issue in the government of contemporary life and this cannot help but have an impact on gender issues.

Risk as consciousness, experience and culture

The analysis of risk as it is experienced is the principal focus of a third approach to which we now turn. Earlier in this introduction we referred to various studies of risk as part of the experience of men's and women's everyday lives. In such work there may often be some hints of governmentality inspired thinking. Thus, Teela Sanders' (2004) research focuses on the array of risks perceived and prioritized by women sex workers. Risks associated with health might be considered a priority concern by various public health programmes for which sex work is highly relevant. However, Sanders found that the women ranked health rather low on the hierarchy of risks because they had confidence in the security techniques with which they worked. 'House rules' governing such matters as condom use were rigorously enforced, and customers were usually compliant with these. In addition, the women regarded the skills they had developed in assertiveness as adequate for dealing with most problems in this respect. Male violence was considered more of a risk, although this had likewise given rise to defence techniques in which they had confidence, even though a sizeable proportion of the sex workers had experienced violence at the hands of their clients. In Sanders' research, emotional risks were found to have caused the greatest concern, and these too had produced defences. For example, the risk that sex work would interfere with the meaningfulness of non-commercial sexual relations could be governed by refusing customers access to certain practices, such as kissing on the mouth or genitals. Perhaps what is striking about such work is that such analysis *is not* carried out in the literature, and this indicates the need for governmental analyses to examine the ways that gendered techniques of the self are generated out of everyday life. But Teela Sanders' work is representative of a third theoretical approach to risk.

Neither governmentality analyses nor the risk society thesis is well suited to analysing the ways that personal and group decisions are made as to *what* constitutes a risk significant enough to prioritize. Here the questions concern: why some problems and not others are recognized as risks; which of these risks should be regarded as crucial and which of lesser concern; how risks are to be weighed up and balanced against other risks; what constraints operate when one is living with and attempting to manage risks; and, in a sense, what risks *mean* in such contexts. Risk is not simply to be understood in terms of expert categories and governmental programmes, but as Mary Douglas (1986; 1992) has stressed, it has to be seen in terms of cultural meanings and situated understandings.

To return briefly to the issue of women's fear of crime, Warr (1985) attempted to get behind the observation of women's apparently 'irrational' fear of crime by conducting interviews that probed beyond the kinds of questions asked in mass surveys. One key finding was that women's responses are linked with the magnitude of the crime rather than simply its probability, and that linked to a fear of robbery and even relatively minor crimes is a fear that turned these into major concerns – the fear of sexual assault. Thus, while for men, these threats, at worst, signified physical violence, and often merely a minor financial nuisance, for women, the level of fear was great because for them, such crimes were associated with the risk of sexual assault. In short, the meaning of crime risk – and thus the perception and management of its magnitude – is highly gendered, whereas this is not registered in the surface interpretations that link supposedly 'objective' to 'subjective' risk.

Similar issues relate to risks in other fields. Refusal to conform to expert definitions of how to govern one's exposure to sexually transmitted diseases (STDs), for example, may not be due to fecklessness or ignorance, but to a careful consideration of the effectiveness of risk-management techniques such as was performed by Sanders' sex workers. Under other circumstances, refusal may be due to other situated meanings of risk management. With respect to precautions related to HIV risks, to require condom use by one's partner may imply a lack of trust. Conversely refusal or 'failure' to take precautions can be understood as an expression of trust, a statement of love or sometimes a source of risk-taking excitement (Rhodes and Cusick 2000; Linneman 2000). Sean Slavin and his colleagues (2004: 45) illustrate this precisely through a participant in their study, Andrew, who 'speaks of deciding not to treat his HIV positive partner as "other" within the relationship. His sense of security in relation to risk shifts away from practical HIV prevention entirely and is constituted within the relationship'. Risk, in this sense 'others' those people who can be thus classified, and this may be regarded as a significant cost against which any benefits have to be offset. For those governing through health policies, objective risk appears as the inescapable focus, and yet for many people it is one thing among many, something with an emotional price tag and something that changes its meaning when imbricated with social and cultural experiences. Said Andrew 'I knew if I was going to have a relationship with X, I wanted things to be easier than having to treat him as different and see all the different things about him. It's like, well, if it makes it easier, I'll catch it (HIV)'.

Perhaps we have inadvertently focused too much on sexualized relations in this latter discussion, since gender issues are clearly important in all manner of risk fields. Consider, for example, levels of concern with respect to environmental risk issues related to nuclear power. These concerns appear to be more pronounced for women than for men. Rather than these reflecting stereotyped assumptions about lower thresholds of anxiety or ignorance among women, evidence suggests that this has to do with how the risk is framed. For men, the question appears more manageable because the risks appear as a question of science and technology, whereas for women, it appears both less manageable and more concerning because it is regarded as an environmental problem and especially as one affecting family and relationships (Davidson and Freudenberg 1996). In this respect, Christina Palmer (2003) has pointed to the relevance of the 'white male effect'. White males tend to rank health and technology risks as low because they endorse an individualist and hierarchic world view, whereas those other social categories with more egalitarian and collective world views tend to perceive such risks as high. With respect to yet other kinds of risks, Lois (2005) has identified what she refers to as a 'gendered confidence pattern' in which men tend to exhibit less trepidation in high-risk rescue settings. She attributes this to cultural and group stereotypes about men's superior rescue ability, to general beliefs that men are 'emotionally stronger' and to the greater familiarity of men with such kinds of hazardous situations.[8] In other words, judgements about whom or what is risky, which risks take priority and even whether risks themselves appear as more important than relationships may be based on gendered assumptions that are not transparently obvious. As Deborah Lupton (1999b: 119) suggests, such 'judgements of "riskiness" are founded in stereotypes, local knowledges, cultural mythologies and other systems of meaning that individuals begin to learn from childhood as part of their acculturation into society'.

This does not imply that such formulations of risk awareness and management are voluntary in any simple fashion. Again, one of the important contributions of the study of risk as consciousness and experience is to bring home the role of power in the definition of risks and their governance. Tim Rhodes' (1997) work on HIV risks and drug use, for example, has stressed the role of 'negotiated outcomes' in contexts where gendered risks are at issue.

> Constraints on some women's attempts at condom negotiation were particularly evident when the initiation of protected sex was perceived as carrying with it greater risks than unprotected sex. As was described, suggesting the use of a condom could mean that 'He would not be happy. I'd get into trouble . . .' (the example showing) that differential perceptions of 'risk acceptability' may be socially organized by gender, particularly as far as sexual behaviour is concerned.
>
> (Rhodes 1997: 220)

Equally, the example serves to illustrate that the identification of risks themselves is a complex gendered process, in which the implementation of techniques to reduce one set of risks creates new gendered risks whose implications outweigh those of the 'original' risk.

---

8 While it may appear that this risk stereotyping of women, where positive values are concerned, is merely a 'subjective' issue, a question of preferences, its consequences have been historically significant. In the 19th century it was widely accepted that women should not enter the ranks of speculators – supposedly they were neither emotionally nor mentally robust enough to be exposed to such risk taking. It followed that if were women licensed to take on such risky business, the vital activities of financial dealings on the stock market would not function as rationally and effectively as the economy required. In other words, such risks were regarded as inherently masculine in the sense that their governance required powers of rational calculation under stress that women were assumed not to possess (Weber 1978, O'Malley 2004). On these grounds, it was well into the 20th century before many stock markets allowed women to enter the profitable domain of financial risk taking.

RISK TAKING

Much of the discussion of risk thus far may be seen as negative, in which risk is constituted in terms of restrictions on freedom in the name of harm reduction. Yet risk is also understood as productive in all three approaches outlined above. For example, Beck's thesis mentions the rise of share market and financial risk taking as part of the new risk consciousness, and considers the global financial system and its permeation into everyday life as a modernization risk in its own right. Likewise, the governmentality literature has registered the fact that the last quarter of the 20th century saw the rise of an apparently contradictory requirement that people, businesses and even government departments should not only be more risk conscious, but should *take* more risks in order to be inventive, creative and profitable (O'Malley 1992). In the Reagan/Thatcher years the idea was promoted that the welfare state (the 'no-risk society') took away all exposure to risk, and thus stifled individual initiative and business enterprise. It was claimed that people had become 'dependant' and needed to become 'active' on their own behalf, spurred on both by the risks attendant with failure and the profitable possibilities created by risky enterprise. Such an approach to risk is, arguably, not only *not* statistical, but is *anti*-statistical because it involves imagination and creativity rather than statistical calculation based on data relating to past events (Bernstein 1998).[9] And if this governmental emphasis on risk taking seems to contradict the demand that we become more prudent in governing predictable harms, this is not how governmental regimes have represented things. Rather, the view promoted is that we must build up our knowledge of risks, hone our choice-making skills and make informed decisions about which risks to take and which to minimize.

This development has been registered in more culturally and experientially oriented work on risk. For instance, risk taking of the sort epitomized by 'masculinist' extreme sports – or 'edgework' as Steven Lyng and Rick Matthews describe it in this book – has come to be valorized for the masses rather than being regarded as the preserve of a small minority of men (Simon 2002). But such analyses of risk taking are not restricted to the impact of changing foci on risk culturally or governmentally. When discussing the activities of women drug dealers, Barbara Denton (2001: 121–24) voices a concern that much of the literature on women and risk renders them vulnerable or disempowered victims, and mobilizes problematic stereotypes with

9 It is easy to forget that in many respects risk, as opposed to risk taking, is a very conservative technology. Predictions based on risk statistics will only work as long as the past repeats the future in relevant respects: innovation is the enemy of risk but at the heart of risk taking. In addition, the two can be contrasted in light of Beck's (1992:49) observation that risk is negation, merely telling us what not to do. Conversely, risk taking always implies a focus on what is possible.

respect to risk taking. Thus, for example, Marsha Rosenbaum (1981: 50) has argued that:

> Men and women differ in their attitude toward risk. For male addicts, particularly at the beginning of their career with heroin or at the beginning of each new run, the daily overcoming of risk and chaos makes this life exciting and alluring . . . heroin is deemed a rewarding feeling for a hard half-day's work . . . on a subjective level, women disdain the riskiness of the heroin lifestyle. It is not surprising that women derive no positive status from engaging in risk.

As Sandra Walklate (1997) has pointed out and Susan Bachelor explores at length in the present collection, such views accord closely with a malestream assumption that women should not be risk takers, and that any who expose themselves to risk are simply feckless. Denton (2001: 123) directly challenges this view of women as risk avoiders; the women drug dealers with whom she worked often opted for risky modes of work – ranging widely from passing forged cheques to cat burglary – even when other options for making money were available. The women in Denton's study recounted their deeds in detail, specifically pointing to the thrill that risk taking generated – one of the 'seductions of crime' to which Jack Katz (1988) draws attention (while at the same time Katz problematically suggests that this is less relevant to women). Perhaps Katz (1988: 246–47) is right when he claims that men's risk taking can be understood in terms of 'distinctively male forms of action and ways of being', such as collective gambling, drinking and fighting – an issue interrogated by Lyng and Matthews in this volume. But there is no licence to move from this to wider generalization about women as risk avoiders. As Susan Bachelor argues in her contribution to this volume, it is often the case that young women approach risk in stereotypically 'female' ways, because of the influence of dominant cultural imageries. But by the same token, *some* young women, who she describes as 'teenage fighters' do engage in violence for its risk-excitement stimulations, although older women tend to regard such activities as a source of shame or embarrassment.

Of course, Bachelor does not assume that all men, let alone all young men, will share a positive orientation toward risk taking and violence. The point, rather, is to consider more closely how risk taking is gendered, while at the same time not adopting crude binaries that fix masculinity and femininity into implausible stereotypes and assume uniformity within gender categories. Though Bachelor examines gender and age, and also by implication gender and class, it's probably fair to say that research on risk and gender is sufficiently underdeveloped to the extent that consideration of more complex permutations is immanent. In this respect, there has been little exploration of the ways in which the risk/gender nexus connects to, and interacts with, other forms of inequality. As we pointed out earlier, the risk exists not only in combination with gender but simultaneously with race, ethnicity, class and sexuality. If risk and gender has yet to be as extensively studied as current theoretical concerns suggest is necessary, this must be all the more true for questions of risk, gender and intersectionality of this kind.

CONCLUSIONS: WHY RISK AND GENDER?

Our overview has highlighted the emergent literature on gender and risk and offered some suggestions for how theorists can more directly examine a variety of risk/gender nexuses. While feminist scholarship has devoted considerable attention to analyzing inequality and explaining shifts in social governance, less focused thought is given to the gendered nature and effects of risk governance. Given that risk is productive, scholars ought to be attentive to the processes through which risk discourses fracture and create gendered subjectivities and to how risk regimes produce inequalities, undermine gains and reconfigure social and individual problems. Risk, for example, can be conceived of as a mechanism that produces structural gender inequality and/ or forms of gender discrimination.

When thinking of risk in terms of experience and consciousness, gender issues have been rather more to the forefront than for other considerations of risk. Even so, some of the most influential writings in this respect – such as the edgework literature and the work of the risk society school – have, until now, either failed to make explicit the ways that risk experience is gendered, or have made direct deductions based on abstract notions of rational choice rather than drawing on evidence of how differently gendered subjects constitute and confront risk. While these vital points have been amply illustrated in the studies we have examined, we think there is a further and less predictable contribution that gender analysis can bring to the understanding of risk.

As commentators (Lupton 1999b; Garland 2003) in the risk literature have noted, the three main theoretical literatures on risk – cultural, governmental and risk society – have tended to ignore each other, apart from offering mutual critiques of variably constructive character. However, as we have tried to show, by shifting the focus to questions of gender and risk (and the same is probably true for the even more neglected subject of race and risk) the disputes between these various approaches to risk become of lesser concern, and the constructive possibilities of integrating them become apparent. For example, mapping women's experiences and their culturally informed understandings and ranking of risks can be regarded in a governmental light, providing insight into how and why individuals adopt certain techniques of the self, or to apply certain material techniques, in order to manage risks. Thus a gendered mapping of 'risk consciousness' can be linked back to a broader risk society approach (as Tulloch and Lupton (2003) show), taking it beyond the self-imposed limitations of merely imputing forms of risk consciousness from the broader social setting.

By focusing on the risk/gender nexus, scholars can assess how various gendered subjectivities and categories are constituted by risk thinking. Gender scholars are well positioned to reflect on the multiple ways that gender, in concert with other forms of inequality, informs risk, on how 'risk' is perceived from gendered subject positions and on the impact and perceived legitimacy of such perceptions. The gendered nature of risk has important social, political and economic implications. A close examination of risk practices will enhance our understanding of how gendered knowledges inform institutional practices aimed at the prevention, minimization and management of risk, and how these practices differently effect men and women. Risk scholarship can be mobilized by scholars interested in theorizing and documenting the production of various forms of inequality.

The chapters in this collection offer nuanced understandings of how risk perceptions, knowledges and practices can generate inequalities in a host of social and institutional practices including health, social and legal services and violence prevention, to name just a few. The integration of gender and risk analyses can open new spaces for thinking about how the characterisation of social problems and groups of people in terms of risk are influenced by gender and about how different communities think about and respond to 'risk'. In so doing, future scholarship can demonstrate how gendered knowledges inform risk practices and thus the (re)organization of social, economic and political regimes.

REFERENCES

Adkins, L. (2002) 'Risk, sexuality and economy' *British Journal of Sociology* 53: 19–40.
Barry, A., T. Osborne and N. Rose (1993) 'Liberalism, Neo-Liberalism and Governmentality: An Introduction' *Economy and Society* 22: 265–266.
Beck, U. (1992) *Risk Society: Toward a New Modernity*, New York: Sage.
Beck, U. (1994) 'The Reinvention of Politics: Towards a Theory of Reflexive Modernization', in U. Beck, A. Giddens, and S. Lash (eds) *Reflexive Modernization*, Cambridge: Polity Press, pp 1–55.
Beck, U. (1999) *World Risk Society*, London: Polity Press.
Beck, U. and G. Beck-Gernsheim (2002) *Individualization*, London: Sage.
Bernstein, P. (1998) *Against the Gods: The Remarkable Story of Risk*, New York: Wiley.
Breslin, F., J. Polzer, E. MacEachen, B. Morrongiello and H. Shannon (2007) 'Workplace injury or "part of the job"? Towards a gendered understanding of injuries and complaints among young workers' *Social Science and Medicine* 64: 782–793.
Campbell, A. (2005) 'Keeping the "lady" safe: the regulation of femininity through crime prevention literature' *Critical Criminology* 13: 119–140.
Castel, R. (1991) 'From Dangerousness to Risk', in G. Burchell, C. Gordon and

P. Miller (eds) *The Foucault Effect. Studies in Governmentality*, London: Harvester/ Wheatsheaf, pp 281–298.

Chan, W. and G. Rigakos (2002) 'Risk, crime and gender' *British Journal of Criminology* 42: 743–761.

Condon, M. (2001) 'Gendering the pension promise in Canada. Risk, financial markets and neo-liberalism' *Social and Legal Studies* 10: 83–103.

Condon, M. (2002) 'Privatizing pension risk: Gender, law and financial markets' in J. Fudge and B. Cossman (eds) *Privatization. Law and the Challenge to Feminism*, Toronto: University of Toronto Press, pp 128–167.

Cutter, S., J. Tiefenbacher and W. Solecki (1992) 'En-gendered fears: femininity and technological risk-perception' *Industrial and Environmental Crisis Quarterly* 6: 5–22.

Davidson, D. and W. Freudenberg (1996) 'Gender and environmental concerns' *Environmental Behaviour* 28: 302–39.

Denton, B. (2001) *Dealing: Women in the Drug Economy*, Sydney: University of New South Wales Press.

Douglas, M. (1986) *Risk Acceptability According to the Social Sciences*, London: Routledge and Kegan Paul.

Douglas, M. (1992) *Risk and Danger. Essays in Cultural Theory,* London: Routledge.

Ewald, F. (1991) 'Insurance and Risk', in G. Burchell, C. Gordon, and P. Miller (eds) *The Foucault Effect. Studies in Governmentality*, London: Harvester/Wheatsheaf, pp 197–210.

Garland, D. (1996) 'The Limits of the Sovereign State: Strategies of Crime Control in Contemporary Society' *British Journal of Criminology* 36: 445–471.

Garland, D. (2003) 'The rise of risk' in R. Ericson and A. Doyle (eds) *Risk and Morality*, Toronto: University of Toronto Press.

Greco, M. (1993) 'Psychosomatic subjects and the duty to be well' *Economy and Society* 22, pp 357–72.

Green, E., D. Thompson and F. Griffiths (2002) 'Narratives of risk. Women at midlife, medical "experts" and health technologies' *Health, Risk and Society* 4: 273–86.

Gustafson, P. (1998) 'Gender differences in risk perception: Theoretical and methodological perspectives' *Risk Analysis* 18: 805–811.

Haggerty, K. (2003) 'From risk to precaution: The rationalities of personal crime prevention' in R. Ericson and A. Doyle (eds) *Risk and Morality*, Toronto: University of Toronto Press, pp 193–214.

Hannah-Moffat, K. (1999) 'Moral agent or actuarial subject. Risk and Canadian women's imprisonment' *Theoretical Criminology* 3: 71–95.

Hannah-Moffat, K. (2004a) 'Criminogenic Neeed and the Transformative Risk Subject: Hybridizations of Risk/Need in Penality' *Punishment and Society* 7: 29–51.

Hannah-Moffat, K. (2004b) 'Losing Ground: Gendered Knowledges, Parole Risk, and Responsibility' *Social Politics* 11: 363–385.

Hannah-Moffat, K. and M. Shaw (eds) (2000) *An Ideal Prison: Critical Essays on Women's Imprisonment in Canada*, Halifax: Fernwood Publishing.

Harding, S. (1991) *Whose Science? Whose Knowledge? Thinking From Women's Lives*, Ithica: Cornell University Press.

Holgate, A. (1989) 'Sexual harassment as a determinant of women's fear of rape', *Australian Journal of Sex, Marriage & Family* 10: 21– 28.

Humpheys, L. (1970) *Tearoom Trade: Impersonal Sex in Public Places*, New York: Aldine de Gruyter.

Katz, J. (1988) *Seductions of Crime*, New York: Basic Books.

Kemshall, H. (2003) *Understanding Risk in Criminal Justice,* Maidenhead: Open University Press.

Linneman, T. (2000) 'Risk and masculinities in the everyday lives of gay men' in P. Nardi (ed.) *Gay Masculinities*, New York: Sage, pp 83–100.

Lois, J. (2005) 'Gender and emotion management in the stages of edgework' in S. Lyng (ed.) *Edgework. The Sociology of Risk Taking*, London: Routledge pp 117–52.

Lupton, D. (1999a) 'Risk and the ontology of pregnant embodiment' in D. Lupton (ed.) *Risk and Sociocultural Theory*, Cambridge: Cambridge University Press, pp 59–85.

Lupton, D. (1999b) *Risk*, London: Routledge.

Lyng, S. (1990) 'Edgework: Voluntary risk taking' *American Journal of Sociology* 95: 851–86.

Maurutto, P. and K. Hannah-Moffat (2005) 'Retrofitting risk and restructuring penal control' *British Journal of Criminology* 45: 1–17.

Miller, E. (1991) 'Assessing the risk of inattention to class, race/ethnicity and gender: comment on Lyng' *American Journal of Sociology* 96: 1530–1534.

Miller, P. and N. Rose (1990) 'Governing economic life' *Economy and Society* 19: 1–31.

O'Malley, P. (1992) 'Risk, Power and Crime Prevention' *Economy and Society* 21:252–75.

O'Malley, P. (2004) *Risk, Uncertainty and Government*, London: Cavendish/Glasshouse.

Palmer, C. (2003) 'Risk perception: another look at the "white male" effect' *Health, Risk and Society* 5: 71–83.

Parton, N. (1996) *Social Theory, Social Change and Social Work: The state of welfare*, London: Routledge.

Rapp, R. (1995) 'Risky business: genetic counselling in a shifting world', in R. Rapp and S. Schneider (eds) *Articulating Human Histories*, Berkeley: University of California Press, pp 175–87.

Ridge, D. (2004) ' "It was an incredible thrill". The social meanings of dynamics of younger gay men's experience of barebacking' *Sexualities* 7: 259–79.

Rhodes, T. (1997) 'Risk theory in epidemic times: sex, drugs and the social organization of "risk behaviour" ' *Sociology of Health and Illness* 19: 208–227.

Rhodes, T. and L. Cusick (2000) Love and intimacy in relationship risk management. HIV positive people and their sexual partners' *Sociology of Health and Illness* 22: 1–26.

Rose, N., P. O'Malley, and M. Valverde, (2006) 'Governmentality' *Annual Review of Law and Social Science* 2: 83–104.

Rosenbaum, M. (1981) *Women on Heroin*, New Jersey: Rutgers University Press.

Ruhl, L. (1999) 'Liberal governance and prenatal care. Risk and regulation in pregnancy' *Economy and Society* 28:91–117.

Sanders, T. (2004) 'A continuum of risk? The management of health, physical and emotional risks by female sex workers'. *Sociology of Health and Illness* 26: 557–567.

Schubert, R., M. Gysler, M. Brown, H. Brachinger (2000) 'Gender specific attitudes toward risk and ambiguity: an experimental investigation'. Unpublished paper. Centre for Economic Research. Zurich: Swiss Federal Institute of Technology.

Simon, J. (1987) 'The Emergence of a Risk Society: Insurance, Law, and the State' *Socialist Review* 95: 61–89.

Simon, J. (1988) 'The ideological effects of actuarial practices' *Law and Society Review* 22: 771–800.

Simon, J. (2002) 'Taking risks: Extreme sports and the embrace of risk in advanced liberal societies' in T. Baker and J. Simon (eds) *Embracing Risk. The Changing Culture of Insurance and Responsibility*, Chicago: University of Chicago Press, pp 177–208.

Slavin, S., S. Kippax and K. Race (1998) *The Sex Culture Project Report*, Sydney: National Centre in HIV Social Research. UNSW.

Slavin, S., J. Richters and S. Kippax (2004) 'Understandings of risk among HIV seroconverters in Sydney' *Health, Risk and Society* 6:14–27.

Stanko E. (1990) 'When Precaution is Normal: A Feminist Critique of Crime Prevention', in L. Gelsthorpe and A. Morris (eds) *Feminist Perspectives in Criminology*, Milton Keynes: Open University Press, pp 123–148.

Stanko, E, (1997) 'Safety talk: conceptualising women's risk assessment as a technology of the soul' in *Theoretical criminology: an international journal* 1(4), pp 479–499.

Tulloch, J. and D. Lupton (2003) *Risk and Everyday Life*, London: Sage.

Valverde, M. (1999) 'The harms of sex and the risks of breasts. Obscenity and indecency in Canadian law' *Social and Legal Studies* 8: 181–97.

Waldby, C. (1996) *AIDS and the Body politic: Biomedicine and Sexual Difference*, London: Routledge.

Walklate, S. (1997) 'Risk and criminal victimization: a modernist dilemma?' *British Journal of Criminology* 37: 235–46.

Walklate, S. (2002) 'Gendering Crime Prevention: exploring the tensions between policy and process', in G. Hughes, E. McLaughlin and J. Muncie (eds) *Crime Prevention and Community Safety: New Directions*, London: Sage, pp 58–76.

Warr, M. (1985) 'Fear of rape among urban women' *Social Problems 32:* 238–250.

Weber, M. (1978) 'The Stock Exchange', in W. Runciman (ed.) *Max Weber: Selections in Translation*, Cambridge: Cambridge University Press, pp 374–377.

Weir, L. (1996) 'Recent Developments in the Government of Pregnancy' *Economy and Society* 25, pp 372–392.

Weir, L. (2006) *Pregnancy, Risk and Biopolitics: On the threshold of the living subject*, London: Routledge.

Wynne, B. (1996) 'May the sheep safely graze? A reflexive view of the expert-lay knowledge divide', in S. Lash and B. Wynne (eds) *Risk, Environment and Modernity*, New York: Sage, pp 44–83.

Chapter 2

From familial disease to 'genetic risk'

Harnessing women's labour in the (co)production of scientific knowledge about breast cancer

Jessica Polzer* and Ann Robertson†

INTRODUCTION – THE GENETICIZATION OF HEALTH RISK

Over the last two decades, life in Western societies has come to be characterized by a prevailing consciousness of 'risk' (Beck 1992). As in other areas of life, risk has become the dominant way to describe, organize and practise health, and it is a central organizing concept in public health practices that focus on screening and early detection of disease (Lupton 1995, 1999; Petersen and Lupton 1996). Alongside this entrenchment in our consciousness of risks to health, genetics has emerged as a dominant mode of thinking about health, disease and personal identity at the beginning of the 21st century (Fox Keller 2000; Nelkin 1992). It is often asserted that the genetics 'revolution', marked by the completion of the Human Genome Project (which in 2000 succeeded in sequencing the entire human genome before its projected timeline), will fundamentally transform how biomedical research is conducted and how health care is practised and organized (Bunton and Petersen 2005; Gottweis 2005).

One of the most significant effects of the sequencing of the human genome has been the identification of a number of genetic mutations that are implicated in the development of adult onset disease.[1] In 1994 and 1995, scientists

* Assistant Professor, Department of Women's Studies and Feminist Research and the Faculty of Health Sciences, University of Western Ontario
† Professor, Department of Public Health Sciences, University of Toronto

1 This chapter does not include a consideration of *prenatal* genetic testing which has been covered extensively elsewhere (Lippman 1991; Markens, Browner, and Press 1999; Rapp 1998). Predictive genetic testing refers to testing healthy adults whose family history puts them at increased risk of inheriting a disease, such as breast cancer. Unlike predictive genetic testing for multifactorial conditions such as cancer, prenatal genetic testing has a richer history of feminist analysis and more *direct* implications for reproductive decision making.

identified 'BRCA1' and 'BRCA2', two genes that, when mutated, increase the probability that a woman will develop an inherited form of breast cancer at some point during her lifetime (Miki *et al* 1994; Wooster *et al* 1995). Although inherited forms of breast cancer account for only about 5 to 10 per cent of all breast cancers (Heisey *et al* 1999), mutations in either the BRCA1 or BRCA2 genes have been found to significantly increase an individual's susceptibility to breast and ovarian cancer.[2]

As genetic mutations continue to be implicated in the development of particular diseases, the notion of health risk is becoming increasingly 'geneticized' (Lippman 1991; 2000). Abby Lippman, who coined the term, describes geneticization as:

> the increasing tendenc[y] to make distinctions between people on the basis of what one believes are genetic differences, to view most disorders, behaviors and physiological variations as determined (wholly or in part) by genes, and . . . comprises ways both of thinking and of doing, applying genetic technologies to diagnose, treat and categorize conditions previously identified in other ways.
>
> (Lippman, 2000: 33)

The ways in which risks to health are becoming geneticized is clear in the recent emergence of predictive genetic testing clinics that provide individuals with risk information concerning their genetically-based, hereditary susceptibility for disease. These health-related services, while often referred to as 'clinics', are distinct from traditional medical services in that they provide individuals not with diagnostic information or therapeutic services, but with information regarding one's genetic susceptibility to disease at some future time. The identification of mutations in the BRCA1 and BRCA2 genes has made it possible to offer predictive genetic testing to women with a strong family history of breast cancer in order to assess their inherited susceptibility to breast cancer. First introduced in Ontario, Canada in 1995, by May 2000 BRCA1/2 mutation testing had become listed as a provincially insured health service for women whose family histories of breast cancer suggested a possible hereditary component. This move was hailed as a victory by some women with family histories of breast cancer who at the time were demanding their rights to genetic testing services (Abraham 1999).

As genetic testing services for late onset disorders becomes more widely available, a growing body of research has examined genetic testing from the

---

2 The BRCA1 and BRCA2 genes are tumour-suppressor genes that normally function to inhibit cell growth. The estimates of the increases in breast cancer risk conferred by BRCA1/2 mutations are inconsistent across studies and range from 56–85 per cent (Heisey, Carroll, Warner, McCready, and Goel 1999).

viewpoint of those being tested. A good deal of this research focuses on the accuracy of lay perceptions of genetic risk (e.g. Bluman *et al* 2003; Watson *et al* 1999), the factors that influence decision making about genetic testing (Bouchard *et al* 2004; Cox 2003; Halbert 2004; Jacobsen, Valdimarsdottir, Brown, and Offit 1997), and/or the psychological effects of genetic testing and genetic risk information (Bish *et al* 2002; Di Prospero *et al* 2001; Dorval *et al* 2000; Hutson 2003; Pasacreta 1999; Schwartz *et al* 2002). With some notable exceptions (Gibbon 2002; Cox 2003), these studies tend to situate individuals as passive recipients of genetic risk information and privilege a conception of the individual as autonomous, disembodied and rationally guided (Petersen 1998; 1999). Such studies tend to overlook that individuals draw upon their own experiential knowledge in formulating their interpretations of genetic risk assessment and screening (d'Agincourt-Canning 2005), with such knowledge inevitably influenced by the multiple social contexts (familial, community, national) in which individuals are located. Furthermore, assumptions of individual autonomy are particularly misguided when one considers that genetic testing is pursued within the context of gendered familial responsibilities. Within this familial context, decisions to accept testing are influenced by the duty or obligation one feels to inform family members of genetic mutations that they may have passed on (d'Agincourt-Canning 2001; Hallowell 1999; Polzer 2005).

In contrast to the body of literature that situates women as passive recipients of expert genetic information, other studies have sought to understand the meaning and significance of hereditary risk for individuals with family histories of disease in the context of their everyday lives (Cox and McKellin 1999; d'Agincourt-Canning 2001; 2005; Gibbon 2002; Parsons and Atkinson 1992). This research illustrates that individuals do not translate statements about genetic risk unproblematically, but actively interpret risk information in ways that have personal meaning. Other studies have focused on the process of genetic testing itself and the specific components through which knowledge of genetic risk is produced and made visible (Atkinson, Parsons, and Featherstone 2001; Prior *et al* 2002; Nukaga and Cambrosio 1997). By showing how knowledge of genetic risk is constructed and interpreted through the use of visualization techniques and inscription devices (such as the pedigree or family tree), these studies contest the assumption that the practice of genetic testing reveals an already-existing, objective reality.

While there has been research both on the individual meaning of hereditary risk, and on the techniques through which knowledge of genetic risk is constructed, the study upon which the present chapter is based is one of the first to address how women's understandings and experiences of their inherited susceptibility to breast cancer are shaped by techniques of visualization, such as the pedigree, and the genetic testing process more generally. Given that breast cancer is typically seen as a 'dread disease' for women (Reagan 1997), it is curious that there have been few studies that focus on the gendered aspects, and gendering effects, of discourses on genetic risk for breast cancer. One exception is provided by Gibbon's (2002) ethnographic study of BRCA1/2 mutation testing which shows how the process of genetic testing is dependent on the actions of women themselves who, through their participation in genetic testing, involve themselves in re-writing their family histories of breast cancer. This study points out how women are implicated in processes of scientific knowledge production and geneticization. Such processes, Gibbon argues, do not work in a linear, top-down manner but, rather, are collaborative processes that require the active involvement of women. Also, d'Agincourt-Canning's (2001) study suggests that predictive genetic testing for hereditary breast cancer risk invokes particular gendered responsibilities, such as the disclosure of genetic risk information to family members, with the 'burdens of this task falling primarily on women' (p. 231).

Alongside these examples, we offer this chapter as a contribution to the growing area of research that focuses on the gendered nature of discourses on genetic risk for breast cancer. Based on the findings of a qualitative study of women undergoing BRCA1/2 mutation testing, we focus on the *production of knowledge* about genetic risk for breast cancer as a gendered activity that operates through women's desires to take charge of their health in light of their family histories of breast cancer. We begin the chapter by situating the study theoretically, and by describing how, prior to genetic testing, the women in this study were already engaged in a particular kind of self-care through their participation in a broad spectrum of risk management activities. We then go on to explore how the process of genetic testing capitalizes on women's (already present) desires to take charge of their health and harnesses their energies towards particular ends. First, we explore how genetic testing enlists the labour of women who, as part of their will to gain knowledge about their genetic susceptibility to breast cancer, engage in the work necessary to gather and compile information about disease in their families in a form that is interpretable by genetics professionals. We also draw attention to the difficult, emotional nature of these information-gathering practices. Second, we consider how this labour sets up the possibility for the clinical construction of the pedigree, or family tree, which authorizes the women's family histories of breast cancer and transforms them into visual evidence of 'genetic risk'. We conclude the chapter with some thoughts on how this knowledge production process presumes and reinforces gendered responsibilities for health in the context of the family, and creates new obligations for women in the production of knowledge concerning their 'genetic risk' for breast cancer. In addition, we consider how the will to genetic self-knowledge can be understood in light of recent shifts in the politics of women's health.

GENETIC GOVERNANCE AND THE ETHICAL
SUBJECT OF GENETIC RISK

Our analysis is situated within contemporary social theories of risk that regard risk discourse as a neoliberal strategy of governance that shifts power away from direct state intervention toward generating conditions that facilitate self-regulation (Rose 1996). From the perspective of governmentality, neoliberal political rationalities are seen to govern through the specification of particular kinds of citizen-subjects who are 'active individuals seeking to "enterprise themselves", to maximise their quality of life through acts of choice' (Rose 1996: 57).

As with risk discourses generally, discourses on health risk operate as neoliberal technologies of governance that rely on and reproduce enterprising subjects who are invited to 'freely' govern themselves through 'processes of endless self-examination, self-care and self-improvement' in order to maintain their health and well-being (Petersen, 1997: 194). As a formula of rule that seeks to responsibilize individuals through their exercise of freedom, neoliberal practices of governance operate through technologies of the self – that is, through the various practices that individuals carry out in their everyday lives in order to make choices, improve themselves and attain a certain state of being. These technologies of the self:

> permit individuals to effect by their own means, or with the help of others, a certain number of operations on their own bodies and souls, thoughts, conduct, and way of being, so as to transform themselves in order to attain a certain state of happiness, purity, wisdom, perfection, or immortality.
> (Foucault 1994b: 225)

Rose (2001) suggests that emerging forms of biological knowledge are fundamentally *ethopolitical* insofar as they exert their influence by engendering particular kinds of ethical relations or 'self-techniques by which human beings should judge themselves and act upon themselves to make themselves better than they are' (Rose 2001: 18). It is in this sense that predictive genetic testing can be viewed as a neoliberal technology of governance that operates through the capacities of individuals themselves who act as agents of their own self-regulation. As a technology of the self, predictive genetic testing invites/incites women to take up a particular set of ethical relations with themselves and their biological relatives. Following Foucault, we use the term 'ethical' here to emphasize the relations that one freely establishes with oneself (Foucault 1985; Rabinow 1994).[3] Rather than placing analytic emphasis

---

3 Foucault's ethics are concerned with investigating the relations that one freely establishes with oneself and others through the lenses of four domains or categories: (i) the 'ethical substance',

on moral laws or universal codes of conduct, this approach to ethical analysis is concerned with the *practices* that individuals use as part of their everyday lives to evaluate and change themselves (Bernauer and Rasmussen 1984; Valverde and White-Mair, 1999).

By situating predictive genetic testing as a technology of the self that privileges particular ethical self-relations, this analysis considers how participation in predictive genetic testing comprises part of the ethical work (*askesis*) (Foucault 1985; Rabinow 1994) that women with family histories of breast cancer perform on themselves in order to cultivate themselves as (pro)active managers of their genetic risks for breast cancer. In the remainder of this chapter we focus specifically on two techniques that comprised predictive genetic testing – the completion of the family history forms and the (re)presentation of familial disease in the form of the pedigree. Through an examination of how women interact with these techniques of governance, we illustrate how predictive genetic testing for breast cancer not only reinforces personal responsibility for health but also inserts women and their family members into circuits of genetic research and scientific knowledge production about breast cancer.

THE STUDY

The work described here was part of a larger study that explored how women with family histories of breast cancer understood and experienced their inherited susceptibility to breast cancer, and how these understandings and experiences shifted as they went through the process of genetic testing. Study participants were recruited from 2001 to 2002 through a familial breast cancer clinic located in a major urban centre in Canada. At the time of data collection, the clinic provided genetic counselling and testing services two days weekly to women who were referred for BRCA1/2 testing and who met the eligibility criteria set by the provincial health insurance plan.

Twenty-four in-depth interviews were conducted with women who agreed to take part in the study at two to three points in time (before genetic counselling, after genetic counselling, after test results were received) in order to learn how their understandings and experiences related to their inherited susceptibility to breast cancer changed (or not) as they went through the

or, 'the way that the individual has to constitute this or that part of himself as the prime material of his moral conduct' (Foucault 1985: 26); (ii) the 'mode of subjectivation', or the way in which people are invited to recognise their moral obligations to act upon themselves (or others); (iii) the 'askesis', or the work that one performs on oneself in order to transform oneself into the ethical subject of one's behaviour; (iv) the 'telos', or 'final cause' or ends that both inform and that are sought through the ethical work one conducts on oneself, with the telos acting backward as motivation, cause and goal (Foucault 1985; Rabinow 1994).

genetic testing process. All of the women in the sample had family histories of breast cancer, a prerequisite for referral to the clinic.[4] The women's ages ranged from 30 to 45 years, with most of the women in their mid-30s. Seven of the nine women had children, with the children's ages ranging from five years to early 20s. The study sample was ethnically diverse, reflecting the ethnic diversity of the urban centre where the study was conducted.

After being referred to the clinic, the women were sent a Family History Questionnaire (FHQ) which they then completed and returned to the clinic. In addition to information about one's own cancer and pregnancy history, the FHQ asked the women for information about dates of birth/death and cancer histories (e.g. type of cancer, age at diagnosis) for their siblings, parents, and maternal and paternal cousins and grandparents. Prior to the first genetic counselling appointment, a genetic counsellor reviewed the FHQ and ordered additional records if necessary in order to construct a woman's pedigree (i.e. family tree) and assess her eligibility for genetic testing. Two of the nine study participants were judged to be ineligible for genetic testing. Of the seven study participants who were eligible for testing, two declined testing and one, although eligible for testing, took nearly one year to complete her FHQ and thus did not complete a third interview during the data collection period. Of the four remaining participants who underwent blood testing within the one-year study recruitment period, three tested negative and one tested positive for a BRCA2 mutation.

The interview data were analysed using standard interpretive techniques (Holstein and Gubrium 1994; Strauss and Corbin 1990) to develop descriptive codes and analytic categories grounded in the women's own words. These analytic categories were then interpreted from the perspective of governmentality (Dean 1999; Foucault 1991) in order to generate theoretical themes that captured how the process of predictive genetic testing invited/incited the women in this study to (re)make themselves into ethical subjects of risk. The analysis illustrates how, through the process of predictive genetic testing, the women in this study sought to transform themselves from 'active participants in health' into '(pro)active managers of genetic risk' (Polzer 2006). Briefly put, in light of their knowledge that breast cancer was a disease in their families and was therefore a threat to their own well-being, the women in this study were already participating in a spectrum of risk management activities (e.g. breast screening, lifestyle modifications) before they attended genetic counselling. These risk management activities constituted the ethical work through which they made themselves into active participants who took charge of their health in light of their family histories of disease. As women who were already engaged in such ethical work, genetic testing was approached as a unique 'opportunity' for genetic self-knowledge, as one more thing they

4 The criteria are listed in the Ontario Medical Association's physician referral guide at http://www.oma.org/pcomm/omr/nov/01genetics.htm.

could do to take charge of their health in order to bring their susceptibility to breast cancer within their own individual control. Above and beyond what they were already doing, acquiring knowledge of their genetic risk was seen to enable them to exercise a more precise control over their health by expanding their 'options' for risk management (e.g. by providing access to MRI screening)[5] and by helping them to fine-tune and channel their risk management efforts in ways that would optimize their chances of early detection and survival. While acquiring genetic risk information was not seen to ultimately influence whether or not they would get breast cancer, it was seen to facilitate the ways in which they could be active participants in their health, both in the present and in the future. From the theoretical perspective previously described, this will to (biological) self-knowledge (Foucault 1994c) is viewed as constituting an integral part of the ethical work through which the women in this study were able to (re)make themselves into (pro)active managers of their 'genetic risk' for breast cancer (Polzer 2006).

With this transformation in subjectivity as a backdrop, the remainder of the chapter focuses on the specific techniques through which knowledge of genetic risk was produced, and through which this shift in subjectivity was accomplished. First, we illustrate how completing the family history forms capitalizes on the women's desires to be active participants in their health, and enlists women's labour in gathering details of familial disease. Then, we consider how the pedigree transforms familial disease into evidence of 'genetic risk', (re)presenting familial disease in a visuospatial map of biological risk relations. Last, we discuss the women's participation in genetic testing, and their collaboration in knowledge production, in terms of their will to genetic self-knowledge.

ENLISTING WOMEN'S LABOUR IN THE PRODUCTION OF KNOWLEDGE OF 'GENETIC RISK'

Congruent with their already-established desires to be active participants in their health, the completion of the family history forms actively involved the women in the process of compiling the information necessary for the clinicians to assess whether or not the observed pattern of disease in their families was suggestive of a hereditary form of breast cancer. In order to complete the family history forms required by the clinic, the women in this study actively worked to collect and compile their family histories, and to transform these oral histories (based on the memories of their relatives and

---

5 Preliminary studies suggest that, in BRCA1 and BRCA2 mutation carriers, MRI is more sensitive for detecting breast cancers than other screening methods on their own, although it is unclear whether this early detection affects mortality (Warner and Causer 2005).

stories communicated through 'word of mouth') into written lists. Except for Elaine, who refused to ask her relatives for assistance as this would be considered disrespectful by her Chinese elders, all of the women in the study attempted to recruit the help of older (usually female) family members to complete the FHQ, as they typically did not know the specific details about their relatives' cancer histories.

Completing the FHQ was rarely a straightforward process. Logistical difficulties were encountered when the women had to recruit the help of family members who lived overseas or with whom they had had little or no previous contact. This laborious process of fact-gathering was also emotionally difficult as some of the study participants had to initiate discussions with relatives (some of whom were not known personally) about the details of their cancer experiences and/or what they knew about other cancers in the family.[6]

> ... it's a little bit uncomfortable to bring this up ... I feel *it makes it a little bit awkward asking them about, you know, 'well what did your mother die of?'* and because they live all over the world ... you don't keep in touch with them ALL the time so we're not that close and just to go and bring that up that's why I asked my sister's help because she was more in contact with them than I am and she felt that she's more able to push the subject ... in THAT sense.
>
> (Annie)[7]

Through these discussions, the women would at times learn about 'new' instances of cancer in their families, that is cases of cancer that, until that point, were not known to them. Particularly for those women who felt especially vulnerable to breast cancer, this process of 'form-filling' was a reminder that breast cancer was indeed a threat to their health. This was the case for Larissa whose fears of getting cancer intensified as she learned of three additional cases of breast cancer in her family:

> R: ... there were three other aunts that also died of breast cancer. .... I thought it was just my grandmother and my mom. But apparently on my grandmother's side ... ALL her sisters died of breast cancer.

---

6 The emotions that were elicited by the process of gathering information about familial disease are noteworthy in order to describe the difficulties associated with the construction of the clinical family history. The emotional aspects related to the production of knowledge about genetic risk should be distinguished from traditional sociological conceptions of 'emotional labour' that focus on the commodification of emotion in the service industry (Hochschild 1983).

7 Quoted text in CAPS indicates verbal emphasis made by the study participants during the research interviews. *Italicized* text indicates passages of transcribed speech that the authors wish to emphasize.

I: So what was it like to find out that new information?

R: Scary. . . . *Even more scary*. Actually to be honest with you I was shocked. I was very sombre throughout the whole day and I was like 'Whoa!' [whispering] I only thought. . . one person. Now when you find out there's been more than one then your chances are a little higher.

(Larissa)

Despite the emotional and logistical difficulties of completing the family history forms, the process of unearthing information about cancer in the family was embraced by almost all of the study participants who felt that this provided them with a clinically endorsed licence to speak about and to learn the 'truth' of breast cancer in their families. This desire to know and to speak about disease in the family is understandable given that, prior to their involvement in genetic testing, the knowledge the study participants had about breast cancer in their families was acquired in a largely *silent* manner. Breast cancer was typically an unspeakable topic within the study participants' families and, as such, the study participants had formed their understandings of their own susceptibility in relation to their experiences of directly witnessing suffering or hearing stories about family members who had suffered with and died of cancer in the past:

My mom never talked about [breast cancer]. Never. Even when she had it. . . . She just didn't [whispering] . . . she didn't talk about it [whispering]. . . . when my aunt [died] – like 20 years ago – I only heard about it when she died.

(Kyra)

By helping to reveal what was once concealed, filling out the family history forms can be seen as a confessional device[8] through which the details of disease in the family are elicited by the women who seek to break their family's silence on breast cancer. In an ethnographic study of a breast cancer genetics clinic in the United Kingdom, Gibbon (2002) similarly comments on how establishing the clinical family history sets in motion a process whereby women see themselves as helping to reveal the family's secrets of disease:

. . . the production of the clinical family history, the clinical encounter itself and concomitant screening and monitoring procedures are seen by

---

8 Foucault specifically elaborated on the pastoral technique of 'the confession' – developed by the Jews and taken up later by Western Christianity – through which individuals were incited not only to *know* the truth of themselves, but also to *speak* the truth about themselves (Foucault 1994a).

many as part of a quite literal uncovering of what was commonly felt to be a 'deadly silence'.

(Gibbon, 2002: 449)

As an injunction to instigate discussions about cancer in the family, the family history forms, although seemingly mundane and neutral, play an important role in the production of knowledge about 'genetic risk'. In addition to enrolling women in the information-gathering labour necessary for the production of knowledge concerning their genetic risk, the family history forms codify and categorize familial experiences of disease in ways that render them interpretable by genetics professionals. Thus, the truth that is spoken through the confession of one's family history of disease does not speak for itself, as it must interpreted by a genetic counsellor who authorises, validates and completes the truth of 'genetic risk' (Foucault 1978: 66–7).

But unlike the traditional dyadic notion of the confession, which involves a (spiritual) guide and the confessing individual, the 'truth' of familial disease is not revealed by the woman alone who offers forth her own secret confessions. Rather, this truth is brought to light through the woman's efforts to incite her family members to speak about disease in the family. Indeed, because the completion of the family history forms necessarily requires the involvement of the woman and her relatives, the clinical family history and the subsequent pedigree are brought into existence through an entire network of familial relationships. It is through this complex network of relationships – between a woman, her family members, and genetics clinicians and scientists – that the clinical family history and the subsequent pedigree are produced, and through which knowledge of 'genetic risk' emerges as a particular form of 'truth' about susceptibility to future disease.

THE (CO)PRODUCTION OF VISUAL EVIDENCE OF 'GENETIC RISK'

While establishing the clinical family histories of breast cancer required the labour of the women and their family members to complete the family history forms, it was through the pedigree that 'genetic risk' was effectively made 'legible to an observing eye' (Armstrong 1983: 1). In other words, just as the family history forms made the unspeakable speakable, the pedigree made the invisible visible.

Whereas the family history forms served to collect information about past instances of breast cancer among the participants' blood relatives, the pedigree further transformed this information by re-presenting it within a perceptual grid that summarized and rendered visible all instances of familial cancer in a genetic map. As suggested by the following quotes, the pedigree, or 'family tree' as some of the women referred to it, provided a new way of seeing and understanding their own susceptibility to breast cancer:

> The one thing that I found when I went [to the clinic] *is the way they made the family tree put things so [much] more in perspective. I mean you see it on paper* and you see 'okay, yeah, this person and that and that and THAT.' And then . . . you know? It puts it more in perspective.
>
> (Annie)

This spatial representation of breast cancer in their families was at times likened by the study participants to seeing their family histories in 'black and white'. For a few women, being presented with this visual evidence of their susceptibility to disease in the form of the pedigree heightened their concerns and fears about getting breast cancer:

> *It was in black and white.* Like you can think about it and then when it's all down on paper [small chuckle] you're going well 'Wow! Oh my God! It's all there.'. . . My mum's sisters had breast cancer. And then her brother had pancreatic cancer. And then her sister that is probably close to her eighties has a daughter [who] has had problems with melanoma. . . . So the pancreatic and the melanoma and then the three breast cancers . . . to me *it was like just arrows pointing to the BRCA2.*
>
> (Kyra)

By (re)presenting the women's family histories of disease in a familiar visual format resembling a family tree, the pedigree convincingly revealed to the women the 'truth' of their genetic risk. In the present study, the women tended not to question how the pedigree (re)presented their family histories of breast cancer. Rather, they tended to emphasize the educational aspects of genetic counselling. Some of the women remarked how, in light of the pedigree and genetic counselling, they could finally understand how breast cancer 'worked' in their families, how they could 'trace' the pattern of breast cancer through their families:

> . . . it's AMAZING how you see things differently now. Cuz like I said . . . before [counseling] . . . you're blind. You don't know. You know there's something there but you really don't know. But NOW I have a vision. Wait a minute! *I can see how things work.* . . . I know HOW it's inherited . . . . I get these genes.
>
> (Larissa)

I thought I was fairly knowledgeable but I came out of there thinking 'Wow! I didn't know THAT!' I mean just in terms of looking at my family tree I thought 'well . . . both families have had cancer I'm . . .

maybe in trouble here', you know? And *then when we started to trace it out and looked at the TYPES of cancer and where the connections . . .* and all that sort of stuff I realised it wasn't a concern but I understood WHY.

(Chantelle)

By visibly displaying what women with family histories of breast cancer already know to be true (that they might or will get breast cancer), the pedigree comprises a particularly seductive technique of governance. Prior *et al* (2002) note how the process of genetic testing transforms family stories of disease into visual 'evidence' of genetic risk, evidence that is not simply revealed but is rather produced through a long and complex process involving multiple techniques and interpretations:

> Finding evidence of cancer-predisposing mutations in individuals is a complex and multi-stage process. At each stage there is a potential for seeing and assessing a risk in many different ways and from a number of standpoints. . . . Initial risk assessments are based on loosely described family histories. These histories need to be firmed up as data using observations drawn from a variety of sources – including cancer registries. Validated data can then be turned into evidence using either pencil and paper diagrams or pedigree-drawing software . . . *Only after that is it plausible to consider the possibility of molecular testing, for in the absence of a suitable history it is unlikely that one would ever find a cancer-predisposing mutation.*
>
> (Prior *et al* 2002: 256, emphasis added)

In addition to rendering genetic risk visible, the truth of genetic risk revealed by the pedigree is difficult to contest because it was constructed on the basis of the completed family history forms, the details of which were produced through the labour of the women themselves and their family members. With this in mind, while the power of the pedigree to transcribe family histories of disease into maps of genetic risk is clear, it is important not to overlook the largely invisible 'social work' (Lindee 2003) that the women themselves did to render the details of their family histories of cancer in a format that was interpretable by the genetic counsellors, that is, to make possible the production of the pedigree. As Lindee (2003) tells us, even the most complex aspects of molecular genetics are grounded in the 'social complexity of the pedigree' and are made possible by extracting information from individuals and families:

> Finding any gene requires extracting words and blood from people . . . The blood and the narrative are embedded in a larger narrative, a pedigree documenting family history, a causal model documenting the nature of a genetic defect based on inheritance patterns revealed in the pedigree

... the first point of translation, is the pedigree, and producing a pedigree is unquestionably social work.

(p. 51)

Indeed, during the post-counselling interviews, some of the women explicitly noted how the pedigree was collaboratively produced by them and the clinic staff. For example, Annie describes the pedigree as a valuable and collaboratively-produced document, resulting from her own labour, the labours of her relatives who assisted her in getting the necessary information, and the labours of the clinicians who used the information to construct a pedigree and assess her eligibility for testing:

> ... I'll pass [the pedigree] on to my children and to my sisters because I think it's a valuable document. It's very helpful ... it's a permanent record of the family history ... it really puts into perspective exactly WHO had WHAT and ... *as a result of a lot of research that I had done ... You know, so this is good. I've done the research and they've done this work for me* so that's great ... Yeah it just summarises the whole story.
>
> (Annie)

Studies that focus exclusively on the pedigree as an inscription device inadvertently reproduce a (gendered) division of labour in which the 'real' work of knowledge production (about breast cancer in this case) is assumed to lie primarily with the scientific work that is conducted in the (public) clinic and laboratory settings. Overlooking the social work that women and their families do to reconstruct their family histories of cancer thus erases the (private) labours that make possible the production of the pedigree and clinical estimates of genetic risk. In relation to this point, one participant in this study felt that, by leaving out certain details she had provided on her family history forms, the pedigree did not properly acknowledge the work that she did to bring her family history of disease to light:

> I'll show you the [pedigree]. I gave [the counsellor] a whole list and ... [rustling papers] and they didn't work on that. *Like all that work I did? They didn't work on that.* ... All she gave me was this [she shows a hand drawn pedigree]. ... There's WAY more people with cancer in my family than that. ... there's all these people that had cancer ... that wasn't even in there but it was on my written form. So I was quite disappointed in that.
>
> (Celia)

By acknowledging the work that the women and their family members do in the production of knowledge about genetic risk, it is possible to understand how the family history forms and the pedigree together transform experiences of disease-in-the-family into visual evidence of 'genetic risk'. The pedigree has been conceptualized as a 'boundary object' (Atkinson, Parsons, and Featherstone 2001) that crosses social spaces and disciplines and enables genetic clinicians and laboratory scientists to co-construct scientific knowledge (Nukaga 2002). This study further suggests that the family history forms can be seen as a boundary object that enables clinicians to interface with women and their families who provide the 'raw data' – that is, their experiences of disease – from which the clinical family histories and the pedigree are derived. By extension, as the traditional caregivers and health providers in the family, women who pursue genetic testing services might be considered boundary workers who usefully link their families (who provide a resource of family history information) with clinical and scientific spheres of knowledge production about genetic risk for breast cancer.

THE WILL TO GENETIC SELF-KNOWLEDGE

Already inspired to bring to light the family's secrets of cancer, the active participant in health seeks out genetic testing as a unique opportunity for genetic self-knowledge and as one more thing she can do to take charge of her health. In turn, the process of genetic testing invites/incites the active participant in health to gather and compile her family's experiences of disease as part of the ethical work that she must do to (pro)actively manage her genetically inherited risks for breast cancer, and to take (better) care of herself and her family.

In this study, this will to biological self-knowledge was a moral imperative, for there was little if any consideration in the study participants' accounts that they might obtain knowledge about their genetic risk and then *not* guide their actions on the basis of that knowledge. Because the women in this study viewed gaining knowledge about their genetic risk as desirable precisely for its ability to optimize their chances for early detection and to expand their future risk management 'options' (e.g. MRI screening), it seemed incomprehensible to most of them why someone would deny such an opportunity for knowledge.[9] While the study participants supported one's *hypothetical* choice not to know their genetic risk, most of them could not understand why, *realistically speaking*, someone would not want this knowledge. To refuse knowledge about one's genetic susceptibility was seen by most of the women in this study as morally suspect, as denying oneself the opportunity to become 'empowered' with information about one's biological potential for disease, and to learn how to expand one's risk management activities:

---

9 This attitude was less forcefully expressed by the two women who were eligible for and refused genetic testing.

. . . it's almost an ignorant mind set of people who wouldn't go [to genetic testing]. Anybody who has the opportunity to go should go. And anybody who says 'I'd rather not know' or . . . 'If there's something wrong with me I don't wanna deal with it' or 'If I have to wait for the test results I'm gonna become anxious' . . . all I can say is 'You go . . . and you find out'.

(Chantelle)

[it's like someone] saying 'I know you know something REALLY important about my health and about my chances of getting [breast cancer] but I just don't wanna know' . . . that to me is just . . . *it's willful blindness or something.*

(Ingrid)

This analysis regards participation in genetic testing as part of the ethical work that women with family histories of breast cancer do to maintain a sense of control over their susceptibility to disease. From this point of view it is understandable why, in the present study, the women who were ineligible for testing, rather than being relieved that their family histories were not suggestive of a hereditary form of breast cancer, were left feeling disappointed and frustrated. For example, Ingrid felt that, by not making the test openly available to *all* women, the eligibility criteria deprived some women of information that could inform their preventive actions:

. . . [when told I was ineligible] I felt badly for women in general. Because [the clinicians] have the KNOWLEDGE! It's really like saying 'Listen we could tell you if you come walkin' across that road whether or not you're gonna' get hit. We just CAN'T tell you.'. . . *I just think it's a shame that that's the state of our medical research . . . that people are deprived of that information.*

(Ingrid)

In this sense, ineligibility for genetic testing was understood as effectively suppressing a woman's will to obtain knowledge in order to exert (further) control over her health. For women who live with a constant awareness of breast cancer and who are highly invested in managing their risks, being ineligible for genetic testing is not necessarily good news as this is seen to suppress their will to acquire genetic self-knowledge, and to deny them the opportunity to construct themselves as morally competent citizens who use genetic risk information to guide their future risk management strategies. In his thoughtful essay on the government of genetic risks, Lemke (2005) suggests that the will to biological knowledge reflects new standards for evaluating moral competence in a genetic age, and therefore questions the extent to which individuals truly 'choose' to know or not to know their genetic risk:

. . . the use of genetic diagnosis is not up to individual freedom or personal choice. The will not to know about your genetic make-up or risk profile could be regarded as no will at all: the sign of a deficient or illegitimate will . . . We might witness a process in which it will be more and more problematic to opt against genetic information and the transmission of this knowledge since this might be seen as an objective witness for lacking moral competence or as an indisputable fact of irrational behaviour.

(Lemke, 2005: 100, emphasis added)

Similar to Lemke's point, the extent to which genetic screening, and risk technologies more generally, uphold individual choice and autonomy has been challenged by others who point out the close relationship between genetic risk and responsibility (e.g. Chadwick 1999; d'Agincourt-Canning 2001; Hallowell 1999; Petersen 1998, 1999). Previous research has shown that an individual's decision to pursue genetic testing often rests in the responsibility she feels to her family members to 'pass on' knowledge about genetic risk so that they too can manage their risks for cancer appropriately (Polzer 2005). Furthermore, the present study suggests that the moral responsibility to obtain knowledge about genetic risk is in part informed by one's past experiences of witnessing the suffering and death of mothers, aunts and other female relatives at a time when women had little information and fewer options available to them for screening and treatment. Under such circumstances, some of the study participants found it extremely difficult to comprehend how any woman today can justify denying an opportunity for knowledge about *how she herself* might alter her present conduct in order to either prevent breast cancer altogether or optimize her chances for survival should she be diagnosed with breast cancer in the future.

The will to genetic self-knowledge observed in this study emerges within a shifting terrain in the politics of health in the 21st century. In the 1970s, the women's health movement called for collective action to challenge patriarchal health care systems through consciousness raising and by making women more active in demanding greater choices in health care. This provides a meaningful historical context for understanding the desire of the women in this study to take matters of health into their own hands by pursing knowledge about their genetic risks for breast cancer. As Robertson (2001) implies, demands for knowledge that expand one's 'options' for self-surveillance and risk management are ironic yet not completely surprising:

It would appear that women, generally, have 'voluntarily' taken up certain practices of self-surveillance and self-governance (e.g. breast self-examination, annual mammograms, lifestyle management) in order to manage their health risks. It is ironical – although, perhaps not entirely surprising – to reflect that the notion of 'Our Bodies, Our Selves' (representing a political intention, on the part of the women's health movement, for women to 're-own' their bodies – that is, to remove them from the clinical gaze) appears to have shifted, within 30 years, to the notion of 'Our Bodies, Our Enemies' (representing a turning back of the clinical gaze on oneself, a 'swallowing of the Panopticon').

(303)

It is reasonable to assert, then, that the women's health movement, which openly encouraged women to become more knowledgeable about their bodies, has provided a fertile ground for a neoliberal mode of genetic governance to take hold and have meaning in women's everyday lives. Within the politics of health of the 21st century, women are increasingly called upon to take charge of their health though acts of 'choice' and self-regulation. As Lippman (2000) suggests, a 'dangerous synergy' exists between risk and choice as technologies increasingly filter women's choices through the lens of risk.

As one such technology, predictive genetic testing for hereditary breast cancer risk operates through the willingness of women themselves who are compelled to 'find out' about their genetic risks in light of their family histories of disease, and to engage in the labour that makes possible the production of such knowledge. Insofar as knowledge about genetic risk is understood to facilitate choice and expand women's 'options' for risk management, collaboration in knowledge production about genetic risk itself can be seen as a gendered responsibility that emerges within ethopolitical modes of genetic governance.

CONCLUSION

Using predictive genetic testing for hereditary breast cancer as an example, our general concern in this chapter has been to explore how emerging forms of knowledge about genetic risk for breast cancer presume and further specify particular kinds of self-regulating subjects. Specifically, we explored how the production of knowledge concerning genetic risk for breast cancer is a gendered activity, one that capitalizes on women's desires to be active participants in their health (in light of their family histories of cancer), harnesses women's labour in the production of scientific knowledge about their genetic risks, and that enables women to (re)make themselves into ethical subjects of (genetic) risk. We have also suggested that participation in scientific knowledge production about breast cancer emerges as a particular form of gendered responsibility, where such participation is tied to increasing and facilitating one's health 'choices' and 'options'.

We have argued in this chapter that, as a neoliberal strategy of genetic governance, predictive genetic testing for hereditary breast cancer operates through, and necessarily relies on, the energies of women themselves who actively work to reveal the details of their family histories of disease. While previous research has shown how the pedigree makes genetic risk visible (Prior *et al* 2002) and renders a particular truth about susceptibility to disease (Nukaga and Cambrosio 1997), we suggest that the pedigree is a collaborative product that is realized through the labour the women themselves do to investigate, unearth and compile information about their family members' experiences with cancer, both living and deceased. Future research should also consider in further detail the gendering effects of predictive genetic testing for breast cancer. For example, as predictive genetic technologies become more mainstream, it will be important to examine critically how predictive genetic testing, in effect, (re)inserts women (and their bodies) into a broader and a potentially more intense network of technological gazes. Although this study focused specifically on breast cancer, a disease which mainly affects women, critical attention should be given to the ways in which women, as traditional caregivers and health care providers in the family, are 'naturally' implicated in strategies of genetic governance that operate *through* the family, itself re-conceived as an object of, and resource for, knowledge about genetic risk.

ACKNOWLEDGMENTS

Warm thanks are extended to the women who participated in this study and to the clinic staff who supported the study and assisted with recruitment. This study was supported by a Social Sciences and Humanities Research Council (SSHRC) Doctoral Fellowship and a National Cancer Institute of Canada (NCIC) Studentship. We gratefully acknowledge Silja Samerski for her comments on a previous version of this chapter.

REFERENCES

Abraham, C. (1999, August 27) 'Tenacious woman scores medical victory' *The Toronto Star*.

Armstrong, D. (1983) *Political Anatomy of the Body: Medical Knowledge in Britain in the Twentieth Century*, Cambridge: Cambridge University Press.

Atkinson, P., Parsons, E., and Featherstone, K. (2001) 'Professional constructions of family and kinship in medical genetics' *New Genetics and Society* 20(1), 5–24.

Beck, U. (1992) *Risk Society: Towards a New Modernity*, London: Sage.

Bernauer, J., and Rasmussen, D. (eds) (1984) *The Final Foucault*, London: The MIT Press.

Bish, A., Sutton, S., Jacobs, C., Levene, S., Ramirez, A., and Hodgson, S. (2002) 'Changes in psychological distress after cancer genetic counselling: A comparison of affected and unaffected women' *British Journal of Cancer* 86, 43–50.

Bluman, L. G., Rimer, B. K., Sterba, K. R., Lancaster, J., Clark, S., Borstelmann, N., Iglehart, J. D., and Winer, E. P. (2003) 'Attitudes, knowledge, risk perceptions and decision-making among women with breast and/or ovarian cancer considering testing for BRCA1 and BRCA2 and their spouses' *Psycho-Oncology* 12, 410–27.

Bouchard, L., Blancquaert, I., Eisinger, F., Foulkes, W. D., Evans, G., Sobol, H., and Julian-Reynier, C. (2004) 'Prevention and genetic testing for breast cancer: Variations in medical decisions' *Social Science and Medicine* 58, 1085–96.

Bunton, R. and Petersen, A. (2005) *Genetic Governance: Health, Risk and Ethics in the Biotech Era*, London: Routledge.

Chadwick, R. (1999) 'Genetics, choice and responsibility' *Health, Risk and Society* 1(3), 293–300.

Cox, S., and McKellin, W. (1999) ' "There's this thing in our family": Predictive testing and the construction of risk for Huntington Disease' *Sociology of Health and Illness* 21(5), 622–46.

Cox, S. (2003) 'Stories in decisions: How at-risk individuals decide to request predictive testing for Huntington Disease' *Qualitative Sociology* 26(2), 257–80.

d'Agincourt-Canning, L. (2001) 'Experiences of genetic risk: Disclosure and the gendering of responsibility' *Bioethics* 15(3), 231–47.

d'Agincourt-Canning, L. (2005) 'The effect of experiential knowledge on construction of risk perception in hereditary breast/ovarian cancer' *Journal of Genetic Counseling* 14(1), 55–69.

Dean, M. (1999) *Governmentality: Power and Rule in Modern Society*, London: Sage Publications.

Di Prospero, L. S., Seminsky, M., Honeyford, J., Doan, B., Franssen, E., Meschino, W., Chart, P., and Warner, E. (2001) 'Psychosocial issues following a positive result of genetic testing for BRCA1 and BRCA2 mutations: findings from a focus group and a needs-assessment survey' *CMAJ Canadian Medical Association Journal* 164(7), 1005–1009.

Dorval, M., Patenaude, A., Schneider, K., Kieffer, S., DiGianni, L., Kalkbrenner, K., Bromberg, J., Basili, L., Calzone, K., Stopfer, J., Weber, B., and Garber, J. E. (2000) 'Anticipated versus actual emotional reactions to disclosure of results of genetic tests for cancer susceptibility: Findings from p53 and BRCA1 testing programs' *Journal of Clinical Oncology* 18(10), 2135–42.

Foucault, M. (1978) *The History of Sexuality: An Introduction*, New York: Random House, Inc.

Foucault, M. (1985) *The Use of Pleasure*, New York: Random House, Inc.

Foucault, M. (1991) 'Governmentality' in G. Burchell and C. Gordon and P. Miller (eds) *The Foucault Effect: Studies in Governmentality*, London: Harvester Wheatsheaf.

Foucault, M. (1994a) 'The ethics of the concern for self as a practice of freedom' in P. Rabinow (ed.) *Michel Foucault: Ethics, Subjectivity and Truth. Essential Works of Foucault, 1954–1984*, New York: The New Press.

Foucault, M. (1994b) 'Technologies of the Self' in P. Rabinow (ed.) *Michel Foucault: Ethics, Subjectivity and Truth*, New York: Pantheon Books.

Foucault, M. (1994c) 'The Will to Knowledge' in P. Rabinow (ed.) *Michel Foucault: Ethics, Subjectivity and Truth*, New York: Pantheon Books.

Fox Keller, E. (2000) *The Century of the Gene*, Cambridge: Harvard University Press

Gibbon, S. (2002) 'Re-examining geneticization: Family trees in breast cancer genetics' *Science as Culture* 11(4), 429–57.

Gottweis, H. (2005) 'Governing genomics in the 21st century: Between risk and uncertainty' *New Genetics and Society* 24(2), 176–93.

Halbert, C. (2004) 'Decisions and outcomes of genetic testing for inherited breast cancer risk' *Annals of Oncology* 15(Supplement 1), i35–i39.

Hallowell, N. (1999) 'Doing the right thing: genetic risk and responsibility' *Sociology of Health and Illness* 21(5), 597–621.

Heisey, R. E., Carroll, J. C., Warner, E., McCready, D. R., and Goel, V. (1999) 'Hereditary breast cancer: Identifying and managing BRCA1 and BRCA2 carriers' *Canadian Family Physician* 45 (January), 114–124.

Holstein, J., and Gubrium, J. (1994) 'Phenomenology, ethnomethodology, and interpretive practice' in N. K. Denzin and Y. S. Lincoln (eds) *Handbook of Qualitative Research*, Thousand Oaks: Sage.

Hochschild, A. (1983) *The Managed Heart*, Berkeley: University of California Press.

Hutson, S. P. (2003) 'Attitudes and psychological impact of genetic testing, genetic counseling, and breast cancer risk assessment among women at increased risk' *Oncology Nursing Forum* 30(2 part 1), 241–46.

Jacobsen, P. B., Valdimarsdottir, H. B., Brown, K. L., and Offit, K. (1997) 'Decision-making about genetic testing among women at familial risk for breast cancer' *Psychosomatic Medicine* 59(5), 459–66.

Lemke, T. (2005) 'From eugenics to the government of genetic risks' *Genetic Governance: Health, Risk and Ethics in the Biotech Era*, London: Routledge.

Lindee, S. (2003) 'Provenance and the pedigree: Victor McKusick's fieldwork with the old order Amish' in A. Goodman, D. Heath and S. Lindee (eds) *Genetic Nature/Culture: Anthropology and Science Beyond the Two-Culture Divide*, Berkeley: University of California Press.

Lippman, A. (1991) 'Prenatal genetic testing and screening: Constructing needs and reinforcing inequities' *American Journal of Law and Medicine* XVII(1, 2), 15–50.

Lippman, A. (2000) *Geneticization and the Canadian Biotechnology Strategy: The marketing of women's health*, paper presented at the The Gender of Genetic Futures: The Canadian Biotechnology, Women and Health, York University, Toronto, ON. February 11–12.

Lupton, D. (1995) *The Imperative of Health: Public Health and the Regulated Body*, London: Sage.

Lupton, D. (1999) *Risk*, London: Routledge.

Markens, S., Browner, C. H., and Press, N. (1999) ' "Because of the risks": How US pregnant women account for refusing prenatal screening' *Social Science and Medicine* 49, 359–69.

Miki, Y., Swensen, D., Shattuck-Eidens, D., *et al* (1994) 'A strong candidate for the breast and ovarian cancer susceptibility gene BRCA1' *Science* 266, 66–71.

Nelkin, D. (1992) 'The social power of genetic information' in D. J. Kevles and L. Hood (eds) *The Code of Codes: Scientific and Social Issues in the Human Genome Project* Cambridge: Harvard University Press.

Nukaga, Y. (2002) 'Between tradition and innovation in new genetics: the continuity of medical pedigrees and the development of combination work in the case of Huntington's disease' *New Genetics and Society* 21(1), 39–64.

Nukaga, Y., and Cambrosio, A. (1997) 'Medical pedigrees and the visual production of family disease in Canadian and Japanese genetic counselling practice' in M. Elston (ed.) *The sociology of medical science and technology*, Oxford: Blackwell

Parsons, E., and Atkinson, P. (1992) 'Lay constructions of genetic risk' *Sociology of Health and Illness* 14(4), 438–55.

Pasacreta, J. V. (1999) 'Psychosocial issues associated with increased breast and ovarian cancer risk: findings from focus groups' *Archives of Psychiatric Nursing* 13(3), 127–36.

Petersen, A. (1999) 'Public health, the new genetics and subjectivity' in A. Petersen and I. Barns and J. Dudley and P. Harris (eds) *Poststructuralism, Citizenship and Social Policy*, London: Routledge.

Petersen, A. (1998) 'The new genetics and the politics of public health' *Critical Public Health* 8(1), 59–71.

Petersen, A. (1997) 'Risk, governance and the new public health' in A. Petersen and R. Bunton (eds) *Foucault, Health and Medicine*, London: Routledge.

Petersen, A., and Lupton, D. (1996) *The New Public Health: Health and Self in the Age of Risk*, London: Sage.

Polzer, J. (2006) 'From active participant in health to (pro)active manager of genetic risk: (Re)Making the ethical subject of risk in the age of genetics', unpublished PhD Dissertation, University of Toronto.

Polzer, J. (2005) 'Choice as responsibility: Genetic testing as citizenship through familial obligation and the management of risk' in R. Bunton and A. Petersen (eds) *Genetic Governance: Health, Risk and Ethics in the Biotech Era*, London: Taylor and Francis.

Prior, L., Wood, F., Gray, J., Pill, R., and Hughes, D. (2002) 'Making risk visible: The role of images in the assessment of (cancer) genetic risk' *Health, Risk and Society* 4(3), 241–58.

Rabinow, P. (1994) 'Introduction' in P. Rabinow (ed.) *Ethics, Subjectivity and Truth: Essential Works of Foucault, 1954–1984, Volume I*, New York: The New York Press.

Rapp, R. (1998) 'Refusing prenatal diagnosis: The uneven meanings of bioscience in a multiculturalworld' in R. Davis-Floyd and J. Dumit (eds) *Cyborg Babies: From techno-sex to techno-tots*, London: Routledge.

Reagan, L. (1997) 'Engendering the dread disease: Women, men and cancer' *American Journal of Public Health* 87(11), 1779–87.

Robertson, A. (2001) 'Biotechnology, political rationality and discourses on health risk' *Health* 5(3), 293–309.

Rose, N. (1996) 'Governing "advanced" liberal democracies' in A. Barry and T. Osborne and N. Rose (eds) *Foucault and Political Reason: Liberalism, neo-liberalism and rationalities of government*, Chicago: University of Chicago Press.

Rose, N. (2001) 'The politics of life itself' *Theory, Culture and Society* 18(6), 1–30.

Schwartz, M. D., Peshkin, B. N., Hughes, C., Main, D., Isaacs, C., and Lerman, C. (2002) 'Impact of BRCA1/BRCA2 mutation testing on psychologic distress in a clinic-based sample' *Journal of Clinical Oncology* 20(2), 514–520.

Strauss, A., and Corbin, J. (1990) *Basics of Qualitative Research: Grounded Theory Procedures and Techniques*, Newbury Park: Sage.

Valverde, M., and White-Mair, K. (1999) ' "One day at a time" and other slogans for everyday life: The ethical practices of Alcoholics Anonymous' *Sociology* 33(2), 393–410.

Warner, E., and Causer, P. (2005) 'MRI surveillance for hereditary breast-cancer risk' *The Lancet* 365, 1747–49.

Watson, M., Lloyd, S., Davidson, J., Meyer, L., Eeles, R., Ebbs, S., and Murday, V.

(1999) 'The impact of genetic counselling on risk perception and mental health in women with a family history of breast cancer' *British Journal of Cancer* 79(5/6), 868–74.

Wooster, R., Bignell, J., Lancaster, J., et al., (1995) 'Identification of the breast cancer susceptibility gene BRCA2' *Nature* 378, 789–792.

Chapter 3

The 'decision trap'

How genetic counselling transforms pregnant women into managers of foetal risk profiles

Silja Samerski

Ms C sits opposite the genetic counsellor. She is pregnant in her fourth month. A fully fledged physician with extra training in human genetics, the counsellor is an expert on congenital disorders, genetic defects and biostatistics.[1] Between them on the table are charts, diagrams and graphs. Behind them is a one-and-a-half hour educational session on the statistical distribution of birth defects, Mendelian inheritance, chromosomal aberrations and their ominous portents of the unborn child's future. Because of her age and her disabled[2] cousin, Ms C's gynaecologist had diagnosed her 'at risk' and suggested she undergo an amniocentesis. But since an amniocentesis carries new risks and can only provide reasons for terminating the pregnancy, the physician did not want to recommend it. Instead he asked Ms C to figure out what to do. Thus he sent her to the geneticist to enable her to make an 'informed choice'. In the genetic counselling clinic, the young physician gave her the input he considered necessary for her decision-making task: he ascertained her risk status, added a few more risks she had been unaware of, then listed her options – which basically boiled down to having the test or not – and finally spelled out the chances and risks associated with each option. Ms C found out that being pregnant means having to make decisions in the shadow of risk: Either she takes the risk of delivering a disabled child, the counsellor tells her, or she accepts the risk of inducing a miscarriage. And if the amniocentesis does not provide the green light she hopes for, she will have to consider terminating the pregnancy. But all this is for her and her husband

---

1 Hence, in contrast to North America, genetic counselling in Germany has long been dominated by male human geneticists. Since the 1990s, however, more and more women have been entering the field so that today a considerable number of counsellors are female. Among the five genetic counsellors whom I observed for my study there was only one woman. This ratio is not representative. The counsellor of the session I chose for this article was male. I can infer from the other counselling sessions I observed that as far as my argument on risk is concerned the sex of the counsellor is irrelevant.

2 In German: 'behindert', a term commonly used by counsellors and clients.

to decide, as the genetic counsellor repeatedly clarifies: 'You have to make the decision, since we do not bear the consequences.'

Ms C is caught in a trap which I call the 'decision trap'. She is being urged to make an informed choice and to take the associated risks. This decision trap is paradigmatic for the contemporary service economy. The more hopeless the situation the more experts insist on the client's autonomy and self-responsibility. Mushrooming counselling services train people to make their own decisions and to thereby accept the hazards of the 'technological society' (Ellul 1964) as risks they have deliberately chosen. Any event can be turned into a risk by using probability theory to link what *is* with what *might be*. Since 'there is no risk in reality,' as Francois Ewald clarifies, 'anything *can* be a risk' (Ewald 1991: 199).[3] What may have once been an unforeseeable misfortune calling for aid and assistance or a social evil provoking political protest is now professionally imputed to clients as an individual risk.

Risk generates 'an obligation to act in the present in relation to the potential future that now comes into view' (Novas and Rose 2000: 486). It creates the illusion that by following professionally prescribed conduct it is possible to seize hold of the future. Various counselling rituals foster this illusion and call upon clients to make informed decisions and then be responsible for all possible consequences. Just as the geneticist burdens his pregnant client with decisions she must make on her risk-labelled pregnancy, so the general practitioner exhorts a healthy pensioner to choose between his age-related risk of prostate cancer and regular checkups – but the eventual follow-up treatment might leave him with impotence and incontinence and has no proven preventive effect. The vocational advisor warns the dismissed cabinetmaker of his high risk of becoming a long-term unemployed worker and incites him to undergo training measures to optimize his labour profile – while the wood industry transfers its workshops to China. The less people are able actually to determine their fate, the more they are trained to be aware of their risks and to feel responsible for what happens to them.

Taking the example of prenatal genetic counselling, I will analyse the symbolic function of professional education in risk awareness and decision making. I will show how clients are led into the 'decision trap' which forces them to choose between pre-calculated risks, and imposes on them a managerial rationality. In the case of prenatal counselling, the expert's lessons

---

3 Ewald's work focuses on a concept of risk which is based on probability theory and the technologies of insurance. In colloquial language, risk is often used as a synonym of danger or daring. In contrast to other languages such as English, French or Italian, the term 'risk' existed in the German language well into the 20th century only in the contexts of business and insurance. See the entry for 'Risiko' in the *Deutsche Fremdwörterbuch*, Berlin 1971. Therefore in German it is easier to distinguish between the technical term 'risk,' which is defined and calculated by experts, and the colloquial 'danger' referring to a concrete, tangible threat. For reasons of clarity, I will stay with this distinction.

surreptitiously transform the expectant mother into a manager of a foetal risk profile. Therefore, rather than investigating the content of the information, I focus on its symbolic effects: What does the geneticist informing Ms C about her 'basic risk' for a disabled child tell her about herself and her unborn child? When he invites her to weigh statistical risks in order to make a personal decision fraught with consequences, what does he tell her to do? And what does this say about our contemporary understanding of autonomy and responsibility? I will draw on a previous study in which I analyse genetic counselling as a lesson in managerial decision making (Samerski 2002). During this study I observed and recorded 30 genetic counselling sessions in three different counselling centres in Germany.[4]

Prenatal genetic counselling is only one example among the various educational programmes that rub people's noses into risk thinking; but it is undoubtedly a very glaring one: Like most genetic counsellors' clients, Ms C is pregnant. The risk curves and probability calculations directly clash with her delicate condition of expecting a baby. She is worried about the well-being of her coming child – and the geneticist saddles her with risks and offers risk management strategies which question the continuation of her pregnancy. But in the end, it is she who has to make a decision. The counsellor tries to bridge the chasm between his statistical constructs and her concrete situation. He tries to spell out his knowledge in words that sound meaningful to her. Technical terms mutate into popular scientific notions loaded with colloquial meaning. An abstract probability turns into a personal threat, and the correlation between genotype and phenotype gells into an illustrative 'gene for'. Thus, the educational session with a geneticist exemplifies how the call for risk management reinterprets deliberation and autonomy. And it illustrates how the professional imposition of this new 'autonomy' deeply disables women, especially when they become mothers.

THE PATHOGENIC EFFECTS OF DOCTOR-ATTRIBUTED RISKS

A statistician's statement about the high risk of having an accident in the bathroom does not make feelings run high. A genetic counsellor's warning of an increased risk for a heart attack or a disabled child, however, transforms a healthy woman into a needy patient. A risk attributed by a doctor has dramatic, indeed pathogenic effects.

In the 1970s, authors such as Ivan Illich (Illich 1976) and Eliot Freidson (Freidson 1970) identified the medical establishment as a major threat to a healthy life. Demigods in white subjected their patients to risky interventions,

---

4 All quotations are taken directly from my transcripts. Translations by Nancy Joyce.

prescribed pills with damaging side effects, and recruited further clients by medicalizing life from the cradle to the grave. Today, patients endanger not only their health with bizarre diagnostic and treatment methods but also their future with statistical soothsaying. Waiting rooms at doctors' offices are packed with people who are in the best of health but who have been labelled 'at risk'. Screening procedures sift through cohorts of healthy people who have been classified into various risk groups in order to pick out those unfortunates who are not yet aware of a prostate tumour or a lump in their breast.[5] How has it been possible to create in healthy citizens such an intense desire for experts and machines to prove that they are (probably) right in feeling healthy? How could this pathogenic diagnosis ever have become a need?

In the 19th century, when anything from horse kicks to the size of behinds was counted and statistically registered,[6] the sociologist and statistician Adolphe Quételet pointed out that the statistical laws that govern society and the masses cannot be applied to the individual. 'These laws have, depending on how they have been determined, nothing personal about them, which is why they can only be applied to individuals with certain restrictions. Applying them to an individual would be as erroneous as using a mortality table to determine the day when a certain person will die' (in Ewald 1993: 196). More than 100 years later, however, we have grown used to regarding probabilities as personal predictions. Every consultation with a doctor today is potentially loaded with frightening risks. From a snowballing mass of data, statisticians calculate probabilities which allow them to predict the frequency with which something will happen in the artificial population from which the sample has been drawn. As soon as they find their way into clinical practice, however, these frequencies become threatening risks.[7] At the patient's bedside or in the office, patients rightly expect their doctor to say something concrete and tangible about them. When their doctor attributes a risk to them, they

---

5 A considerable number of those shattered by a positive test result submit to unpleasant and even harmful interventions only to learn that their test results were wrong. But even for those whose suspected breast or prostate tumour is verified, it does not mean they were the lucky ones: Many would more likely have died with it than from it. On the havoc wrought by professionals who are not aware of the pitfalls of interpreting test results and misunderstanding statistics, see Gigerenzer 2002; on the danger of cancer prevention programmes, see Weymayr and Koch 2003.

6 About the history of probability and statistics, see Gigerenzer *et al* 1989, Hacking 1990.

7 Patricia Kaufert and John O'Neil have analysed how risk mutated from a statistical frequency to a concrete threat when Canadian physicians tried to convince the Inuit to give up births at home. Taking a seemingly objective mortality rate, the doctor declares that traditional midwifery is too risky. But taken out of its original epidemiological context, this rate becomes an empty 'pseudo rate'. And for the Inuit, this risk is meaningless anyway: 'For the woman, risk is the occasional threat of danger in childbirth accepted as part of a natural process' (Kaufert and O'Neil 1993: 50). But a 'risk' which seems to objectify a threat to health and life allows no objection: 'The physician dismisses her claims as irrelevant for a definition of risk which is objective, scientific, expressible in numbers' (ibid: 50).

inevitably understand it as a diagnosis, a personal threat which then hangs over their present-day lives like a Damoclean sword.[8] But by definition a risk does not refer to a concrete person but to a constructed case; never to the 'I' or 'you' in a colloquial statement, but always to a case taken from a statistical population. 'In statistical affairs . . . the first care before all else is to lose sight of the man taken in isolation in order to consider him only as a fraction of the species. It is necessary to strip him of his individuality to arrive at the elimination of all accidental effects that individuality can introduce into the question.' (Poisson, S.-D. *et al* 1835, in Hacking 1990: 81).

In the age of population curves, rain probabilities, and genetic soothsaying, awareness of the restricted meaning of statistical calculations has waned. Doctors lump statistical probabilities together with a diagnosis or a personal danger, giving the appearance of concreteness to an abstract frequency. This epidemic misunderstanding of statistical probabilities as personal threats transforms healthy people into patients suffering from a new iatrogenic disease: risk anxiety. Once an attested risk for breast cancer or a heart attack has unleashed fantasies about suffering and early death, pseudo-patients find it difficult to recover their peace of mind. Though free of illness, they live under the shadow of medical prophecies. Doctors cannot dispel their patients' new fears, they can merely suggest different strategies for risk management. Prophylactic pill popping, dietary orders, prescribed physical exercises, and above all regular screening and monitoring are supposed to guard against the evil conjured up by statistical calculations.

PRENATAL CARE AS RISK MANAGEMENT

Nowhere has risk-thinking in medicine been so powerful and symbolically efficacious as in prenatal care. Pregnancy is a unique state of uncertainty, the embodiment of the 'not yet'. But, as historian Barbara Duden has shown, historically 'pregnancy', in contrast to today, never referred to a provable physiological state. Instead, it meant the somatic stance of a woman who expected a child (Duden 1993; 1998; Duden *et al* 2002). Thus, only women could know about and experience being pregnant; it could not be professionally diagnosed. Duden concludes that historically 'pregnancy' never existed, 'but rather women who felt pregnant' (Duden 2002: 64; *my translation, S.S.*). The now antiquated German expression 'being in good hope' ('in guter

---

8 Taking the example of benign lumps in the breasts, Sandra Gifford describes how physicians treat risk factors as 'objective clinical signs of disease' (Gifford 1986: 222). According to Lorna Weir, 'clinical risk', that is, risk at the bedside or in the doctor's office, is a chimera: it puts together heterogeneous concepts such as clinical diagnosis and treatment with statistical frequencies. It 'acts upon individual bodies' (Weir 1996: 374) but is generated through epidemiological knowledge.

Hoffnung sein') emphasizes this particular stance on the part of the pregnant woman: her attitude toward the child she is expecting.

Modern medicine has transformed this gendered somatic stance into an objectified state ascribed to women by experts. Today, a woman is mostly declared 'pregnant' by a test-strip or a gynaecologist on the grounds of hormone level and ultrasound scan. She then becomes the uterine environment of a developmental process which has to be professionally managed. Each time she visits the gynaecologist, the patient's interior is scanned by ultrasound and she is encouraged to wrongly believe that the visualisation of measured values on the screen is a picture of her unborn (Duden 1993). Handbooks and glossy brochures display the developmental stages of a foetus, and the accompanying texts warn expectant mothers to avoid alcohol, cigarettes and stress in order to minimize the risks involved in foetal growth. The technological reconstruction of reality demands doubting one's own corporeality. As Barbara Duden has formulated it poignantly, women are stripped of their skin; they are disembodied (Duden 1993).

A modern woman diagnosed pregnant cannot be in 'good hope' anymore, but is instead talked into a state of 'bad expectation'. Everything that could possibly happen is ascribed to her as a frightening risk which she can either accept or guard against. The simple fact that she is pregnant carries the 'basic risk' that the child might have some congenital disorder. Her age is fed into a statistical calculation to determine her risk for a child with Down's syndrome. A welter of other risks can follow: The German 'maternity passport',[9] a hand-held pregnancy record, lists 52 potential risk factors that immediately classify a pregnant woman as being 'at risk'. A mother-to-be aged over 35 or under 18, an earlier caesarean, a genetic disease or disability among her relatives, a difficult family situation: the list is broad and vague enough to ensure that most women fall under at least one category. Little wonder that three out of four pregnancies are now diagnosed as being 'at risk'.[10]

Risk mobilizes. In any case, even when there is not much that can be done to prevent the predicted potential disaster, risk creates the need for information and counselling. A growing army of advice givers teach bewildered mothers-to-be how to behave in their new roles as risk carriers. Risk management demands responding to technogene constructs that lie beyond our perception. Therefore, doctors, nurses and counsellors teach their clients that trusting their own senses is deceptive. 'Responsibility is equated with the

9 The 'maternity passport' is a hand-held pregnancy record that captures all medical data, from the mother's blood type and iron level to ultrasound scans and the karyogram. The pregnant woman is supposed to carry it with her at all times as a precaution. It was introduced in 1968; the extent of medical entries has massively grown since then.

10 In 1999, 74 per cent of all pregnant women in the German state of Niedersachsen were diagnosed as being 'at risk'. See Schwarz 2004: 25.

capacity to behave rationally, the term presupposes a calculation of expected benefits and risks, and a decision to follow the path with the greatest possibility of benefit with the least risk' (Ruhl 1999: 96). When pregnancy no longer means expecting a child, but is instead a risk-laden reproductive process, then women are expected to submit to professional guidance. And there they learn that only they are considered responsible if they weigh risks and become managerial decision makers.

GENETIC COUNSELLING

During a woman's pregnancy, prenatal genetic counselling is the most formal and elaborate professional counselling among the various educational services now in demand. From Berlin to San Francisco, the goal and principles of genetic counselling are the same; even the structure of the session and some of the formulations are comparable.[11] What differs is the counsellor's professional background: In North America, a master's degree programme has turned genetic counselling into a growing profession almost completely dominated by women. By contrast, German genetic counsellors are men and women with an MD and a five-year advanced training in molecular biology, genetic epidemiology, chromosome preparation and counselling techniques.

The major clientele of genetic counsellors are pregnant women classified as 'at risk'. As the mesh of prenatal monitoring techniques such as ultrasound and maternal serum screening designed to detect risks becomes tighter, more pregnant women are being labelled 'at risk' and are landing in the genetic counsellor's office. Here a geneticist lectures on different genetic diseases, the probabilities of birth defects, the pregnant woman's location in various risk diagrams and their ominous prognostications about the unborn's future, and lastly, a modern woman's obligation to feel responsible for decision making. The goal of the one-to-two-hour crash course in biostatistics and genetics is not compliance with professionally prescribed conduct, but 'individual assistance in reaching a decision'.[12] Geneticists encourage their clients to make their own decision – after being professionally prepared for it. This decision is a historically unique one: The pregnant woman is being asked in the light of her current risk profile if she wants to keep her pregnancy or to make its continuation conditional upon further test results.

11 See Wertz and Fletcher 1989; Wertz 1995. For genetic counselling in the United States, see the anthropological study of Rapp 1999.
12 Author's translation. The German wording is: 'medizinisch kompetente, individuelle Entscheidungshilfe' (Kommission für Öffentlichkeitsarbeit und ethische Fragen der Gesellschaft für Humangenetik 1996: 129).

The aim of the genetic counselling session has not always been the client's autonomous decision making. Only a few decades ago advice from a geneticist was part of state-sponsored eugenic programmes. The goal of such a session was to prevent the birth of a disabled child. The eugenicist could do nothing more than apply Mendel's rules to the hypothetical pairing of the clients in order to discourage the 'unfit' from having children. Most people had no use for such genetic prognostication, and demand for such consultation was low. This changed drastically in the 1970s when chromosomal checkups from amniotic fluid and the option of terminating pregnancy allowed geneticists to enter the field of prenatal care. Information about the various disabilities and diseases a newborn child might have has since become an everyday part of prenatal care. Genetic counselling was converted from hereditary prognostications into a service industry selling information as indispensable raw material for making informed choices about prenatal test options. It has emerged as a forerunner of the new pedagogical enterprise of educating patients about risk management for their own affairs.

Drawing on my previous study, the remainder of this chapter will return to Ms C. During the genetic education programme, she has learned that she must choose between two risks: on the one hand, the risk of inducing a miscarriage by the puncture and, if she receives a positive test result, the decision whether or not she wishes to terminate the pregnancy; and, on the other hand, if she abstains from testing, the risk of delivering a disabled child and then being accused that it was avoidable. Ms C is stuck in a situation where she can only consent to the lesser evil. Thousands and thousands of women are delivered to the horns of this dilemma every year.[13] They enter the counselling room expecting a child, anxious about its well-being and suspecting that they might have to undergo some additional examinations. And after the session they are burdened with a new task: They have learnt to see their coming child as a risk profile and have been made responsible for its management. Thus, I will analyse how an educational enterprise aiming at responsibility and autonomy surreptitiously turns mothers-to-be into collaborators for the improvement of future populations.

13 There are roughly 50,000 genetic counselling sessions every year in Germany – which also includes non-prenatal genetic counselling – and 70–80,000 foetal karyotyping. See Schmidtke et al 2005. There is widespread consensus among geneticists and physicians that in order to guarantee a client's informed choice any genetic test should be prepared for and followed by genetic counselling. But in fact, many women undergo an amniocentesis without regular genetic counselling. German genetic counsellors mainly deal with special cases, whereas routine prenatal diagnostics is often left to obstetricians. Genetic counselling can be seen as a paradigmatic instance for other less detailed educational sessions such as instruction from an obstetrician or midwife.

The child-to-be as risk profile

During the counselling session, Ms C has been well informed about possibilities, probabilities, and potentialities. The genetic counsellor's expertise enables him to speculate about what might happen. He derives these possibilities from his client's characteristics and traits such as age, test results and ancestry. Thus at the beginning of the counselling session, the counsellor had to interrogate Ms C about her medical history and family. He then constructed a risk profile on the basis of her answers. It was this constructed risk profile that determined the course of the genetic counselling session: It determined Ms C's test options, the information considered necessary for her 'informed decision making', and the counsellor's sense of urgency.

Creating a risk profile

Let me recapitulate the session from the beginning. After having done some formalities, the geneticist starts to ask Ms C a whole series of questions. He wants to know whether she has ever been seriously ill and if this is her first pregnancy. Then he takes her maternity passport and leafs through it, asking in passing if the pregnancy has been normal thus far. The geneticist begins drawing circles and squares on a blank sheet of paper. Slowly he goes through all of Ms C's and her husband's relations, asking about the health of the children and the causes of death for the deceased, searching for potential abnormalities. Anything for which a genetic cause is not professionally ruled out can become a potential threat for the coming child. The early death of a toddler might indicate a genetic disease, miscarriages might be caused by a chromosomal abnormality on the client's or her husband's side, and a disabled relative might have a genetically transmittable disability.

When he has finished sketching the family tree, he draws a bright red ring around the circle, which symbolizes her cousin. 'Otherwise, there is nothing striking', the geneticist concludes after casting one last critical glance at the geometric configuration that is meant to represent Ms C's family. Laying the groundwork for the counselling session, he reads aloud what he has noted down regarding Ms C's profile of distinguishing features: 36 years old, first pregnancy in the 14th week, cousin on the maternal side with a mental disability of unknown origin. This profile is what strikes him as relevant for the rest of the counselling session. From each of these features he then deduces a risk. This risk is nothing more than a probabilistic characteristic of a statistical totality into which the geneticist has placed the woman on the basis of her respective features. Genetic counsellors, however, present this abstract variable as a personal threat; they speak of a 'personal risk' and equate this risk with 'insecurity'.

Since the cause of the disability of Ms C's cousin is unknown, there is not much the counsellor can say about it. By questioning Ms C about his appearance, he tries to figure out if it is a case of Down's syndrome. The fact that the cousin has two healthy siblings calms the expert down, and finally he convinces her to try to ask her relatives – with whom she has lost touch – about any clinical documentation. Most congenital disorders are of unknown origin, he clarifies. But the counselling session has not yet come to an end; on the contrary: the geneticist now reels off his whole counselling programme. Ms C learns that a potential mental disability is only one misfortune among innumerable others that she must reckon with. In the logic of risk, everything is possible as long as it has not been ruled out. Therefore, pregnant women must be informed about all the birth defects ever registered and are to consider them as 'risks' to their own children.

From her positive pregnancy test, the counsellor deduces a 'basic risk'. From his records, he pulls out an illustration showing a white circle with a thin black slice in it. 'Look here,' he says, 'every woman has this so-called basic risk, three to five per cent, that the child might have a congenital disorder.' Then he lists everything a child might be born with: cleft palate, heart defect, mental disability. This risk applies to all pregnant women without exception, he states, and therefore also to Ms C. It also includes genetic diseases which might unexpectedly pop up in one generation. 'It might strike anybody, and that's why it is part of the basic risk,' he helpfully notes.

Routine prenatal testing cannot foresee most congenital disorders. Normally Down's syndrome can be predicted, and that's why the child with the slanted eyes represents the mental retardation that could have been avoided (Marteau and Drake 1995). Hence education about the cytological errors leading to Trisomy 21 and the gloomy prospect of perpetual motherhood is an obligatory chapter of prenatal education. The geneticist shows Ms C a steeply rising risk curve and asks again for her age. He sets the odds at 1:287. This number measures the frequency of children being born with Down's syndrome in the statistical cohort of women aged 36. What can that mean to a pregnant woman who is expecting her first baby?

As cognitive psychologist Gerd Gigerenzer has shown, probabilities are misunderstood by most people, no matter whether they are experts or clients. A weather forecast of 30 per cent chance of rain, for example, is interpreted in bizarre ways (Gigerenzer 2002: 33–34). What it really means is that a meteorologist is the creator of a fictitious tomorrow, which were it to occur a hundred times, would be a rainy day on 30 of them. But to the only real tomorrow that exists, risk is irrelevant. Ms C, however, is concerned about her only real tomorrow, about her child to come. The various risks that have been pinned on her do not add an iota to her knowledge about herself or her unborn child. All the counsellor could do was explain what might happen and put this 'might' in statistical terms. But his colloquial formulations, statements such as 'your risk' and the equation of risk with insecurity or even danger lend the appearance of concreteness to an abstract frequency. The statistical probability boils down to a personal threat, an alleged tangible reality.

The impact of 'genetic risks'

The possible disasters evoked by the counsellor's talk about risk do not threaten Ms C from somewhere outside her, but from within herself. In contrast to environmental or lifestyle risks which are understood as hazards from outside, doctor-attributed risks indicate not only potential disasters in the future, but also bodily 'disorder in the present' (Kavanagh and Broom 1998: 442). As Kavanagh and Broom (1998) have shown with the example of the PAP smear test, risk invites the patient to imagine a threat that is already present within herself. 'Embodied' or 'corporeal risks' transform a healthy person into an ailing patient who considers herself on the verge of a threatening disease. This pathogenic effect of doctor-attested risk is even more powerful when it comes to genetics. In the popular scientific imagination, genes crop up as causes for one's bodily features and personal peculiarities, be it your sibling's blue eyes and blond hair, your daughter's nail-biting habit and your uncle's boozing.[14] Thus, connecting a risk to such genes suggests that the cause of future disaster already lurks in one's own body.

When the counsellor informs Ms C about the various risks she faces as a pregnant woman, he explains to her that genetic diseases not only run in the family, but might also pop up unexpectedly. We all have 'one to ten such recessive genes inside us,' says the counsellor.[15] And suddenly, in the next generation, they might trigger a disease. Ms C learns that she has little agents inside her which might cause suffering and affliction to her offspring. Her child's potential disease might already be pre-programmed inside her. Surprisingly, the counsellor does not explain how she should imagine such a gene. The basic concept of genetics, the gene, is hardly ever explained in genetic counselling sessions. Instead, genetic counsellors univocally equate genes with the antiquated term 'hereditary factors' (German: Erbanlagen), invoking everyday connotations for the sake of plausibility. In the following session when the counsellor explains to his client the causes for cystic fibrosis, she invokes a simple if-then relationship between gene and disease:

> C(ounselor): And there is a gene on chromosome 7. If you have this gene once, you're healthy yourself, it doesn't bother you. Only if the child inherits two mutated genes from father and mother, then the child is sick.

The gene appears as a hidden agent determining one's fate. Tomorrow's disasters seem to be pre-programmed into DNA. But in fact, just like attesting a

---

14 Here I refer to interviews conducted for a research project on the colloquial meaning of the word 'gene' (title: 'Das Alltag-Gen') on which I collaborated with Barbara Duden.

15 German wording: 'Obwohl natürlich auch eins bis zu zehn solcher rezessiver Gene hat haben wir alle in uns, wird geschätzt, und man wird sie nicht alle durchchecken können. Und: Treffen kann uns alle mal was.'

'risk', attributing a 'gene for' means nothing else than placing the testee into a statistical cohort in which the frequency of certain events is higher than average. Even two of the so-called 'severe mutations', once considered the definite cause for cystic fibrosis, do not necessarily lead to the disease (The Cystic Fibrosis Genotype-Phenotype Consortium 1993). But popular scientific gene talk about 'genes which cause diseases' and 'genes for' foster the myth that a genetic test reveals a bodily predisposition or even a pre-programmed fate. 'Genetically caused' seems to be a statement about something which already exists, whereas it is only a shorthand for a probabilistic relation.

The myth of the causal power of genes is reinforced by formulations such as 'gene defect' and 'gene for'. These catchy notions intimate causal factors whereas they are only shorthand for the correlation between a DNA sequence and appearance, between genotype and phenotype (Lewontin 1992; Hubbard and Wald 1993). Except for a few cases, such as Huntington's Chorea where the genetic variation correlates almost 100 per cent with the disease in question, the geneticist can only deduce a probability from a genetic test result.[16] But 'gene talk', that is, the misleading talk about 'genes for', hides the statistical nature of genetic prognostication. Therefore, the diagnosis 'gene for' or 'gene defect' transforms calculated probabilities into physical defects. One's own body becomes the major threat to one's own health.

Risk transforms a probabilistic future into a present threat that must be guarded against. It mobilizes us to act today based on a fictitious tomorrow created by experts. The fullness of the present atrophies under the shadow of a made-up future. With the 'gene for', however, the distinction between what is and what might be collapses completely. Future possibilities turn into present disorders. This way the pregnant woman is made into a resource for risk management; she is turned into a compatible subject of the probabilistic administration of populations.

The expectant mother as manager of a foetal risk profile

My study on genetic counselling (Samerski 2002) focuses on the symbolic effect of the counselling procedure. I did not conduct interviews after the sessions and therefore I do not know what women actually took home in each concrete case. From their faces I could sometimes infer that they were at a loss when they heard about Mendel's rules and probability distributions. But no matter what happened with each woman after she left the clinic: in each of the sessions which I observed, I witnessed a fundamental reinterpretation of

---

16   In her article on the pitfalls of genetic testing, the geneticist Ruth Hubbard gives the example of 'Retinis pigmentosa,' a so-called hereditary disease which affects the retina: Two siblings share the alleged 'gene for' – one is almost blind, another is a truck driver working at night (Hubbard and Lewontin 1996).

the client's situation, if not of her very being. By informing their client about chromosomal aberrations, genetic risks, and the probabilities of birth defects, geneticists reinterpret her pregnancy as a developmental process with different probable outcomes. They anticipate what might happen in terms of probabilities and thereby transform their client's hope for a child into a state of risk that demands monitoring and decision making.

Clients as decision makers

Genetic counsellors rightly reject the accusation that they pressure their clients to undergo tests. The human geneticist Jörg Schmidtke 1995 made it very clear that it is not possible for physicians to set a medical indication for prenatal diagnosis: first of all, because there is no cure. In the event of a positive test result, the woman would have to decide between delivering an 'avoidable' child and terminating the pregnancy; second, because they cannot base advice on risk. Genetic counsellors quickly back off when clients ask them to interpret the risk figures pinned on them. At best, experts insert a sub-clause about statistics in general such as: 'this is only statistics', or 'I mean, it's true . . . In individual cases, when it's you who is affected, then it's one hundred percent for you'. One counsellor explicitly tells his client to see rhyme and reason in the abstract number. After informing her that her risk of delivering a child with Down's syndrome is 1 per cent, he says:

C: This is (–), well, first of all, it's just a number

W(oman): Uh huh (short laugh)

C: And it can be regarded as high or low. This is an entirely personal assessment and rightly so. Yes, some will say it is fortunately low, and another family will say and be just as justified (–) um, that is more than what we can accept. It can be viewed quite differently.

In fact, the principle of 'non-directiveness', celebrated as client-centred and progressive, displays the impossibility of making sense of 'personal risk'. Statistical numbers cannot say anything meaningful about a pregnant woman and her unborn child.[17] Thus, doctors cannot really recommend anything to the new class of 'at risk' patients. If they do not want to act as eugenicists improving the quality of the population or as health economists cutting down the costs of nursing the unfit, they cannot derive a professional 'ought'

---

17 As empirical studies on 'risk perception' and 'risk communication' have shown, the supposed decision makers struggle hard to make sense of numbers that in principle are meaningless for individuals (Kavanagh and Broom 1998; Lippman-Hand and Fraser 1979; Rapp 1999; Zuuren *et al* 1997).

from statistical calculations. In contrast to diagnosis, the major pillar of traditional medical practice, the attribution of risks does not indicate any remedy or treatment. The person diagnosed with a risk is fit as a fiddle; the doctor can only speculate about what *might* happen.

Genetic counselling reveals a fundamental shift in the doctor–patient relationship. For decades, it had been common practice for the 'demigods in white' to prescribe the course of action they considered appropriate according to their professional standards. The patient was expected to comply with the professional's decision. Today, however, doctors appeal to their patient's autonomy. They go through the list of the various examination possibilities, detailing their respective side effects and potential negative after-effects; warn of the possibility of false-positive and false-negative results; insert a sub-clause fundamentally casting doubt on the very point of such examinations; and then leave it up to the woman to select one of the risk-laden options. When medicine turns into the management of risk profiles, professionals pass the buck to their clients. Lacking a valid professional 'ought', the client's will and her preferences become the only legitimate driving force. In the face of risk, the old rule 'doctor knows best' is replaced by the 'patients decide best'.

The decision trap

Without any direct force or pressure, Ms C has been made a decision maker in the prenatal service system. 'Either you do it or you don't; at some point the decision has to be made', as another counsellor put it concisely. Genetic counsellors do not care what their clients decide; what matters to them is that they make an informed choice. Counsellors thus offer the option not merely of taking advantage of prenatal tests, but also of abstaining from them. In genetic counselling the possibility of undergoing amniocentesis and perhaps of aborting the foetus stand as equally weighted alternatives to what until now had not required any decision of the pregnant woman at all: that of bringing her child into the world with no ifs, ands, or buts. In the same way the geneticist calculates the risks a test may involve, he also calculates in advance the risks Ms C exposes herself to should she choose *not* to undergo amniocentesis. In doing so, the counsellor models her future in such a way that any possible outcome can be seen as a consequence of her decision. The visual representation of the decision-making model described here is the decision tree: There are at least two options to choose from, and both have many potential outcomes. This model presents the pregnant woman with a trap: the 'decision trap'.[18] Be it a miscarriage as a result of the amniocentesis

18 There is a whole series of studies analysing the so-called reproductive decision in terms of decision-making theory – that is, according to a model that is supposed to make management decisions calculable, see Frets 1990. This original statistical model of decision making is now

or a child with Down's syndrome – all at once she is responsible even for things that she cannot influence. Simply being pregnant, as unquestionable as that could be a generation or two ago, is no longer possible. The 'decision trap' turns the state of 'expectation' into a 'self-determined decision' to accept the risks of giving birth to a disabled child. Another counsellor explicitly tells his client that nowadays a woman has only herself to blame if she simply gives in to fate. While he does not compel her to take the test, he makes it clear that she should know what she is doing if she chooses not to do so. After informing her of her age-related risk of giving birth to a child with Down's syndrome, he states blankly: 'In any event you know, and if you don't want to simply bow down to fate, you don't have to.'

The client's informed and free choice has been widely accepted as a bulwark against expert and state control. More than that: in market societies, 'individual choice' is considered the epitome of freedom and autonomy. No matter whether vocation, holiday trip, religious practice, girlfriend, lifestyle, or medical treatment – those considered to be self-empowered today are those who can choose what they want in every situation in life. The 'unleashing' from traditional bonds and the choice between a growing number of options is understood as an increase of freedom. At best, this new 'freedom' is discussed as 'ambivalent' because it imposes new 'responsibilities' on the individual (Beck and Beck-Gernsheim 1994; Beck-Gernsheim 1995). This idea of freedom and autonomy, on the one hand, and new individual hazards and responsibilities, on the other hand, underlies most of the literature on the choices demanded by prenatal diagnostics (Gregg 1993; Ruhl 1999). What has been a blind spot so far is the new mentality demanded by these new decisions. In fact, the decision the risk-classified woman has to make resembles an investment decision when speculating on the stock market: she must choose among pre-selected options and be prepared to accept the associated risks.

The kind of decisions taught in genetic counselling sessions stipulate a mentality which until the latter half of the 20th century had been restricted to insurance and business administration. Until then, 'to decide' in the colloquial sense did not mean weighing risks and benefits and choosing the most profitable option. Both the German 'entscheiden' and the English 'to decide' have been used as legal terms and refer to the settlement of a quarrel or the solution of a question. Dictionaries do not list 'choice' as a synonym for 'decision', but 'conclusion' and 'determination'.[19] Then, in the 1970s, reference

propagated as a set of instructions on how decisions in general are supposed to be made, see Hammond *et al* 1999. Professional decision-making aids such as genetic counselling are shaped by this new understanding of decision making. See Samerski 2002.

19 See 'decision' and 'decide' in the Oxford English Dictionary (Oxford 1989) and in The American Heritage Dictionary of the English Language (Boston 1992) as well as 'Entscheidung' and 'entscheiden' in the Deutsches Wörterbuch von Jacob und Wilhelm Grimm

books testify to a striking shift in the semantics of the term. 'Decision' is suddenly explained as a 'choice between options' and detailed entries about 'decision theory' appear which explain decision as the mathematically modelled strategy for the selection of options with maximal expected utility.[20] 'Decision' became the product of applying management techniques.

Genetic counselling can be understood as a ritual which introduces pregnant women to this managerial rationality. They are asked to anticipate their coming child in terms of a distribution of possible outcomes and follow the rationale of decision theory for reducing risks and making the optimal choice. In the following session, the counsellor explicitly invites the woman, who is accompanied by her husband, to subject her pregnancy to a risk-benefit analysis. After he has told them about her risk for having a child with Down's syndrome and held it up against the risk of inducing miscarriage through amniocentesis, he says:

> C: I wanted to make it clear just now that it is always the job of the parents to weigh them. These two risks.
>
> M(an): Hmm.
>
> C: You are in no way obliged . . . to undergo this test. Because it's . . . the parents who decide, the mother . . .
>
> M: Hmm.
>
> C: . . . in particular.

Many women agonize over the decision they are expected to make. In fact, a group of German medical sociologists titled their empirical study on the decision of pregnant women for an amniocentesis 'An impossible decision' (Friedrich *et al* 1998). These women are being asked to follow an abstract rationale which in the end has real and possibly unbearable consequences. She 'enters into a rational seeking of information and choices and finds herself trapped in a nightmare', as the sociologist Barbara Katz Rothman put it poignantly (Rothman 1987: 181).

(Leipzig 1854–1954), Deutsches Wörterbuch of Lutz Mackensen (München 1967 and 1986) and Deutsches Wörterbuch of Hermann Paul (Tübingen 1992).

20 See the successive editions of Der Grosse Brockhaus (e.g. Wiesbaden 1977–1979) and Meyers Enzyklopädisches Lexikon (Mannheim 1971–1979).

CONCLUSION: EDUCATION IN RISK MANAGEMENT AS A NEW SOCIAL TECHNIQUE

Today every conceivable life situation presents a potential need for counselling, from procreation and birth to death and grief. Professional guidance has advanced in the past 50 years to become one of the most important social technologies. Freedom, choice and autonomy have been so redefined that they require scientific input and guidance services to be appropriately exercised. As the cognitive psychologist Gerd Gigerenzer (2002) declared, to be a guide in the contemporary world, sound judgement needs updating. In a technogene world flooded by chances and risks, he says, professional education in statistics is not only a must for survival, but also the key to understanding that probability is the foundation of the world we live in. Enlightened rational human beings have to realize that sensorial certainty is an illusion produced by evolution. Thus they must learn the enlightened manner of weighing benefits and risks.

Under the banner of facilitating 'responsibility' and 'autonomy,' professional power encroaches on deliberation and decision. In contrast to the 'tyranny of experts' (Liebermann 1970), when paternalistic professionals expected compliance from their clients, the goal of teaching decision making is not obedience, but far more subtle, risk-guided self-management. Prenatal genetic counselling is a telling example of this new kind of educational enterprise. It explicitly facilitates an 'informed choice' on the basis of risks where traditionally there had been good hope, but no decision, namely in the advanced stages of pregnancy.

Feminist scholars have generally seen this new demand for decision making as a success in the struggle for emancipation. They honour 'choice' and 'reproductive freedom' as highly desirable values and welcome professional information and access to service options as prerequisites for their realization. My analysis of genetic counselling, however, shows that 'taught decision making' neither increases a woman's autonomy, nor does it bring her closer to her desire: a healthy or at least a 'normal' child.[21] Information on risks and test options assume that there is something to know about the unborn and something to do about its future health. It fosters the myth that the outcome of a pregnancy depends on the pregnant woman's responsible decision making. 'Risk talk, far from limiting or rationalising guilt, actually leads to a proliferation of guilt by assuming responsibility everywhere' (Ruhl 1999: 106). The pregnant woman is invited to take responsibility for a future that can be statistically counted on but is still unknown. This opens up a

---

21 Interviews show that women do not strive for 'perfect' babies, but just want their children to be 'normal'. See Press *et al* 1998.

completely new possibility of victim blaming. No matter what the client has decided, it is always her who made the choice – and took the risk.

By informing the pregnant client about calculable risks, avoidable disabilities, and prenatal test options, the counsellor reframes the client's hope-filled pregnancy. The coming child is transformed into a calculable risk profile that can come into existence only if the woman takes the responsibility for its makeup. This radically changes what it means to become a mother. What is at stake here is not only the client's sanity, but also her care for the child growing within her. The counselled woman is expecting a baby, a 'you' that is coming into existence. As her belly grows, she slowly turns toward the unknown which will become her dearest one. A situation of fundamental cultural meaning has become the gateway for the scientific reinterpretation of 'I' and 'you'. An intimate and particular gendered experience is destroyed by the imputation of technogenous constructs and managerial values. In genetic counselling, a woman's desire to care for her coming child is turned into the duty to weigh risks and benefits, to treat it as a faceless member of statistical totalities.

REFERENCES

Beck, Ulrich and Beck-Gernsheim, Elisabeth (1994) *Riskante Freiheiten. Individualisierung in modernen Gesellschaften*, Frankfurt a.M.
Beck-Gernsheim, Elisabeth (1995) *Welche Gesundheit wollen wir?*, Frankfurt a.M.
Duden, Barbara (1993). *Disembodying Women: Perspectives on Pregnancy and the Unborn*, Cambridge, MA.
Duden, Barbara (1998). 'Die Ungeborenen. Vom Untergang der Geburt im späten 20. Jahrhundert', in Jürgen Schlumbohm, Barbara Duden, Jacques Gélis and Patrice Veit (eds) *Rituale der Geburt. Eine Kulturgeschichte*, München, 149–168.
Duden, Barbara (2002) *Die Gene im Kopf – der Fötus im Bauch*, Hannover.
Duden, Barbara, Schlumbohm, Jürgen, and Veit, Patrice (2002). 'Zwischen "wahrem Wissen" und Prophetie: Konzeptionen des Ungeborenen' in Barbara Duden, Jürgen Schlumbohm and Patrice Veit (eds) *Geschichte des Ungeborenen: Zur Erfahrungs- und Wissenschaftsgeschichte der Schwangerschaft, 17.–20.Jahrhundert*. Göttingen.
Ellul, Jacques (1964) *The Technological Society*, New York.
Ewald, François (1991) 'Insurance and Risk' in G. Burchell, C. Gordon and P. Miller (eds) *The Foucault Effect. Studies in Governmentality*. Chicago, 197–210.
Ewald, François (1993) *Der Vorsorgestaat*, Frankfurt a.M.
Freidson, Eliot (1970) *Profession of Medicine: A Study of the Sociology of Applied Knowledge*, New York.
Frets, P. G. (1990) *The Reproductive Decision After Genetic Counselling*, Rotterdam.
Friedrich, Hannes, Henze, Karl H., and Stemann-Acheampong, Susanne (1998) *Eine unmögliche Entscheidung. Pränataldiagnostik: Ihre psychosozialen Voraussetzungen und Folgen*, Berlin.
Gifford, S. (1986) 'The meaning of lumps; a case study of the ambiguities of risk' in C. R. Janes, R. Stall and S.M. Gifford (eds) *Anthropology and Epidemiology: Interdisciplinary Approaches to the Study of Health and Disease*, Dodrecht, 213–246.

Gigerenzer, Gerd (2002) *Calculated Risks. How to know when numbers deceive you*, New York.

Gigerenzer, Gerd, Swijtink, Zeno, Porter, Theodor, Daston, Lorraine, Beatty, John, and Krüger, Lorenz (1989) *The Empire of Chance. How Probability Changed Science and Everyday Life*, New York.

Gregg, Robin (1993) ' "Choice" as a double-edged sword: information, guilt and mother-blaming in a high-tech age' in *Women & Health* 20(3), 53–73.

Hacking, Ian (1990) *The Taming of Chance*, Cambridge.

Hammond, John S., Keeney, Ralph L., and Raiffa, Howard (1999) *Smart Choices. A Practical Guide to Making Better Decisions*, Boston.

Hubbard, Ruth and Lewontin, Richard C. (1996) 'Pitfalls of Genetic Testing' in *New England Journal of Medicine* 334(18), 1192–1194.

Hubbard, Ruth and Wald, Elijah (1993) *Exploding the Gene Myth. How Genetic Information is Produced and Manipulated by Scientists, Physicians, Employers, Insurance Companies, Educators, and Law Enforcers*, Boston.

Illich, Ivan (1976) *Limits to Medicine. Medical Nemesis: The Expropriation of Health*, London.

Kaufert, Patricia and O'Neil, John (1993) 'Analysis of a Dialogue on Risks in Childbirth. Clinicians, Epidemiologists, and Inuit Women' in M. Lock and S. Lindenbaum (eds) *Knowledge, Power and Practice: the Anthropology of Medicine and Everyday Life*, Berkeley, 32–54.

Kavanagh, A. M. and Broom, D. H. (1998) 'Embodied Risk: My Body, Myself?' in *Social Science and Medicine* 46, 437–444.

Kommission für Öffentlichkeitsarbeit und ethische Fragen der Gesellschaft für Humangenetik e.V.(1996) 'Positionspapier' in *Medizinische Genetik* 8: 125–131.

Lewontin, Richard (1992) 'Genotype and Phenotype' in: Elisabeth A. Lloyd and Evelyn Fox Keller (eds) *Keywords in Evolutionary Biology*, Cambridge, Mass., 137–144.

Liebermann, Jethro K. (1970) *The Tyranny of the Experts. How Professionals are Closing the Open Society*, New York.

Lippman-Hand, A. and Fraser, F. C. (1979) 'Genetic Counselling: The Postcounselling Period: I. Parent's Perception of Uncertainty' in *American Journal of Medical Genetics* 4, 51–71.

Marteau, Theresa M. and Drake, Harriet (1995) 'Attributions for Disability: The Influence of Genetic Screening' in *Social Science and Medicine* 40(8), 1227–1132.

Novas, Carlos and Rose, Nikolas (2000) 'Genetic Risk and the Birth of the Somatic Individual' in *Economy and Society* 29(4), 485–513.

Press, Nancy A., Browner, Carole H., Tran, Diem, Morton, Christine, and Le Master, Barbara (1998) 'Provisional Normalcy and "Perfect Babies": Pregnant Women's Attitudes Toward Disability in the Context of Prenatal Testing' in Sarah Franklin and Helena Ragoné (eds) *Reproducing Reproduction. Kinship, Power and Technological Innovation*, Philadelphia, 46–65.

Rapp, Rayna (1999) *Testing Women, Testing the Fetus. The Social Impact of Amniocentesis in America*, New York.

Rothman, Barbara Katz (1987) *The Tentative Pregnancy. Prenatal Diagnosis and the Future of Motherhood*, New York.

Ruhl, Lealle (1999) 'Liberal Governance and Prenatal Care: Risk and Regulation in Pregnancy' in *Economy and Society* 28(1), 95–117.

Samerski, Silja (2002) *Die verrechnete Hoffnung. Von der selbstbestimmten Entscheidung durch genetische Beratung*, Münster.

Schmidtke, Jörg (1995) 'Die Indikationen zur Pränataldiagnostik müssen neu begründet werden' in *Medizinische Genetik* 1, 49–52.

Schmidtke, Jörg, Pabst, Brigitte, and Nippert, Irmgard (2005) 'DNA-based genetic testing is rising steeply in a national health care system with open access to services: a survey of genetic test use in Germany, 1996–2002' in *Genetic Testing* 9(1), 80–84.

Schwarz, Clarissa M. Schücking Beate (2004) 'Adieu, normale Geburt? Ergebnisse eines Forschungsprojektes' in *Dr.med. Mabuse* 148 (März/April), 22–25.

The Cystic Fibrosis Genotype-Phenotype Consortium (1993) 'Correlation Between Genotype and Phenotype in Patients with Cystic Fibrosis' in *The New England Journal of Medicine* 329(18), 1308–1313.

Weir, Lorna (1996) 'Recent developments in the government of pregnancy' in *Economy and Society* 25(3), 372–392.

Wertz, Dorothy C. (1995) *Ethische Ansichten europäischer und nicht europäischer Genetiker; Ergebnisse einer internationale Umfrage*, Berlin.

Wertz, Dorothy C. and Fletcher, John C. (1989) *Ethics and Human Genetics. A Cross-Cultural Perspective*, Berlin.

Weymayr, Christian and Koch, Klaus (2003) *Mythos Krebsvorsorge. Schaden und Nutzen der Früherkennung*, Frankfurt a.M.

Zuuren, F. J. van, Schie, E. C. M. van, and Baaren, N. K. van (1997) 'Uncertainty in the Information Provided During Genetic Counselling' in *Patient Education and Counselling* 32, 129–139.

Chapter 4

Risk, edgework, and masculinities

Stephen Lyng and Rick Matthews *

One of the most provocative assertions made by risk society theorists is the claim that the traditional categories of identity and location within the contemporary social order – designations based on gender, kinship, class, race, etc. – no longer carry substantial meaning and significance. At work in the risk society are fundamental changes in consciousness and agency, along with institutional rearrangements, which align with the growth of environmental, political and economic risks on a global scale. Risk society theorists argue that risk consciousness and 'institutionalized individualism' are displacing social and cultural differentiations tied to class, race and gender (Beck and Beck-Gernsheim 2002).

Our chapter provides a partial assessment of this thesis by considering the implications of expanding risk consciousness and action for contemporary expressions of gender and gender relations. Of all of the role patterns studied by sociologists, gender would seem to be the best predictor of risk-taking behaviour. Academic researchers and laypersons alike have traditionally perceived inherent gender differences in risk orientation, seeing males predisposed to risk taking and females averse to such behaviour. This perception has been sustained in part by clear evidence of male over-representation in certain kinds of risk-taking activities, such as high-risk sports and occupations, crime and health-related risk behaviours. However, the assumed gender difference in risk-taking propensity has been called into question recently by researchers who have pointed to the routine risks of criminal victimization faced by women in everyday life (Walklate 1997), risk-taking activities specifically dominated by females (e.g., prostitution, see Miller 1986; 1991), and evidence of gender differences in how risks are *managed* but not necessarily in risk-taking inclination (Lois 2005). Thus, the available data on risk practices suggest that males and females may not differ in their predilections to risk taking, but they may be attracted to different types of risk behaviour and may deal with risks in gender-specific ways. If risk consciousness and action are

---

* Carthage College

on the rise in the risk society, it is possible that gender is being 'historically disrupted' (Connell 1995) and substantially reconfigured in this new context.

In this chapter, we explore the relationship between risk agency and gender by focusing on types of risk activities dominated by men. A close examination of the ethnographic data on leisure and occupational risk taking recently conceptualised as 'edgework' (Lyng and Snow 1986; Lyng 1990; 1993; 1998; 2005; Lois 1999; Ferrell *et al* 2001; Holyfield 1997; 1999; 2005; O'Malley and Mugford 1994) reveals that participation in edgework allows men to construct a new form of masculinity, one that is well suited to the political and economic logic of the risk society.

RISK CONSCIOUSNESS AND ACTION IN THE RISK SOCIETY

When the risk society model was first introduced to English-speaking audiences in the early 1990s, the principal theoretical goal was to make sense of structural changes that have been underway in Western societies for two centuries. The publication of the English edition of Ulrich Beck's germinal book *The Risk Society* (1992) introduced a large number of social scientists to a unique vision of immanent change in modern society. Beck (1999) identifies a key cultural change in Western societies that opened the door to deliberate risk taking by major public and private institutions and organizations. With the cultural diffusion of the notion of 'calculable risks', the uncertain and potentially harmful consequences of human decisions were increasingly subjected to formal risk analysis. Consequently, most of the dangers we now face derive from *human* products and practices with what are deemed to be low-probability 'side-effects' presumably outweighed by anticipated benefits. However, as Beck (2002: 3) points out, '[t]he modern world increases the worlds of difference between the language of calculable risks in which we think and act and the world of non-calculable uncertainty that we create with the same speed of its technological developments'.

Beck uncovers one of the great paradoxes of our time: With the advance of science and the expansion of technological and productive capacities, the risks of mass disasters of our own making increase dramatically, with heightened threats of ecological catastrophes, global economic crises and attacks by transnational terrorist networks (Beck 2002: 5). Modern societies 'turn back on themselves', leading to escalating risks of human-made disasters and the increasing erosion of core social institutions. At the centre of this modernization process is a form of human intentionality that is blind to its own unpredictable outcomes. As Scott Lash (2003: 51) notes:

> Science and industry, for all their claims to objectivity, and to being somehow objective and outside of the world, are indeed in the world with

their proper interest-constituted intentionality. The problem here . . . is that what is intended leads to the most extraordinary unintendedness, to side-effects, to unintended consequences.

While Beck and his colleagues call attention to the dangerous unintended consequences of deliberate risk taking at the institutional and organizational levels, it is also important to acknowledge the dangers of increased risk taking by individuals. By many different measures, individuals engage in more risk behaviour today than in any other time in the post-war period. This pattern can be traced in part to the influence of neoliberal political discourse and policies that have shifted responsibility for dealing with adverse life events (unemployment, health crisis, old age, etc.) from collectivities to individuals. The rise of neoliberalism has been incorporated into more recent presentations of the risk society perspective (Beck 1999), but risk society theorists have largely ignored what may be the most obvious form of individual-level risk taking. We refer to voluntary risk-taking activities – high-risk or 'extreme' sports, dangerous occupations, certain criminal activities, risky interpersonal relations and the like – pursued as intrinsically rewarding endeavours and not as means to other desired goals (see Simon 2002; 2005).

These emerging patterns of voluntary risk taking, cutting across many sectors of contemporary social life, have recently generated a line of inquiry focused on the concept of 'edgework'. The post-war period has been a time of expanding opportunities for risk taking: consider the explosive growth in new leisure risk-taking activities such as skydiving, BASE jumping,[1] hang gliding, cliff climbing, white water rafting and similar high-risk pursuits recently designated as 'extreme sports'; the growing public interest in and media attention to high-risk occupations such as police work, firefighting, emergency medical work, search and rescue services, combat soldiering, test piloting; and increasing rates of violent street crime, illicit drug use and promiscuous sexual practices.[2] The increasing popularity of voluntary risk-taking practices in recent decades raises an obvious question – why would any of the participants in these activities voluntarily place themselves in circumstances that hold a high risk for serious injury or death? This core question initially inspired the development of the edgework model of voluntary risk taking, to which we now turn.

1 BASE is an acronym for Buildings (skyscrapers, grain silos), Antennas (television and radio towers), Spans (bridges, trestles), or Earth (cliffs, outcroppings), which designate the range of departure points for clandestine parachute jumps by individuals and small groups. BASE jumping is currently an illegal activity in the US (see Ferrell et al 2001).
2 Rates of street crime, illicit drug use and promiscuous sexual practices have increased over the long term (post-war period) in Western societies, although short-term rates have been more variable.

VOLUNTARY RISK TAKING AS EDGEWORK

In seeking to explain contemporary forms of voluntary risk taking, Lyng (1990) addressed this problem from a theoretical standpoint not previously employed in the study of risk-taking behaviour. Before the 1990s, risk research was dominated by two general approaches: (1) economic models of rational actors making cost/benefit calculations, and (2) psychological theories of intrinsic motivations or personality predispositions to risk taking (see Lyng 1990: 853–854). These approaches tended to explain voluntary risk taking either in terms of abstract categories of 'risks' and 'rewards' or through the quantitative analysis of survey data, psychological scales and related measures of attitudes and sentiments (see Heimer 1988).

Noticeably absent in risk studies was research focusing on two critical dimensions of all risk-taking activities – the actor's immediate experience in negotiating high-risk situations and the broader social context in which this experience emerges. Explaining risk taking in terms of these two dimensions directs attention to the general human motivations involved in risk behaviour, thereby avoiding the tautological reasoning involved in positing a 'tendency to take risks' (i.e., a personality predisposition or intrinsic motivation) as the cause of risk-taking behaviour. It also avoids the equally troublesome concern in rational choice theory with vaguely defined 'rewards' measured against 'costs'. In choosing to emphasize the lived experience of risk taking as revealed in subjects' collectively constructed accounts, we can approach the motivations for this behaviour as a topic of empirical discovery. This theoretical and methodological approach, rooted in phenomenological theory and the participant observation method, treats motivation as an emergent phenomenon situated in pragmatic actions of social actors dealing with challenging and emotionally charged experiences (Lyng 1990; Wacquant 1995; Holyfield 1997; Lois 1999; Ferrell et al 2001, see also Lyng 2005).

Thus, the resulting perspective on risk behaviour inverts the traditional research paradigm in this field: instead of seeing risk taking compelled by an internal need to satisfy urges or attain rewards, the edgework model views risk takers being drawn into these activities by the seductive power of the experience. This seductive power derives from the attraction of a clear and vitally consequential boundary line – an 'edge', as it were – which must be negotiated by the individual risk taker. In the purest expression of edgework, one 'negotiates' the edge by striving to get as close to it as possible without actually crossing it. This usually means managing situations that involve a high risk of death or serious injury, although the edge can assume many different forms (consciousness versus unconsciousness, sanity versus insanity, control versus chaos, etc.).

The ethnographic and participant observational data reveal common experiential patterns that characterize a wide range of edgework activities. In most forms of edgework, participants report time passing either much faster or slower than normal and spatial boundaries collapsing as they approach the edge. For example, rock climbers often describe lengthy periods of time scaling cliffs (sometimes requiring many hours) as seeming to last only a few minutes, while BASE jumpers experience several seconds of freefall from a skyscraper or bridge as lasting an eternity. Similarly, risk takers who conduct edgework with various forms of technology (racing cars or motorcycles, high performance aeroplanes, surgical tools, etc.) commonly describe the apparent dissolution of boundaries between themselves and the technologies under their control, giving them a sense of 'being one with their machines'.

These powerful sensations are accompanied by other strong feelings and emotions. The alterations in the perception of time and space and feelings of mental control over environmental objects lend a 'hyperreal' quality to edgework activities, producing a sense of the experience as deeply authentic and ineffable. Edgework also generates intense emotions that must be managed. Obviously, fear must be overcome, particularly the type of fear that produces a paralysis of action or what edgeworkers often refer to as 'brain lock'. However, the most important challenge in dealing with fear is not necessarily to *overcome* it but to *convert* it into something that is sensually appealing. This is usually achieved by edgeworkers striving for a Zen-like acceptance of fear, in which one remains confident of one's ability to act skilfully and competently even when shaking with fearful apprehension. Succeeding in this effort allows edgeworkers to combine intense bodily arousal with a focused attention and creative responses to the unfolding circumstances of a high-risk situation. This mix of elements very likely explains why most edgeworkers claim that being on the edge is when they feel most alive.

The management of fear and its transformation into corporeal stimulation are associated with other foreground features that contribute to the attractions of the edge. One consequence of edgeworkers' abilities to manage fear is a sense of omnipotence and control. Data collected on a wide range of different high-risk sports and occupations reveal that edgeworkers often see themselves as members of an elite group who possess special powers of control over chaotic situations. They believe that the power to control seemingly uncontrollable circumstances is innately determined, deriving from a basic 'survival skill' that distinguishes true edgeworkers from those who are attracted to risk taking but lack the 'right stuff' (Wolfe 1979) to conduct it successfully.

Possessing these strong feelings of confidence bordering on omnipotence, participants experience an exaggerated sense of self at the edge, which they often describe as their authentic or 'true' self. These feelings of self-determination are also associated with a fully *embodied* sense of self (see Wacquant 1995; Lyng 2004). Although all human action is fundamentally embodied in nature (Frank 1995; Lyng and Franks 2002), the body's role in managing the challenges of risky circumstances is forefronted in the accounts of edgeworkers. These risk takers often refer to the inherent 'wisdom' of their bodies in responding appropriately, immediately and automatically in life-and-death conditions. They regard these responses as essentially instinctive and therefore outside the realm of cognition. As a skydiver in Lyng's (1990: 860) original study reported about his experience of a parachute malfunction: 'I wasn't thinking at all – I just did what I had to do. It was the right thing to do too.'

A second key dimension of voluntary risk taking involves the structural background factors that intertwine with the foreground experience. As a theoretical model built from front to back (in contrast to the back-to-front approach of the traditional paradigm, see Katz 1988), the edgework perspective connects the foreground experience to structural forces shaping the character of everyday social life and the broader social context of edgework practices. Extending the analysis to this level allows us to connect edgework sensations, emotions and skills to the dominant institutional patterns of the risk society.

As indicated above, risk society theorists direct attention to the immanent character of the modernization process. Although the idea of risk emerged within the modern context, the scientific, technological and industrial developments taking place in the era of risk consciousness have become increasing threats to the integrity of modern social relations and institutions. Hence, the modernization process is *reflexive* in that it steadily erodes modern constructions of class, race and gender and the legitimacy of modern social institutions. Beck and his collaborators (2003) refer to this pattern of immanent change in 'late' or 'second' modernity as *reflexive modernization.*

In a particularly insightful essay on the nature of reflexivity in the risk society, Scott Lash (2003) looks at the second modernity in terms of Manuel Castells' (1989) notion of the 'logic of flows'. While the logic of structure governs personal relationships and experience in the first modernity, these domains conform more with the logic of flows in the second modernity: 'Beck's chronic indeterminacy of risk and risk-taking, of living with risk is much more of a piece with, not the determinacy of structure but the partial, the elusive determinacy of flows' (2003: 49). The logic of flows has profound implications for human agency in the risk society.

Lash (2003: 50) notes that one of the most important consequences of reflexive modernization is 'non-linear reflexivity' or the 'increasing independence of agency and structure'. The classic institutions of the state, class, the nuclear family and ethnic group begin to fragment and dissolve in the second modernity, with the subject becoming increasingly 'nomadic' and less constrained by normative prescriptions. In this context, 'the subject must be much more the rule-finder him- or herself' (2003: 53), moving from a position of *reflection* to *reflexivity.*

The meaning of reflexivity in this usage can be found in a particular kind of knowledge and action that is best suited for dealing with the 'totally normal chaos' that actors confront in the second modernity. As determinant judgements become less and less relevant to effective problem solving in the new social reality, actors must make judgements based on knowledge of uncertainty: 'judgment is always a question of uncertainty, of risk; it also leaves the door open much more to innovation' (2003: 53). The concept of non-linear reflexivity has powerful implications for understanding the significance of edgework in the risk society. Consequently, it is worth quoting Lash at some length on this matter.

> Beck often describes today's non-linear reflexivity in terms of, not the 'I think therefore I am', but instead in terms of 'I am I'. 'I think, therefore I am' has to do with reflection. 'I am I' has more to do with reflex . . . Reflexes are indeterminate. They are immediate. They do not in any sense subsume. Reflexivity, Beck notes, is characterized by choice, where previous generations had no such choices. What Beck often omits to say is that this choice must be *fast*, we must – as in reflex – make *quick* decisions . . . The subject relating to today's fragmented institutions instead has moved from a position of reflection to one of being reflexive.
>
> (2003: 51–52)

With the shift from reflection to reflexivity in the fragmented institutional context of late modernity, edgework can now be seen as an experiential 'ideal type' (Weber 1903–17/1949: 90) of human agency in the risk society. In Max Weber's usage, an ideal type functions strictly as a conceptual tool for doing empirical research and advancing sociological theory. It is a heuristic device that accentuates the essential features of a particular social phenomenon, which, when compared to empirical reality, highlights similarities and divergences with the concept. While Weber's ideal type is a conceptual construct, we can conceive of an experiential version of this device, involving types of experience that are accentuated forms of more general experiential patterns. These purified expressions of important social experiences often become sites for identity construction by social actors. We propose that edgework serves such a function in the risk society – one relating most directly to gender identity.

Lash's description of reflexive agency bears a striking similarity to the descriptive material on edgework practices. As noted above, the starting point for all of the sensations, perceptions and skill requirements involved in edgework is the necessity for immediate action to save oneself from death or serious injury. Consequently, one's actions in conducting edgework are reflexive in precisely the sense that Lash describes: one acts automatically, without reflective consciousness. Indeed, the demands of the moment actually *annihilate* the social repository for reflective consciousness – in G. H. Mead's conception, the 'me' involved in imaginative rehearsal of possible responses to the challenge at hand. If the main current of the risk society is to push people from a position of *reflection* to *reflex*, then nowhere is this transition revealed more dramatically than in edgework.

Thus, contextualizing edgework in terms of the risk society gives us a new way to understand the contemporary significance of this practice. Although participation in high-risk sports and other leisure pursuits has increased in recent decades (see Rinehart and Sydnor 2003: 3), these activities have attracted participants and spectators for well over a century in Western societies (Simon 2005). However, today's voluntary risk takers, as compared to those of the early 20th century, are no longer as marginal to the mainstream population as they once were. Often viewed either as an exemplary or deviant activity in an earlier era, edgework has become increasingly normalized in the late modern context. As Jonathan Simon (2005: 206) notes, edgework and 'center work' begin to blur in this context: 'The polarity between institutional life and edgework collapses. Edgework is increasingly what institutions expect of people.'

Our analysis suggests that edgework is best viewed as the archetype of agency in the risk society, but the primary concern of this essay is to inquire into the gendered nature of this new form of agency. The problem of agency should never be addressed in gender-neutral terms. Consequently, we will now consider how the rise of risk agency in recent decades is related to gender and gendering practices.

EDGEWORK – A CASE OF UNIVERSALIZING MALE EXPERIENCE?

While not formally documented through extensive multivariate analysis, there are good reasons to suspect that participation in edgework activities is highly correlated with such variables as gender, age, race and class. These connections are revealed most clearly in the kinds of risk-taking activities emphasised in the initial formulation of the edgework perspective and in recent elaborations of the model. Almost without exception, young white males of middle-class origin predominate among participants in these high-risk leisure and occupational activities. Although we should be cautious about drawing any firm conclusions from the more restrictive empirical evidence of the initial research (see Lyng 1991), the edgework model may reflect a potential bias in privileging the experience of middle-class white males.

In the first formal critique of the edgework approach, Eleanor Miller (1991) expressed exactly this concern in assessing the general analytical utility of the model. Although Miller found strong similarities between the empirical themes reported in the original study of edgework (Lyng 1990) and her own data on the risk experiences of African-American female street hustlers, she perceived a potential distortion relating to the race, gender and class specificity of the qualitative data presented in the initial study. The key problem for Miller is the claim of nomothetic potential for a theoretical framework based on evidence collected on prototypically white male pursuits. To make such a claim is to assign universal human significance to distinctively white, middle-class male experience, which serves to pathologize the risk-taking experiences of females, non-whites, members of the underclass and other minority groups (see also Walklate 1997). Miller points out that the only way to avoid this problem is to broaden the empirical base of the model, to include the risk experiences of a wider range of social groups.

The problems of deriving theoretical generalizations from a limited set of field data must be acknowledged (see Lyng 1991), but it is also important to probe more deeply into Miller's assumptions about 'prototypically' male activities. In attributing male bias in the edgework model to the use of field data on occupational and leisure activities numerically dominated by males, Miller assumes that the males involved in these enterprises are demonstrating 'masculinity', although she never describes the defining elements of this model of masculinity. Consequently, her critique is rooted in the assumption that masculinity is defined by 'what men actually are/do/experience'. As R. W. Connell points out (1995: 69), the uncritical acceptance of this assumption ignores the modern epistemological principle that 'there is no description without a standpoint', which means that supposed 'neutral' gender descriptions themselves depend upon presuppositions about gender. After all, it is at least *theoretically* possible that males involved in some male-dominated activities are actually expressing *femininity* rather than masculinity. For instance, the fact that transvestite groups are uniformly male does not support the claim that transvestite practices represent an expression of masculinity, since transvestites are, by definition, males posing as females.

If we are to avoid the problems associated with essentialist definitions of masculinity in making sense of the relationship between sex and edgework, a different perspective on gender is required for analysing edgework practices. Treating leisure and occupational edgework activities as expressions of male sex predispositions that are discernable through a gender-sensitive analysis of these activities is epistemologically troublesome and theoretically simplistic. By Miller's logic, the way to avoid universalizing the male risk-taking experience is to clearly distinguish female and male risk activities and acknowledge that when females take risks, 'they do so in ways that are often stereotypically feminine (just as Lyng's subjects act in stereotypically masculine ways)' (1991: 1533). A more theoretically fruitful approach would be to invert this logic, as Jack Katz suggests in referring to the strong correlations of sex and race with robbery: 'It is essential, for pursuing the relationship of both sex and race to robbery, that we turn the issue around and ask, first, not what robbery patterns reveal about sex or race, but *what the sex and race patterns reveal about robbery*, that is, about what people are trying to do when they do stickup' (1988: 238, emphasis in original). Thus, as an alternative to focusing on sex-specific predispositions (whether biologically and socially based) expressed in voluntary risk taking, it is possible to reverse the approach and ask, 'what does the sex ratio in high-risk sports and occupations reveal about these forms of edgework – about what males are trying to do when they do edgework?' In the next section, we use this alternative approach to explore the connection between masculinity and edgework in contemporary Western society.

GENDER PROJECTS AND THE SOCIAL CONFIGURATION OF MASCULINITY

In order to avoid the problems relating to unexamined assumptions about 'prototypical' male behaviour, a new approach is required, one that offers a much richer analysis, empirically and theoretically, than the essentialist perspectives on masculinity. Such an approach can be found in the pioneering work of R. W. Connell and others who have followed his lead. Connell (1995; 2000) has advanced a relational perspective on gender that allows us to simultaneously consider 'the different dimensions or structures of gender, the relation between bodies and society, and the patterning or configuration of gender' (Connell 2000: 23–24). There are several advantages in adopting Connell's approach to defining gender and masculinity.

First, such definitions are – to adopt the metaphor Bauman (2000) uses to analyse contemporary society – fluid. As such, we can expect that definitions of masculinity may change over time, both as individual definitions change and – equally important – as institutional definitions change (Connell 1995; 2000; Kimmel 1996; Miller 2001, 2002; Messerschmidt 2000, 2004). Such a definition avoids the problems of being either overly deterministic (i.e., positivist or essentialist) or overly dependent upon localized definitions (i.e., semiotic or post-structuralist). Adopting such a definition allows us to consider not only how one 'does' gender, but also how the broader movement toward a risk society – and all the attendant changes in social institutions – alters the ways in which masculinity is constructed. In this view, masculinity and femininity are not strictly culturally determined, but rather are configured in 'gender projects', which Connell (1995, 2000) defines as practically accomplished constructions of gender that emerge over time through interaction with others, self-reflection, and responses to socially historic features of contemporary life (see also Kimmel 1996; Messerschmidt 2000, 2004). In this sense, gender projects involve agency on the part of the individual while also reflecting the influences of larger social forces.

Second, the relational approach allows us to take account of multiple definitions of masculinity without ignoring larger culturally shared definitions. By acknowledging that there are different ways of doing gender, we can examine, for example, the relationships between different forms of masculinity (Messerschmidt 2000, 2004). As Connell (2000) summarizes, 'different masculinities do not sit side-by-side like dishes on a smorgasbord. There are definite social relations between them. In particular, there are relations of hierarchy, in which some masculinities are dominant while others are subordinated or marginalized' (2000: 10). Thus, hegemonic masculinity may be the culturally idealized form of masculinity, but not necessarily the most common form (or the form to which every masculine project aspires).

Third, the relational approach calls attention to apparent contradictions in gender constructions. If we are to accept the fluid and dynamic nature of gender, we must also accept that there may be contradictions not only within particular gender projects, but also within larger social, cultural or institutional definitions of masculinity. On the most basic level, this may entail acknowledging that some females can adopt masculine characteristics as part of their gender project (Cohen 2005; Gattuso 2005; Miller 1998, 2001, 2002; Mullins et al 2004). For example, by adopting male attitudes and behaviour relating to aggression and violence and constructing an identity typically embraced by males, women may gain access to male privilege (Miller 1998; 2001; Messerschmidt 2004; Mullins et al 2004). In sporting events we can see this in the rise of female participation in sports like boxing, which has increased substantially in the past several years (Cohen 2005). Noting the change, Gattuso (2005: 65) writes that 'the Golden Gloves spawned a female division in 1995 and in New York the number of entrants nearly doubled in each of the first three years'. Consider also changes in female participation in street crimes traditionally dominated by males (Miller 2001; Mullins et al 2004). In regard to violent retaliation among street criminals, Mullins et al (2004: 932) note that:

> the motivations for intragender retaliation seem very similar for men and women: the building and maintaining of street reputations . . . when a woman is shown disrespect or challenged by another woman, a desire for violent payback is common. Thus, as with women who enter masculinized spaces in other social arenas, women on the street appear to have adapted to – and sometimes to have adopted – prevailing masculine attitudes and behaviors vis-à-vis aggression.

Mullins et al (2004) indicate that the women in their study have not adopted violence 'wholesale', in that the violent acts committed by the women were enacted 'less frequently, with less severity, and were more likely (than men) to seek nonviolent modalities of retaliation' (2004: 933). Thus, while female street criminals differ in some important ways from their male counterparts, they recognize that success in the male-dominated spaces of the street requires adopting the retaliatory tactics typical of males.

Finally, referring to the apparent contradictions mentioned above, Connell

(1995: 73) also states that masculinity and femininity are 'always liable to internal contradiction and historical disruption'. This point is supported by Messerschmidt's (2004) research on the gendered nature of adolescent violence and gender projects. He notes that some of the female delinquents are feminine in traditional ways (e.g., through the use of makeup and clothes), while also adopting very masculine characteristics of aggression and violence. He calls this 'bad-girl femininity', wherein certain feminine characteristics are maintained, and others are jettisoned in favour of traditionally masculine ones.

EDGEWORK AND THE MAKING OF MASCULINITY

Armed with an analytical approach to masculinity that gives equal weight to agentic and contextual factors in the expression of maleness in social life, it is now possible to explore the connection between masculinity and the varieties of occupational and leisure edgework dominated by males. When we examine the overwhelming male presence in wide range of 'extreme sports' (skydiving, hang gliding, rock climbing, competitive skateboarding/biking, motocross, etc.) and high-risk occupations (firefighting, police work, combat soldiering, etc.), it is tempting to emphasize the opportunity these pursuits offer for demonstrating 'intrinsic' male character traits – fearlessness, emotional control, action orientation and toughness. However, to succumb to this temptation would result in an uncritical acceptance of ideologically-tinged presuppositions about masculinity. The fact that certain historical and contemporary discourses refer to such qualities in describing the ideal expression of male character does not mean that male edgeworkers hope to realise these masculine ideals. Indeed, an examination of the ethnographic evidence on edgework activities reveals a conspicuous absence of such references by participants (Lyng and Snow 1986; Lyng 1990, 2005).

As an alternative to this ideologically-based approach to explaining male domination of these edgework activities, we focus on the socially constructed nature of masculinity and consider how some varieties of edgework are undertaken as male gender projects. Employing Katz's rhetoric, we ask, 'What are males trying to do when they do edgework?' Posing the problem this way forces us to orient the analysis to the empirical evidence on the edgework experience as opposed to merely speculating about the significance of this experience to male participants.

Constructing masculinity in edgework

Adopting this empirically-based approach leads to an intriguing picture of how masculinity is constructed in edgework practices. As just noted, the claim that males use edgework as a way to demonstrate fearlessness and toughness in the face of great danger is not supported by the evidence. In fact, these traits are often ridiculed by edgeworkers, who see them as valued attributes of a bygone era or qualities imputed to them by uninformed outsiders. A related point is that the edgework approach to negotiating risks incorporates certain elements found in traditional ideological constructions of femininity.[3] For example, in considering the ideological distinction between male rationality and female intuition, it is clear that intuitive judgements are more crucial to successful outcomes in edgework than one's capacities for rational calculation. In the high-risk world of bond trading, for instance, traders explicitly refer to the importance of intuitive judgement and one's 'feel for the market' in successful trading (Abolafia 1996: 236).[4] This connects with another basic distinction emphasized by traditional gender discourses – the gendered opposition between mind and body. The association of mind with masculinity and the body with femininity in these discourses has little relevance to the way that males actually do edgework. As Lyng (2004) points out, edgework is best regarded as a fully embodied practice in which the 'mind' (understood in the Meadian sense) is extinguished by the demand for an 'instinctive' bodily response to saving oneself. Thus, male edgeworkers must learn to trust their bodies to act appropriately in the face of an extreme challenge, much as women in childbirth allow their bodies to 'take over' at a crucial stage in the birthing process.[5]

The intuitive and embodied character of the edgework practices intertwines with other qualities emphasized by ideological constructions of traditional femininity such as emotionality and impulse. In contrast to media presentations of high-risk occupations and sports as dominated by fearless individuals, actual edgeworkers report that fear pervades most aspects of the risk-taking experience (Lyng 1990: 860). The goal in edgework practice is not

3 It should be stressed that our analysis here relies on a clear distinction between gender *discourses* and actual gender *practices*. The masculine and feminine dichotomies emphasized in this section are treated as ideological constructions of gender deriving from a definition of hegemonic masculinity belonging to the early modern period. This does *not* imply that the dichotomous traits discussed here refer to inherent differences between males and females. Such an implication would be inconsistent with the basic logic of our analysis, which is rooted in Connell's (1995) approach to gender and his critique of essentialist perspectives.

4 This idea was expressed especially well by one of Abolafia's (1996: 236) subjects: 'It's a visceral thing. The brain to mouth reflex. Traders cannot put into words what they have done, even though they may be great moneymakers. They have a knack. They can't describe it.'

5 To reiterate an earlier point, we use this illustration to underscore the divergence between the contemporary construction of masculinity in edgework practices and traditional ideological constructions of gender. It is important to note that males employ instinctive/embodied approaches for dealing with challenges in activities traditionally seen as masculine enterprises, such as in military combat activities, contact sports like boxing and similar activities. In other words, by using this particular illustration, we do not mean to imply that embodied responses are inherently feminine.

to *deny* the existence of fear but rather to *transform* it into equally intense feelings of exhilaration. As a general matter, intense emotional experience is highly valued by male edgeworkers, which contradicts the ideologically imputed male predilection for affective neutrality (or anger and rage as the only possible male emotions).

One could also see the male attraction to the impulsive, spontaneous character of edgework as an importation of a putative feminine value into a masculine risk-taking project. When Ralph Turner (1976) introduced the distinction between 'institution' and 'impulse' in describing the range of experiential anchors for the construction of identity, he did not relate this polar distinction to gender specifically. However, traditional discourses on gender do tend to locate male identity in 'institutional' experience, in acts of volition, role behaviour, and the pursuit of institutional goals, while female identity is often consigned to the 'impulse' end of the continuum, where the 'real self' is found in emotional outbursts and spontaneous expressions. Male edgeworkers, however, typically define their core identity in terms of their risk-taking activities (as skydivers, hang-gliders, firefighters, soldiers, etc.) and often speak of discovering their 'real selves' in the spontaneous, impulsive experience of negotiating the edge. This is not surprising when we consider the range of sensations that edgework generates. Participants in most forms of edgework report feelings of self-determination and self-realization and a sense of authenticity in their embodied self-reactions to the challenges at hand. Thus, participants in high-risk activities typically identify most fundamentally with their spontaneous experiences as edgeworkers and only secondarily with normatively constrained experiences associated with their institutional roles.

In privileging intuition, the body, emotionality, and impulse over rationality, the mind, affective neutrality, and restraint, the gender project of male edgeworkers incorporates some traits borrowed from traditional ideologies of femininity. However, further examination of the field data reveals other dimensions of edgework that reflect discourses on traditional masculinity, although the traditional masculine characteristics, like the feminine elements just discussed, appear in reconfigured forms. So, for example, all types of edgework require the use of finely-honed skills and male edgeworkers typically assign high value to skills traditionally possessed by men – the ability to operate sophisticated technology (aeroplanes, racing cars or motorcycles, etc.) and athletic abilities (flying one's body in freefall, mountain climbing skills, etc.). Thus, the skill-orientation of male edgeworkers emphasizes abilities traditionally valorized by males and, in this sense, it does not distinguish edgework from other skilful pursuits like craft occupations or hobbies dominated by males. What *is* distinctive about the skill-orientation of edgeworkers, however, is its extension beyond the activity-specific skills involved in particular forms of risk taking to encompass a special ability that edgeworkers regard as an innate capacity – the 'survival skill' described above, labelled as 'the right stuff' in the test-pilot subculture (Wolfe 1979) or 'mental toughness' in certain athletic forms of edgework (i.e., endurance running).

In looking at the specific aptitudes involved in this basic survival capacity, we find additional evidence of abilities emphasized by traditional discourses on masculinity. At its core, the survival skill is rooted in a putative male desire to *control* one's environment (see Walklate 1997: 41), including the emotional and mental environment of one's self-system (i.e., avoiding fear-induced 'brain lock' and focusing one's attention) and objects of the external environment confronted at the edge (a form of technology, an aspect of nature, etc.). In edgework, however, the need to control one's environment is pushed to an extreme degree, to the point of seeking *control over the seemingly uncontrollable* (Lyng 1990: 872). According to Ellen Langer (1975), the sense of controlling the seemingly uncontrollable, which is a common psychological outcome of using skills in situations where outcomes are actually chance-determined, produces powerful feelings of mastery and competence. This could very well explain the empowering character of edgework and the sense of omnipotence it produces in some participants.

So, what are we to make of the curious mixture of traditionally feminine and masculine elements that males incorporate into their edgework practices? For one thing, it is clear that in managing risks, males are much more creative in their gendering strategies than some analysts might assume. The unique combination of skills and dispositions in dealing with risks reflects a degree of flexibility not fully appreciated by those who assert that males manage risks 'in ways that are *stereotypically . . .* male' (Miller 1991, emphasis added). Of course, the same can be said for females as well, as witnessed in the flexible combination of traditional feminine and masculine characteristics exhibited in the 'bad-girl femininity' described by Messerschmidt (2004). Indeed, the edgework masculinity project offers additional empirical support for Messerschmidt's (2004: 37) claim that 'individuals may situationally adopt cross-gender strategies and engage in certain masculine and feminine practices without changing their fundamental gender project, [while] others may construct a specific fundamental gender project . . . that contradicts their bodily sex category'.

In short, it is clear that male edgework practices are highly gendered but our analysis suggests that this pattern can be fully understood only by inverting the standard logic of analysis in gender studies: rather than seeking to explain how male edgeworkers manage risks in masculine ways, we should consider how masculinity is achieved through the management of risks in edgework. However, since the configuration of gender involves both agency *and* social context, accomplishing this goal requires that we examine edgework as a masculine gender project undertaken within the context of the risk society.

The social configuration of masculinity in late modernity

In directing attention now to contextual factors, we return to the general themes introduced at the beginning of this chapter. Incorporating this dimension into the analysis raises the problem of the historicity of the social patterns under analysis, although this problem is not always explicitly addressed. We noted earlier that risk society theorists see fundamental changes taking place in contemporary Western society that may signal an important historical shift. If this perception is valid, it is likely that fundamental social configurations such as gender are being 'historically disrupted' at present (Connell 1995). Old configurations of masculinity and femininity may be giving way to new gender arrangements that align with immanent historical forces of reflexive modernization.

As noted in our earlier description of the risk society, the institutional context of edgework practices, and the gender projects related to these practices, is one in which the 'partial, elusive determinacy of flow' has steadily displaced the 'determinacy of structure' as dominant institutional influence on human agency. Thus, Lash's distinction between reflection and reflexivity may be a useful device for contrasting the construction of gender in the first and second modernity. In the first modernity, gender projects are oriented primarily to a nexus of structure and agency designated by the term 'reflection'. Consequently, patriarchy in the first modernity partly depends on the social alignment of masculinity with the key correlates of reflectivity or reflective action – the male privileging of rationality over intuition, mind over body, affective neutrality over emotionality, constraint over impulse, and control over adaptation (see above). In the structural context of early modernity, configuring masculinity in terms of these qualities confers clear advantages to males in gaining access to valuable resources.

This configuration of masculinity is best conceptualized as a historically-specific form of 'hegemonic masculinity'. As Connell (1995: 77) defines it, hegemonic masculinity refers to 'the configuration of gender practice which embodies the currently accepted answer to the problem of the legitimacy of patriarchy, which guarantees (or is taken to guarantee) the dominant position of men and the subordination of women'. With the ascendancy of reflectivity in the first modernity, the incorporation of reflective capacities into male gender practice establishes this expression of masculinity as hegemonic. It constitutes a configuration of masculinity that clearly legitimates the dominant position of men and the subordination of women. When it could be asserted that men are 'naturally' rational and reflective, emotionally controlled and constrained in their behaviour, while women are 'naturally' irrational and impulsive, emotionally labile and controlled by bodily processes, male dominance of modern institutions and reward structures was assured.

In late modernity, however, agency has become increasingly independent of structure and the logic of flows begins to displace the logic of structure. This means that the capacity for reflective action is less and less relevant to ensuring access to power and privilege. Thus, the association of masculinity with dimensions of reflectivity (rationality, mind, affective neutrality, control, etc.) no longer sustains patriarchal arrangements in the way that it once did. Indeed, patriarchy begins to lose its legitimacy in the transition from early to late modernity as increasing numbers of women reject traditional femininity and incorporate reflectivity into their own gender projects and as changing historical circumstances undermine the male advantage accruing from the appropriation of reflectivity. In this period of declining legitimacy for traditional patriarchy, we would certainly expect to see signs of an important historical disruption of masculinity.

This disruption instigates the transition to a new form of hegemonic masculinity in the risk society, one based on the critical nexus of agency and historical context represented by the term *non-linear reflexivity*. As we have seen, the social reality of the risk society is characterized by great uncertainty and indeterminacy brought about by the reflexive modernization process. The nation state is increasingly undermined by globalization, the security of work declines and employment practices become more flexible, the ascriptive patterns of collective life are eroded, and the internal relations of family life become more complex (Beck *et al* 2003). In this context, 'normal chaos' becomes the daily reality of increasing numbers of people and they must adjust their problem-solving strategies to this new reality. As Lash would say, this kind of environment requires the quickness and indeterminacy of reflex.

We can now understand how edgework emerges as a masculine gender project in the risk society. As an experiential ideal type of non-linear reflexivity – that is, as an accentuated expression of reflexivity (see above), edgework becomes a key focal point for the construction of hegemonic masculinity in the second modernity. We have asserted that edgework is conducted by drawing on one's capacities for reflex action. In fact, all of the skills and sensations associated with edgework are connected to the demand for such action. In negotiating the edge, one must be prepared to 'ad hoc' a response to quickly changing circumstances and resist the temptation to 'think too much' about the evolving situation. The most important skill employed in edgework, the so-called 'survival capacity', is regarded as an innate ability that emerges in reflex responses. Indeed, most of the sensations associated with the edgework experience are direct consequences of reflex action overwhelming reflective consciousness (in Meadian terms, the suppression of the 'me' by the demand for immediate action). As reflective consciousness and the social self (the 'me') are annihilated in the reflex action, an 'acting self' (that mimics the 'I') is left in its wake, producing feelings of self-determination and authenticity, spatial and temporal implosions (feelings of 'oneness' with environmental objects and time passing faster or slower than normal), and a sense that the experience is ineffable (see Lyng 1990: 880–882).

Thus, by constructing masculinity in terms of the consciousness, action and skills required for doing edgework, males provide an 'answer to the problem of the legitimacy of patriarchy' in the developing risk society, a social world in which this kind of reflexive agency is increasingly seen as determining one's chances of success in economic, political and interpersonal endeavours.[6] This is a substantial reconfiguration of masculinity, especially considering that some of its components were previously aligned with the early modern ideological construction of femininity – intuition, embodiment, emotionality and impulse. In the newly evolving system of gender relations, however, claims about the 'natural' capacities of males to 'get a feel for a situation', to draw on their 'instincts' in decision making, to express 'intensity' and 'intense emotions', to 'ad hoc' solutions to problems, and 'thrive on chaos' are becoming more prominent themes in contemporary discourses on masculinity.

Theorizing edgework as a male gender project devoted to the construction of hegemonic masculinity in the risk society raises several important considerations, which we address in concluding the analysis. First, we must remain cognizant of the contingent nature of this project – like all projects, it may or may not lead to the desired goal. As Connell (1995: 76) notes, 'hegemonic masculinity is not a fixed character type . . . It is, rather, the masculinity that occupies the hegemonic position in a given pattern of gender relations, *a position always contestable*' (emphasis added). Although males are over-represented in many forms of edgework, female participants can be found in all high-risk sports and occupations, and some edgework practices are almost entirely dominated by females (i.e., prostitution). Thus, the effort to construct masculinity through edgework activities – and the claim that edgework consciousness, action and skills are distinctively masculine – is likely to be contested by females. Female edgeworkers are not likely to accept the idea that only males can possess 'the right stuff'.

---

6 In support of this assertion, consider the growing body of ethnographic research on stock, bond and commodities trading, especially Abolafia's (1996) work on 'hyper-rational gaming' in the bond trading business. The strategies and actions of these traders, as described by Abolafia and others (Cetina and Bruegger (2000), Zwick (2005), Smith (2005)), can be appropriately classified as forms of reflexive agency. Paul du Gay (1994) sees a similar trend in recent managerial and organizational discourses that call for greater individual risk taking and more flexible organizational forms to counter traditional bureaucratic practices and structures. In the political realm, we could also point to the last US presidential election (2004), in which candidate George W. Bush and John Kerry provided a stark contrast between the 'reflexive' politician whose political decisions are perceived to be based on instinct and gut feelings (Bush) and the 'reflective' politician who relies on deep reflection and reasoned analysis in decision making (Kerry). The fact that Kerry's reflective nature proved to be a major liability in this election could be taken as a sign of the ascendancy of reflexivity in the political domain.

Second, it is important to consider how the edgework masculinity project connects with the primary sites of gender configuration, i.e., its significance for personality development, its incorporation into contemporary discourses and ideologies, and its institutional locations (Connell 1995: 72–73). These problems must be left to future research initiatives, but we can offer some speculative propositions about the institutional locations of edgework practices in the post-war period. It is significant that most of the early research on edgework activities has primarily focused on high-risk, 'extreme' sports and other forms of leisure risk taking. Although high-risk occupations have always existed, the most significant growth in voluntary risk taking in the post-war era has occurred in the leisure domain. One way to account for this pattern is to propose that leisure risk taking may have initially emerged as a response to the structural logic of the first modernity. This accords with the modernist theoretical interpretation of edgework (see Lyng 1990), which views participation in leisure risk taking as a response to the alienating, over-socialized character of early modern institutional life. This response could be seen as intertwining with a male gender project devoted to constructing a form of 'marginal masculinity' (Connell 1995: 81) standing in opposition to the hegemonic masculinity of early modernity.

As early modern institutions and social relations gradually give way to the contextual logic of late modernity, leisure risk taking takes on new significance. Now the contrast between the new leisure pursuits and other institutional realities (work, family, consumption, etc.) become less stark, as uncertainty, chaos and risk taking begin to permeate all aspects of social life. Thus, at some point in the transition from early to late modernity, the masculine prototype constructed through the edgework gender project is no longer marginal but begins to acquire hegemonic potential. In the contemporary context, it increasingly plays a role in ensuring the dominance of men and the subordination of women.

A third and final consideration is the problem of relating the edgework gender project to other expressions of masculinity in addition to the hegemonic form. Connell points out that gender projects devoted to hegemonic masculinity are often undertaken by relatively few men, even though males in general benefit from the patriarchal relations legitimated by these projects. Consequently, 'if a large number of men have some connection with the hegemonic project but do not embody hegemonic masculinity, we need a way of theorizing their specific situation' (Connell 1995: 79). The crucial conceptualization here is the idea of 'complicity' with hegemonic masculinity.

Complicit masculinity consists of gender projects that give males access to the 'patriarchal dividend' without subjecting them to the challenges and risks associated with hegemonic masculinity. It is clear that for most males, involvement in edgework activities is complicit rather than actual. Consider the sizable and growing spectatorship among males for a broad range of high-risk sports (ultimate fighting; racing sports such motocross, auto road racing – most especially NASCAR; and other 'extreme' sports in the genres of professional skateboarding, trick biking, etc.). Similarly, the large male audience for media depictions of risk taking in 'action' films, crime films and similar genres represents another level of complicity with the edgework gender project. By providing material support for these authentic and simulated expressions of edgework practice, many males contribute to the broader ideological dissemination of this form of hegemonic masculinity, even though they do not actively embrace the edgework gender project themselves. This would appear to be a good investment on their part, insofar as it adds to a patriarchal dividend that all males indirectly access.

CONCLUSIONS

This chapter strives for a better understanding of the relationship between risk and gender in the contemporary risk society. The movement toward 'government by risk' has had wide ranging gender-specific consequences for men and women in the late modern era that are just beginning to be addressed by social scientists. We are also beginning to see substantial shifts in thinking about gender differences in risk agency, with many risk analysts now questioning long-held assumptions about males as risk takers and females as risk avoiders. This has opened up new lines of research into the gendered nature of risk taking, which have allowed us to move beyond assumptions about gender differences in risk-taking propensity to focus instead on the different risk management strategies employed by males and females.

These insights notwithstanding, we still confront the empirical reality of a substantial over-representation of males in certain risk-taking activities. This study focuses on a domain of risk taking in which this is the case – forms of leisure, occupational and criminal risk-taking conceptualized as edgework. To make theoretical sense of this pattern, we have argued that male-dominated edgework is best understood as a gendering strategy. Rather than focus on sex-specific predispositions, we have chosen to treat sex and gender as practical accomplishments realised through activities that carry important social, cultural and political significance.

The critical nexus of agency and historical context in the risk society, conceptualised here as non-linear reflexivity, is found experientially in various forms of edgework practice. Thus, in the late modern era, males are drawn to edgework activities in search of the purest possible expression of risk agency and consciousness so that they can master the skills of 'controlling the seemingly uncontrollable'. In taking up the edgework challenge, these males embrace a gender project that is leading to a new archetype of masculinity, one that is well suited to the task of legitimating male power and privilege in the contemporary social order.

REFERENCES

Abolafia, Mitchel Y. (1996) 'Hyper-Rational Gaming' *Journal of Contemporary Ethnography* 25(2): 226–250.

Beck, Ulrich (1992) *The Risk Society*, London: Sage.

Beck, Ulrich (1999) *World Risk Society*, London: Polity Press.

Beck, Ulrich (2002) 'The Silence of Words and Political Dynamics in the World Risk Society' at http://logosonline.home.igc.org/beck.htm.

Beck, Ulrich and Beck-Gernsheim, Elisabeth (2002) *Individualization: Instituitional-ized Individualism and Its Social and Political Consequences*, London: Sage.

Beck, Ulrich, Bonss, Wolfgang and Lau, Christoph (2003) 'The Theory of Reflexive Modernization: Problematic, Hypotheses, and Programme' *Theory, Culture, and Society* 20(2): 1–33.

Bauman, Zygmunt (2000) *Liquid Modernity*, London: Polity Press.

Castells, Manuel (1989) *The Informational City*, Oxford: Blackwell.

Cetina, Karin K. and Bruegger, Urs (2000) 'The Market as an Object of Attachment: Exploring Postsocial Relations in Financial Markets' *Canadian Journal of Sociology* 25(2): 141–168.

Cohen, Leah (2005) *Without Apology: Girls, Women, and the Desire to Fight*. New York: Ransom House.

Connell, R. W. (1995) *Masculinities*, Berkeley: University of California Press.

Connell, R. W. (2000) *The Men and the Boys*, Berkeley: University of California Press.

du Gay, Paul (1994) 'Making Up Managers: Bureaucracy, Enterprise and the Liberal Art of Separation' *British Journal of Sociology* 45(4): 655–674.

Frank, Arthur W. (1995) 'For a Sociology of the Body: An Analytical Review', pp. 36–102 in M. Featherstone, M. Hepworth, and B. S. Turner (eds) *The Body: Social Process and Cultural Theory*, London, UK: Sage.

Ferrell, Jeff, Dragan Milovanovic, and Stephen Lyng (2001) 'Edgework, Media Practices, and the Elongation of Meaning' *Theoretical Criminology* 5(2): 177–202.

Gattuso, John (2005) 'Petronelli Boxing Gym' J. Gattuso (ed.) in *Shadowboxers: Sweat, Sacrifice, and the Will to Survive in America's Boxing Gyms*, Stone Creek Publications.

Heimer, Carol A. (1988) 'Social Structure, Psychology and the Estimation of Risk' *Annual Review of Sociology* 14: 495–519.

Holyfield, Lori (1997) 'Generating Excitement: Experienced Emotion in Commercial Leisure' in Rebecca J. Erickson and Beverley Cuthbertson-Johnson (eds) *Social Perspectives on Emotion*, Vol. 4, Greenwich, CT: JAI Press.

Holyfield, Lori (1999) 'Manufactured Adventure: The Buying and Selling of Emotions' *Journal of Contemporary Ethnography* 28(1).

Holyfield, Lori, Jonas, Lilian and Zajicek, Anna (2005) 'Adventure Without Risk Is Like Disneyland' pp 173–86, in S. Lyng (ed.) *Edgework: The Sociology of Risk Taking*, New York: Routledge.

Katz, Jack (1988) *The Seductions of Crime: Moral and Sensual Attractions in Doing Evil*, New York: Basic Books.

Kimmel, Michael (1996) *Manhood in America: A Cultural History*, New York: Free Press.

Langer, Ellen J. (1975) 'The Illusion of Control' *Journal of Personality and Social Psychology* 32: 311–28.

Lash, Scott (2003) 'Reflexivity as Non-linearity' *Theory, Culture, and Society* 20(2): 49–57.

Lois, Jennifer (1999) 'Socialization to Heroism: Individualism and Collectivism in a Voluntary Search and Rescue Group' *Social Psychology Quarterly* 62 (2): 117–135.

Lois, Jennifer (2005) 'Gender and Emotion Management in the Stages of Edgework', pp. 177–152 in S. Lyng (ed.) *Edgework: The Sociology of Risk Taking*, New York: Routledge.

Lyng, Stephen (1990) 'Edgework: A Social Psychological Analysis of Voluntary Risk Taking' *American Journal of Sociology* 95: 851–86.

Lyng, Stephen (1991) 'Response to Miller' *American Journal of Sociology* 96(6): 1534.

Lyng, Stephen (1993) 'Disfunctional Risk Taking: Criminal Behavior as Edgework'. pp. 107–30 in N. Bell and R. Bell (eds) *Adolescent Risk Taking*, London: Sage.

Lyng, Stephen (1998) 'Dangerous Methods: Risk Taking and the Research Process' pp. 221–51 in J. Ferrell and M. S. Hamm (eds) *Ethnography at the Edge: Crime, Deviance, and Field Research*, Boston: Northeastern University Press.

Lyng, Stephen (2004) 'Crime, Edgework, and Corporeal Transaction' *Theoretical Criminology* 8(3): 359–75.

Lyng, Stephen (2005) 'Sociology at the Edge: Social Theory and Voluntary Risk Taking', pp. 17–49 in S. Lyng (ed.) *Edgework: The Sociology of Risk Taking*, New York: Routledge.

Lyng, Stephen and Franks, David D. (2002) *Sociology and the Real World*, Boulder, CO: Rowman and Littlefield.

Lyng Stephen and Snow, David A. (1986) 'Vocabularies of Motive and High Risk Behavior: The Case of Skydiving', pp. 157–79 in E. J. Lawler (ed.) *Advances in Group Processes*, vol. 3, Greenwich, Conn.: JAI.

Messerschmidt, James (2000) *Nine Lives: Adolescent Masculinities, the Body and Violence*, Boulder, CO: Westview.

Messerschmidt, James (2004) *Flesh and Blood: Adolescent Gender Diversity and Violence*, New York: Roman and Littlefield.

Miller, Eleanor M. (1986) *Street Woman: Women in the Political Economy*, Philadelphia: Temple University Press.

Miller, Eleanor M. (1991) 'Assessing the Risk of Inattention to Class, Race/Ethnicity, and Gender: Comment on Lyng' *American Journal of Sociology* 96(6): 1530–34.

Miller, Jodi (1998) 'Up it Up: Gender and the Accomplishment of Street Robbery' *Criminology* 36(1): 37–66.

Miller, Jodi (2001) *One of the Guys: Girls, Gangs and Gender*, Oxford: Oxford University Press.

Miller, Jodi (2002) 'The Strengths and Limits of "Doing Gender" for Understanding Street Crime', *Theoretical Criminology* 6: 433–60.

Mullins, C., Ricard Wright, and Bruce Jacobs (2004) 'Gender, Street-life, and Criminal Retaliation' *Criminology* 42(4): 911–40.

O'Malley, Pat and Stephen Mugford (1994) 'Crime, Excitement, and Modernity', pp. 189–211 in G. Barak (ed.) *Varieties of Criminology*, Westport, CT: Praeger.

Rinehart, Robert and Sydnor, Synthia (2003) 'Proem', pp. 1–17 in R.E. Rinehart and S. Sydnor (eds) *To the Extreme: Alternative Sports, Inside and Out*, New York: SUNY Press.

Simon, Jonathan (2005) 'Edgework and Insurance in Risk Societies: Some Notes on Victorian Lawyers and Mountaineers', pp. 203–26 in S. Lyng (ed.) *Edgework: The Sociology of Risk Taking*, New York: Routledge.

Simon, Jonathan (2002) 'Taking Risks: Extreme Sports and the Embrace of Risk in Advanced Liberal Societies', pp. 177–208 in T. Baker and J. Simon (eds) *Embracing Risk: The Changing Culture of Insurance and Responsibility*, Chicago: University of Chicago Press.

Smith, Charles W. (2005) 'Financial Edgework: Trading in Market Currents', pp. 187–200 in S. Lyng (ed.) *Edgework: The Sociology of Risk Taking*, New York: Routledge.

Turner, Ralph H. (1976) 'The Real Self: From Institution to Impulse' *American Journal of Sociology* 81: 989–1016.

Wacquant, Loic J. D. (1995) 'The Pugilistic Point of View: How Boxers Think and Feel About Their Trade' *Theory and Society* 24: 489–535.

Walklate, Sandra (1997) 'Risk and Criminal Victimization: A Modernist Dilemma?' *British Journal of Criminology* 37(1): 35–46.

Weber, Max (1903–1917/1949) *The Methodology of the Social Sciences*, Edward Shils and Henry Finch (eds), New York: Free Press.

Wolfe, Tom (1979) *The Right Stuff*, New York: Farrar, Straus, and Giroux.

Zwick, Detlev (2005) 'Where the Action Is: Internet Stock Trading as Edgework' *Journal of Computer-Mediated Communication* 11(1), article 2 at http://jcmc.indiana.edu/vol11/issue1/zwick.html.

Chapter 5

Engaging in a culture of barebacking

Gay men and the risk of HIV prevention

Kane Race[1]

To love, to want, to have sex with someone of the same sex is a gendered risk. To understand how this is so, it is necessary to approach gender, not as a biological property of bodies, nor merely as the social expression of certain biological characteristics, but as a regulatory system organized around the presumption of heterosexuality. This presumption, which queer theorists have termed heteronormativity (Berlant and Warner 1998), entails certain naturalized beliefs: that there are two sexes, male and female; that men are sexually active and not passive; that women are nurturing and receptive; that sex is private, conjugal and procreative; and that desire follows from biological sex and is directed toward the opposite sex.[2] The threat of violence, abuse and ridicule – as well as more mundane forces, like everyday prejudice and administration – constrain the range of relations, affective formations and futures that are available to gendered subjects.[3] In this sense, HIV is not the biggest risk that impacts gay life, nor necessarily the most physically threatening, but the regulatory system of sex/gender certainly makes HIV more of a risk than it ought to be.

The regulatory system of sex/gender has severely impeded responses to HIV/ AIDS. Legislation forbidding the use of State funds for purposes thought to promote homosexuality has criminally obstructed effective HIV education.[4]

---

1 Dean Murphy drew my attention to textual materials used in this analysis and provided opportunities to present and develop this research. I would also like to thank David Halperin, Susan Kippax, Marsha Rosengarten and Niamh Stephenson for reading and commenting on earlier versions of this article and Adrian Kerr for enduring the writing of it.
2 This regulatory system does not merely constrain the social performance of gender roles. As Judith Butler has shown, the social frame of gender organizes the considerable variety of chromosomal, genetic and anatomical configurations within and among each individual according to the binary logic of male or female. That is, the biological sexes of male and female are an effect of this process of gendering. Butler 1990.
3 For a sociological discussion that describes this process and how it's contended in the gay male context see Eribon 2004.
4 The Helms Amendment in the US and section 28 of the Local Government Act 1988 in Britain blocked State funding for educational programmes that 'promote homosexuality', hamstringing HIV education targeting gay men. See generally Patton 1990.

The vain hope to ensure a drug-free nation in countries like the United States has similarly blocked interventions proven to reduce HIV transmission such as needle and syringe exchange programmes, with disastrous effects. Anti-drug norms are not the same as sex and gender norms, but the parallel is clear: the virulent investment in the norm has involved an abandonment of bodies as they are lived, and the epidemic has spread unnecessarily. This is why, from the outset, HIV prevention activists have found it necessary to risk a practical distinction between normative morality and the embodied ethics of HIV prevention. Where moral reactionaries condemned homosexuality outright, activists pointed to the possibility of preventing HIV transmission through the use of condoms and the avoidance of quite specific practices such as unprotected sex. Where conservatives denounced addicts and objected to the institution of needle exchanges, harm reduction practitioners appealed to the possibility of modifying injecting practice and the public health objective of HIV prevention. In this sense, a tension between normative morality and an ethic of care grounded in embodied practice is a defining feature of HIV politics, and those who are interested in responding effectively to the epidemic must remain alive to the ways in which the propagation of certain normative ideals compromises the ability to engage effectively (Race, forthcoming).

This chapter contributes to the analysis of the encounter between normative morality and embodied ethics in the field of HIV/AIDS by considering the phenomenon of barebacking, a term that emerged in Western gay culture in 1996 after over a decade of unprecedented behavioural change on the part of gay communities, and which sought to revalue anal sex without condoms as an erotic practice. The focus of the article is on how risk discourse produces certain risk subjectivities in gay sexual subjects; and on the question of how to engage with a practice that understands itself as a transgression of existing norms. The basic argument is that in making themselves, and being made, the subjects of a (hetero)normative social order, gay men are led to interpret their sexual practice as intentional deviance regardless of HIV risk, and this leads to a misrecognition of the preventive possibilities of their practice. I use the frame of Foucault's later work on ethics, care of the self, and the use of pleasure to emphasize the social and political aspects of these processes of subject formation.[5] In so doing, I am trying to signal the importance of fostering

---

5 Foucault posits a distinction between normative morality and ethics in order to draw attention to historical processes of subject formation (that is, the processes through which subjects come to recognize themselves as subjects of a particular moral code) in Foucault 1984. I read this work as providing conceptual resources for withstanding and responding to the debilitating effects of specific disciplinary configurations. For an illuminating discussion of the significance of this distinction in gay life and politics see Halperin 1995. For an earlier empirical application of this distinction to HIV prevention see Race 2003. Jonathan Simon uses a similar distinction to identify different conceptions and practices of risk in the neoliberal

a relation to HIV that is based, not on moral compliance, but on a careful consideration of other bodies – their attributes, differences and capacities.

In the first part of the chapter I consider the work of an HIV-positive cultural producer who, in the effort to constitute a collective background to his practice of HIV risk reduction, found himself in breach of normative stipulations that require sex to be private and individual, and gay anal sex to be covered over and domesticated, irrespective of HIV risk. Barebacking, which is the name his practice took on as it attempted to achieve a public face, became charged with moral transgression rather than HIV prevention. By comparing barebacking to more recent constructions of unprotected sex, I show how the process of devising public and personal strategies of HIV prevention is confounded by gendered norms.[6] In the second part of the chapter I extend this analysis to the practices of HIV social science. I argue that social science is intimately involved in the production of barebacking since it invites sexual subjects to (mis)recognize themselves as purely intentional individuals, either virtuous or deviant. Here we can see how normative discourses of HIV risk and sexuality intersect with neoliberal discourses which stipulate a (tacitly gendered) model of the self that is rational, calculating, independent, in control, and decisional. By concentrating on gay men's moral intentions while ignoring the circumstances of sex, HIV social science invokes and produces a neoliberal sexual actor who finds himself embracing HIV risk. In the last part of the chapter I discuss briefly how 'barebacking' has been responded to in Australia. If risk cannot be understood outside the ways that it is known (Dean 1999), then barebacking raises a methodological question about *how to engage* with 'illicit' bodily practices, and this question applies equally to each of the domains I consider: media representation, scientific practice, and HIV policy.

It is by now a truism in HIV social commentary to attribute barebacking (understood as a paradigmatic instance of wanton risk) to some problematic aspect of masculinity, ascribed to gay men (or to *some* gay men – the same ones, no doubt, who spend such spectacularly long hours at the gym) and then to explain ongoing HIV transmissions in these terms.[7] And certainly

context, with interesting parallels. Simon 2002. Of course, ethical practices are not unrelated to norms, and they may well instate their own norms (the safe sex norm is an obvious example). My hope is that, by attending to social processes of subject formation, and the question of how the body is – what happens to it – as it incorporates given norms, some practical alternatives and viable responses to the current predicament will emerge.

6 For a wide-ranging discussion of how the strategy of self-abjection may assist gay men's efforts around HIV prevention (which has informed and encouraged my work here) see Halperin (2007).

7 For a lively rebuttal of some of the more common forms of scapegoating that confound gay men's HIV prevention see Rofes 1998. For queer readings of bodybuilding that reflect the complexity of gendered counterpractice see Halperin 1995, and Morrison 2001.

the vernacular of barebacking, with its intonations of macho adventure and rugged individualism, would appear to support this view. But this interpretation too quickly assumes that 'risk' is the *only* appeal of unprotected anal sex and that gender can be linked straightforwardly to some quality of desire in relation to risk. Gay men enjoy anal sex, including anal sex without condoms, for all sorts of reasons, very few of which are determined by the fact that it has been found to be a route of HIV transmission. Historically speaking, the 'risk' has befallen the practice, rather than generating it. Further, how does one 'gender' a man's desire for his partner to come inside him, 'regardless of the risks', for the intimacy, trust or 'giving over' this expresses? Is it masculine or feminine? Should it be linked to the sex of the subject (male), the purported gender of the sexual position (feminine-receptive), or the affect it expresses (and then, which aspect? the supposedly masculine enthusiasm for risk? or the supposedly feminine relation of self-surrender?)? Or should it be read in terms of the violation of hegemonic masculinity that Leo Bersani thinks male homosexuality expresses (Bersani 1988)? And then, how is that particular desire to be gendered? Further, is it the same desire as that which animates the insertive partner (also a barebacker) who, say, experiences difficulties with condoms but believes himself relatively safe in adopting this sexual position? Who simply prefers the sensation of sex without condoms? And what if (as is the case in most reported acts of barebacking) one or both of the partners knows themselves to be HIV-positive, and believes their partner is too (Adam 2005)? What value is risk conferring here? Is barebacking always risky? Does the belief, in a given instance, that it is (or is not) make a difference to our theory of gendered risk? Indeed, what can we usefully say about gender or risk here, except that the complexity of sex constantly undoes and reworks its coordinates? Perhaps the language of barebacking tells us more about the cultural terms in which a valued but multiply censured practice has been defended and asserted than anything definitive about gendered desire. This is why, in what follows, I treat gender, not as an attribute that is given and that predisposes people to risk, but as a norm that complicates and limits self-care among those whose sexuality it stigmatizes. Indeed, I would maintain that the most important frame for understanding barebacking is not gender, understood in the categorical sense, but rather sexuality, understood as a regulatory system that works in and through gender, but that is not reducible to it and frequently challenged unpredictably by it.

RISK, ETHICS AND *AUTOPORNOGRAPHY*

In his book *Autopornography*, the HIV-positive gay porn star, writer and sex advocate Scott O'Hara gives a frank and amiable account of his sexual experience during the first phase of the AIDS epidemic in North America (O'Hara 1997a). He describes periods of abstinence; of limiting his sexual practice to certain acts (both alone and with particular partners); of using condoms for anal sex (on one occasion he describes this as 'kinky' and 'hot'); and also of unprotected sex. He describes times when he has no libido at all, some of which coincide with periods of illness, and he describes a time after 1994 when his libido returns, when he realizes 'there were other HIVers out there with whom I didn't need to worry about transmission; men who didn't worry about isolating bodily fluids' (1997a: 129). Despite his upfront sexual manner and sexual articulacy, O'Hara relates how he found it difficult to raise the subject of AIDS with potential sex partners, such that he'd 'essentially given up sex rather than learn[ed] to discuss it' (1997a:127). In 1994, he gets an 'HIV+' tattoo on his left bicep (which he refers to as the most visible spot on his body save his forehead) and surrounds it with a 'tasteful little circlet of swimming spermatozoa'. These steps are taken in an attempt to ensure that the sex he has is safe or at least better informed with respect to HIV transmission. For example, on one occasion he describes a sexual encounter with a 'redneck' where he avoids doing anything risky (even oral sex) because it is too dark to see his tattoo. He suggests they jerk each other off in a scene he describes as 'really exciting' (1997a: 200).

Although not all gay men are porn stars or poets, O'Hara's thinking here is typical of the concerns and innovations expressed by many HIV-positive gay men.[8] He takes care not to put HIV-negative men at risk, and because of his preference for sex without condoms he tries to ensure his sexual partners are other likely HIV-positive men. He describes the risk of sexually transmitted infections and 'possibly other things that are transmissible among HIVers too', but he places little emphasis on these possibilities. 'I assume my partner has the same deductive facilities that I have so I grant him the right to make his own decisions about what precautions he thinks are appropriate' (1997a: 201). O'Hara is alert to the way in which risk and health discourses can be used to naturalize and promote certain moral regimes. At one point, he voices his suspicion that the medical profession's fixation on these dangers 'has more to do with its longstanding distaste for gay sex than on scientific research. You know: Anal Sex – Icky! Dirty!' Believing some doctors to be 'only too happy to make whatever judgments they can to stop people from having dirty, messy sex', he suggests 'people just need to learn what their own personal safety guidelines are. I doubt the medical profession will offer much realistic help along those lines, so it's up to us to use our noggins' (1997a: 202).

Elsewhere, however, these risks play a more material role in O'Hara's sexual negotiations with other HIV-positive men: 'Nowadays when I make an agreement with a man that we'll fuck uncovered, it's an extreme declaration

---

8 For qualitative evidence to this effect, see Barry Adam's rigorous analysis in Adam 2005. An important early study of practices of safety outside the condom code exists in Rosengarten *et al* 2000.

of trust, knowing that there are potentially lethal diseases that we could be passing back and forth – crypto, meningitis, hepatitis – and we think it's worth the risk.' Though he reports only four instances of this sort of occasion, 'each time stands out, diamond sharp, in my memory, more because of the trust shared than because the sex was extra special' (1997a: 202).[9] Without particularly wishing to object to these instances, it is worth observing that if the stakes of intimacy can be raised in this way it would seem the risks have made some impression.

O'Hara's account is a valuable record of some of the ways gay men have negotiated different and sometimes contradictory formations of sex, infection, risk, responsibility and intimacy. He provides a candid and unapologetic account of the variable positions in which he finds himself as a gendered subject of medical, sexual and romantic discourses. Perhaps what is most confronting in O'Hara's writings for those concerned with HIV prevention is his refusal to subordinate his self-esteem to the prerogatives of HIV prevention. While he never endorses recklessness on the part of HIV-positive individuals, he is not prepared to let public health imperatives determine his self-conception as a gay man with a particular relation to HIV:

> I've become somewhat notorious, over the past year, for my positions on HIV. To put it briefly as possible: I can't quite believe it's a curse. I'm not trying to out-Louise Ms. Hay, but in my life, AIDS has been an undeniable blessing. It woke me up to what was important; it let me know that NOW was the time to do it. And – this is the part that upsets people – it also gives me the freedom to behave 'irresponsibly'. I look at the HIV negative people around me, and I pity them. They live their lives in constant fear of infection: mustn't do this, mustn't do that, mustn't take risks. They can't see past that simple 'avoidance of infection,' which has come to be their ultimate goal. They believe that AIDS = death sentence. Well, I'm sorry, but I was quite possibly infected in 1981, and I'm in pretty good health 15 years later. If that's a death sentence, I guess life in a prison of negativity sounds a lot worse. My life is so much more carefree than theirs, so much more 'considered,' that I shake my head and count myself lucky to have been infected. Risk taking is the essence of life, and people who spend their entire lives trying to eliminate risk from their lives are . . . well, they're not my kind of people. I know a couple of people who have self-consciously made the decision to seroconvert; I admire them tremendously, because it takes a considerable amount of self-confidence and self-knowledge to make a decision that flies in the

9 Elsewhere he writes of his HIV+ partner 'When I tell Chris – lovingly – that I want to feel him shoot inside me, unprotected, it indicates a level of trust, of cohesion, that I don't think is achievable when both partners are primarily concerned with preventing the exchange of bodily fluids' (O'Hara 1997b).

face of every medical and journalistic opinion in the world. I applaud this sort of independence. These men are, I might add, some of the most inventive sex partners I've been with. No surprise.

(1997a:129)

It is illustrative of O'Hara's position as a minoritized sexual and medical subject that his sexual practice entails practices of cultural production. In order to create a viable context for his life he found himself contending forces that would keep both homosexuality and the realities of HIV isolated and private. Though he spent most of his career writing, discussing and practising sex, at the heart of O'Hara's work as a cultural producer is a conviction that there is nothing very special about it. In the preface to *Autopornography* he writes 'sex is really not the all important subject that my writing would seem to imply' though he admits to having had a 'one-string harp for the past decade':

All I want is for sex and porn to take their proper places in life, alongside eating and writing letters – enjoyable activities, not for everyone perhaps, but normal, beneficial, and quite, quite harmless to children. Nothing to get excited about.

(1997a: ix)

For O'Hara, sex is a field of friendly sociability and ordinary belonging. Indeed, when he wants to convey his attitude to sex in his later videos, he does something very unusual in gay porn: he smiles.

In 1993, O'Hara established *Steam* magazine, a publication he edited and billed as a 'Quarterly Journal for Men'. He distributed the first issue free at the March on Washington though later editions came in at a heftier $5.95. The magazine featured accounts of his and other writers' sexual experiences, as well as reports on bathhouses and other areas where gay men meet for sex, and various commentary and writings on sexual matters. Among the contents were regular discussions of HIV issues, though these were not restricted to unexamined rehearsals of public health mantra. The magazine grew to include a literary element, with excerpts of work from writers, scholars and activists such as Samuel R. Delany, Eric Rofes and Pat Califia. *Steam* contributed to what had become a flourishing public culture around sexuality in the United States and elsewhere, only one of a multitude of circulars, events, meeting places, conferences, performances, parties and collections that offered alternatives to the authorised construction of sex as rightfully situated in the home, between man and wife, in the context of conjugal intimacy. The magazine was explicit about how it wanted to link sex and public culture:

We encourage writers, photographers, film-makers, artists, and everyone else to work in the field of sexual expression – not because it's necessarily about Public Sex, but because the more public our sexuality becomes – via, for instance, artwork that deals with it – the less upset society will be with our 'flaunting' our sex in public.

(O'Hara 1993)

Like other projects of this sort, the magazine hoped to reverse the damaging disinformation of privacy and shame that produces and suffocates subordinate sexualities. Thus whatever problems one might have with the way O'Hara positions HIV seroconversion in the passage cited at length above (where it appears almost as a rite of passage naturalized by gendered constructions of risk, bravado and independence) one can also appreciate the way he helped activate a public setting in which such issues could be debated and collectively and actively negotiated.

I have opened this chapter with a discussion of Scott O'Hara's work as a way into some of the contemporary dimensions of sex and HIV prevention among gay men. O'Hara's discourse is familiar in terms of a certain approach to sex that one encounters in some urban and non-urban gay cultures in various parts of the world – one that I believe to be of some value. In beginning this chapter with O'Hara's work I do not wish to overstate or lionize his celebrity or cast him as exemplary, since to do so would be to frame him in terms of some norm or ideality when what I seek is a more ethical engagement with the corpus of material from which his work is drawn. Indeed I find myself in the curious position of wanting at once to affirm and resist O'Hara's authority. O'Hara was only one of the voices that began to speak and write of the pleasures of unprotected sex at about the time that Highly Active Antiretroviral Therapy ('HAART') was made available in the West (in 1996).[10] These accounts typically referred to unprotected penetrative sex between HIV-positive men, something that is safe with respect to HIV transmission and whose physical sensations are largely taken for granted by much of the population. But since they breached established norms around safe sex and the use of condoms, these declarations were subject to attack. I want to affirm such accounts in the sense that they represent creative and situated negotiations of the relations between sex, HIV risk, experimentation and care. They contribute to a larger project of collective self-improvization and engagement that has been crucial to the success of HIV prevention, and from which the original invention of 'safe sex' sprang. As feminist literature has shown, knowledge does not merely flow in a top-down direction. Against the pessimism of epidemiological risk categories (which deterministically

---

10 HAART was a term coined to denote combination therapy involving a new class of drugs, protease inhibitors, publicized at the 1996 International AIDS Conference in Vancouver. Where it is made available (it still reaches only a tiny proportion of the world's HIV-infected population), HAART is celebrated as converting HIV/AIDS from a fatal condition to a chronic manageable illness.

linked risk to certain social categories and 'promiscuity'), safe sex drew on the lived experience of gay sexuality, the biological modes of viral transmission, and the interruptive practices of condoms and non-penetrative sex to establish new protocols of safety.[11] Similarly, in attending to the situated experience of sex and risk, accounts such as O'Hara's mobilize lay knowledge in the construction of viable intimate practices that avoid HIV transmission. Rather than positioning 'risk' and 'safety' as practices that are set once and for all, they tackle the more difficult and intensive work of conceiving HIV risk as subject to a relational dynamic that involves intimate negotiation between two or more persons as well as changing technologies and conditions.[12] They approach risk as a matter of subjective responsiveness and interpersonal sense-making rather than pre-emptive legislation by technocrats. The authority to define risk and safe practice is wrestled away from medical monopoly and opened up onto a public and popularly accessible sphere. This approach has great value for those who wish to promote some movement around HIV prevention.

But O'Hara's account also illustrates some of the risks of liberal, or neoliberal, self-accounting when it comes to the collective responsibility for HIV prevention. His attempt to make sense of his AIDS diagnosis and reject a patient or victim identity sets off alarm bells for the example it might set to both HIV-positive and HIV-negative men with respect to HIV prevention. Such alarm has grown to define whole agendas of HIV education in the era of HAART, particularly in the United States, with materials now routinely depicting the more gruesome aspects of treatment side-effects in campaigns that explicitly aim to devalue HIV-positive experience in the eyes of the gay public and which sometimes seem to be nothing more than a concerted attempt at re-victimization. One of the values of O'Hara's account is the way it illustrates how this discourse (of positive value) preceded the introduction of HAART and drew elements from prior discourses of positive self-empowerment and long-term survivorship. His perspective on risk is embedded within a shared experience of long-term survival that preceded HAART but was of course unknown at the beginning of the AIDS crisis. Today, the conflict between discourses of positive self-empowerment and discourses of HIV prevention is aggravated by the improved prospects of living with HIV in the context of HAART availability and represents a major impasse in contemporary gay responses to the epidemic.

Thus apart from the sociological insight and ethical complexity that a consideration of O'Hara's work offers in respect of HIV-positive sexual practice, another reason for citing him here is that O'Hara is often associated and

---

11 See Escoffier 1999, Patton 1990.
12 For a detailed theoretical discussion of the relation between HIV medical technologies and sexual practice see Rosengarten (forthcoming).

sometimes even attributed authorship of a specific valuation of unprotected anal sex known as 'barebacking'. Indeed he comes close to claiming this authority for himself when he says in a 1997 opinion piece that he was 'probably the first person to make a public Declaration of Intent to Engage in Unsafe Sex in a national publication' (O'Hara, 1997b).[13] Barebacking emerged in the context of a series of accounts of this sort that provoked outrage both within and outside the gay press, such that it soon took on the sense of an 'erotically charged, premeditated act' with little reference to the question of serostatus (and in some instances at least a highly sensationalized investment in risk on the part of HIV-negative men) (Rofes 1998).[14] I am interested in the conditions in which self-accounts such as O'Hara's can be taken to amount to a defiant and indiscriminate intentionality with respect to HIV transmission and the sense in which those conditions can be understood as disciplinary.[15] I want to suggest that barebacking can be approached as the outcome of a fractious encounter between normative publicity and embodied ethics in which the latter were basically misrecognized by the former.[16] O'Hara's is a fortuitous instance because of the ethical care (and also self-regard) that can be found in his sexual practice. By tracking the different forms his discourse takes as it moves from one scene of publicity to another we can see how barebacking takes on a life of its own and how this investment in unprotected anal intercourse depends on an encounter between normative apprehension and a defensive response to this apprehension, such that the desire for condomless sex materializes, if only very occasionally, as a defiant intent to have *unsafe* sex. To make its (perfectly viable) claim around HIV-positive sexuality, barebacking reached for what is perhaps the most available language to defend a practice under attack: the language of individual rights and entitlements. This had the effect of framing sex as a property or entitlement rather than a relation between people, promoting what some have analysed as a presumptive (rather than malicious) disregard of the other within barebacking discourse (Adam 2005). It is O'Hara's defensive, individualized citation of the norm and the way it encourages us to relate to sex as an abstract property or entitlement rather than a

---

13 This piece appears in the mainstream gay publication *The Advocate* and refers to a 1995 editorial in *Steam* magazine, 'Exit the Rubberman' which thematically resembles the passage quoted at length above, though it adopts even more strident tones. I am grateful to Eric Rofes for finding me a copy of 'Exit the Rubberman'.
14 Rofes provides a vital and engaged account of this moment in the North American context.
15 I use this term in Foucault's sense to refer to the process, peculiar to modern societies, of distributing behaviour around a given norm and producing it in terms of normal or abnormal individuality. I want to emphasize the categorical and individualizing elements of this process of subject formation, whereby subjects are led to assess their individuality against norms of HIV prevention (here, the condom code). See Foucault 1977.
16 My understanding of publicity as a gendered phenomenon is derived from Warner 2002. See Chapter 4.

relational field that I wish to resist. Thus I propose to use O'Hara's writings and their circulation as an entry point into a broader analysis of the normative conditions in which gay sex involving HIV-positive subjects becomes uncovered.

Some insight into these conditions can be gleaned from an article that appeared in the *San Francisco Chronicle* in February 2006, entitled 'The Same Sex Scene: A Serosorting Story'(Heredia 2006). Despite the inflammatory reaction to barebacking in 1997, an apparent decline in the rate of new infections in San Francisco by 2006 despite increases in so-called 'risk practice'[17] led some authorities to embrace what they call 'serosorting' – the practice of selecting sexual partners on the basis of sharing the same HIV status. This is of course the same practice that people like O'Hara were promoting in the furore over barebacking, though now made respectable some 10 years later with a scientific designation (the bitter irony of which is certainly understated by one man interviewed for this article who says, 'I was doing serosorting before they had a word for it. Now, they're saying it is an effective prevention strategy, which is great.') But where barebacking scandalized by virtue of its apparent association with promiscuity and casual sex, serosorting is normalized by means of a conjugal frame that promises 'an intimacy previously missing'.[18] Barebacking and serosorting clearly overlap, and may actually refer to the same practice, but they proclaim quite different positions in the field of sexual morality, revealing how risk discourse is filtered through and enforces already moralized categories. By paying attention to the terms in which serosorting is endorsed for a mainstream audience we can gain insight into some of the forces that mediate the intelligibility of gay sex in relation to HIV prevention.

Serosorting is constructed in the article as a form of mutual support ('leaning on each other') in the context of chronic illness, with the added spin-off of HIV containment. The story opens with a 'waiting room romance', at the clinic where two long-term HIV survivors meet and fall in love. The article usefully frames serosorting in terms of the contemporary pressures that bear on HIV-positive subjectivity, with the HIV-positive individuals interviewed speaking of the stresses associated with the fear of infecting others, the challenges of disclosing HIV status to new partners, and the advantages of negotiating elements of long-term chronic illness in relation with someone who knows what to expect and who is going through something similar. For these individuals, seroconcordant relations are one way of resolving such concerns. A San Francisco couples therapist is quoted:

---

17 That is risk, as reified in the practice of unprotected anal intercourse.
18 The by-line of the article reads: 'Dating within the HIV-positive or negative population has reduced the HIV infection rate in San Francisco. It also allows for an intimacy previously missing.' See Berlant 1997, on the politics of intimacy in the neo-conservative US.

> I don't think HIV positive men are hooking up to help the community
> ... I think they are doing it so they don't have to use condoms and
> so they can circumvent that HIV coming-out process. They don't want
> to have to hide their meds [medications]. Physiologically there are
> changes in their bodies they can't hide. In serosorting they're looking for
> somebody who doesn't have issues with these things.

These comments have the merit of constructing serosorting as a question of
pleasure and convenience for HIV-positive men, casting it as a reasonable
response to current configurations of risk, responsibility, pleasure, health and
new technology.

But when serosorting is seized upon as a public HIV prevention strategy,
something funny happens. The story quotes interview material from Lee, a
44-year-old part-time usher who 'prefers to only date HIV-positive men
because he would rather have sex without condoms'. The emergence of
HIV dating sites on the internet and the high proportion of HIV-positive
gay men in San Francisco are cited as conditions that enable him to disclose
his HIV status easily. The inclusion of Lee is noteworthy because his sex
life does not adhere strictly to an ideal of long-term conjugal commitment.
But Lee is drawn in the heterosexual imagery of 'dating' ('I exclusively
date HIV-positive guys'), and is pictured spending time with his partners
engaging in couple-like activities such as 'finding entertainment in the
community that is low-cost or free'. Meanwhile, James and Brian, the
feature couple of the article, are monogamous. The article probes their
intimate life:

> The couple's sex life has evolved. At first they had sex without condoms.
> But after a couple of years together, [Brian] decided he didn't want to
> risk giving [James] his strain of the HIV virus, a particularly nasty type
> that is hard to treat. Instead they enjoy kissing, petting, preening and
> massaging each other ... 'To be in love with somebody and having a
> fulfilling life you're not missing out on anything not having penetrative
> sex,' James said.

The article closes with the couple gently caressing and snuggling on the
couch, highlighting their 'matching titanium rings'. 'The only time we're
apart is when we're on our way to getting together,' says Brian.

The construction of serosorting in this article brings home the importance
of attending to the ways in which practices involving minoritized sex and
HIV are normatively grasped. Where barebacking is misrecognized as intentional recklessness such that the practical ethics informing the practice are
lost, serosorting is celebrated in conventional terms that invisibilize gay
practices and cultures of casual sex. It is telling that the valorization of
serosorting in this piece rests on the ultimate erasure of gay anal sex as well as

an invocation of matrimonial norms. A normative investment in segregation also becomes apparent with one interview cited: 'Seroselecting is like choosing somebody who is in the same church, like being Episcopalian or Methodist and wanting to marry an Episcopalian or Methodist ... They just get it, you don't have to explain.' There are times in this discourse when serosorting appears to be nothing more than an intricate device through which gay men might be shepherded into normative modes of relationship, sorted by HIV status. The narrative betrays a phobia around the very idea of HIV-positive people as actively sexual, which it attempts to contain by appealing to normative forms of intimacy (Crimp 1992). But this characteristic only indicates a more immediate problem for HIV prevention workers who must come up with realistic strategies adapted to the practical contexts in which gay sex occurs. While the discourse of serosorting references a widely accessible (and widely accessed) culture of casual sex, it offers a somewhat sanitized version that does not exactly correspond with the sexual culture in which most 'serosorting' takes place. In all the talk around serosorting there is little attention to the relational or situational contexts of gay sex or their practical contingencies. While it is possible that the apparent anonymity of the internet may make it easier for some HIV-positive men to disclose their status when seeking sex online, it remains the case that disclosure is rare in most of the contexts in which casual gay sex occurs, and there are considerable obstacles and practical difficulties around disclosure for HIV-positive gay men.[19] Meanwhile in social research a surprising number of HIV-negative men indicate rarely knowingly having sex with an HIV-positive partner, an expectation that does not reflect reality, and it seems that few HIV-negative men are clued into the sometimes very subtle attempts of HIV-positive men to negotiate seroconcordant unprotected sex (many of which do not involve spoken disclosure of HIV status).[20] In this sense, the discourse of serosorting may promote a certain brand of wishful thinking that is much more difficult to effect in practice. While after two decades of AIDS it seems important to find ways in which gay men can safely enjoy unprotected anal sex (including in casual contexts), the uncovering of gay sex within serosorting discourse is premised upon a normative misrecognition of much gay sexual practice and promotes this same misrecognition *within* it, raising its own set of challenges and risks.

The appearance of the internet in this narrative dramatizes some of the paradoxes of normative exposure for HIV-positive subjects and brings us back to the discussion of O'Hara. For while norms of individual responsibility would seem to require that HIV-positive subjects advertise their status

19 Even in San Francisco. See Sheon and Crosby 2004.
20 For a lucid illustration of this point see Adam 2005. His observations are borne out by survey data in Australia. See VanDeVen *et al* 2001, 36–7.

when seeking sex online, it is just such an advertisement that HIV prevention advocates fret over when they suggest that the internet 'causes' unsafe sex. In the context of barebacking the internet was often said to cause risk by virtue of the visibility it gave to HIV-positive sex but in the context of serosorting it has become an icon of responsibility. The terms of risk become identifiable with the terms of responsibility here, insofar as both anticipate some level of abstract self-publicity around HIV. It is noteworthy, for example, that O'Hara cites national publicity as the context for his 'Declaration of Intent'. The norms of abstract personhood that inhere in the national public sphere lead him to discount the relational or embodied contexts of his practice in favour of an assertion of his individual entitlement.[21] O'Hara's self-disclosure can similarly be understood to involve a certain 'taking' of responsibility. His sexual practice is taken in normative terms to be 'irresponsible', though a more detailed account shows that it is carefully considered. Normative constructions of responsibility work here to undercut ethical relations to the self and others and spectacularize them as risk. At this moment, we can see how risk and responsibility enter into a zone of indistinction for HIV subjects and it becomes apparent that barebacking and serosorting run the same range of risks, alternatively grasped – a major misrecognition of minor practices of corporeal responsibility.[22] Perhaps what needs to be contended with here is the normative infrastructure that turns minor instances of self-disclosure into advertisements.

In this context, it is useful to consider the editorial discourse of another infamous 'zine that formed part of this public culture in terms of the distance it takes from some of the overtones of O'Hara's discourse. One of the ways that O'Hara's accounts differ from many representations of condomless sex between HIV-positive men that circulated at this time was his willingness to editorialize about HIV-positive status as a viable identity for uninfected men.[23] The *Diseased Pariah News* was a magazine published for, by and about HIV-positive people, and used dark humour and unabashed sexuality to challenge the construction of the HIV-positive as frail, pitiable and desexualized patients.[24] Like *Steam, Diseased Pariah News* worked to construct a counterpublic set of identities and subject positions around sexuality and medicine, in this case primarily among HIV-positive gay men. It took its leave, however, from the exemplary character of the discourse within

21 For more on the risks and paradoxes of mass abstraction for minority subjects see Warner 2002 and Berlant 1997.
22 On zones of indistinction and the politics of exposure see Agamben 1995.
23 Compare the examples cited by Rofes 1998.
24 *Diseased Pariah News* took its name from a cartoon about Delta Airlines refusing to fly known HIV-positive people, in which a man at the ticket counter is asked by the agent, 'Would you like smoking, nonsmoking or the diseased-pariah section?'

which O'Hara effectively advertises his HIV status.[25] As one of the editors, Tom Shearer, put it in the first edition:

> We should warn you that our editorial policy does not include the concept that AIDS is a Wonderful Learning Opportunity and Spiritual Gift From Above. Or a Punishment for our Previous Badness. Nor are we much interested in being icons of noble tragedy, brave and true, stiff upper lips gleaming under our oxygen hoses. We are not saints or devils, just a couple-o-guys who ran into a Danger Penis.
>
> (Shearer 1990)

Diseased Pariah News refutes the demonics of HIV-positive identity, but also its heroics. This had less to do with the magazine's commitment to the imperative of HIV prevention than its access to variable experiences of living with HIV. By setting up a counterpublic scene of HIV-positive revaluation, *Diseased Pariah News* generated a sharp critique of the normative terms of liberal self-representation and its stark alternatives of glamorization or demonization. In other words, it does not follow from O'Hara's example that positive self-representation works against a well-informed response to HIV – quite the contrary. With the introduction of HAART, for example, *Diseased Pariah News* hoped to present an unpopular alternative to the glossy representations of living with HIV that flooded US public culture at that time in the form of pharmaceutical advertisements. As editor Tom Ace put it in 1997: 'Anyone who thinks that we're close to the end of AIDS just isn't involved in what's going on. They don't have friends who failed the drugs. Or friends who have side effects. The drugs are not a walk in the park.'[26]

By considering these media in terms of how they work to construct various public and counterpublic identities and subjectivities, we gain insight into how different risks materialize around HIV and what this has to do with normative publicity. If we consider that bodies only make sense within a disciplinary frame shot through with sex and gender norms, we can ask how a sexed and gendered 'grid of intelligibility' mediates the ways in which various responses to HIV become available,[27] and the difference that different scenes

25 For a preliminary formulation of exemplary power in relation to drugs and mass consumption see Race 2005.

26 Cited in Anonymous 1997. After the death of its founding editors, the final issue of *Diseased Pariah News* (11) was circulated in 1999 and included critical commentary on HAART. Tom Ace, editor of the final edition, wrote 'we're not quitting because protease inhibitors have made DPN obsolete. We emphatically don't believe that AIDS is history (yet)'(36).

27 My use of the term 'grid of intelligibility' is informed by the recent work of Judith Butler, who uses it to show how processes of self-reporting and self-understanding are structured by social norms, in particular sex and gender norms (Butler 2004). Butler situates the concept in relation to processes of recognition and self-recognition: 'Indeed, if we consider that human

of publicity make to the materialization of these norms. What happens as various parties strive to make minority practices (of HIV risk but also HIV prevention) normatively intelligible? What distortions, identities, impasses, advantages, and compromises ensue and how are they negotiated? The combination of minoritized sexuality, mass abstraction and discipline at play here suggests the need to theorize ways in which experience can be grasped as particular, and particularly shared.[28] I am interested therefore in the question of how to engage with barebacking: how one might engage critically with this body of material without inciting the same defiant charge. I want to perform a different relation to the body of material from which O'Hara's voices are drawn – one that is not confined to the dangerous terms of moral denunciation and liberal celebration. This is essentially a methodological question, and in the next section I consider different ways of knowing HIV risk and the different forms of responsibility they produce.

THE DISCIPLINARY PRODUCTION OF INTENT TO ENGAGE IN UNSAFE SEX

I stated above that this analysis concerns the normative conditions in which gay sex involving HIV-positive subjects becomes uncovered. I meant to suggest the ways in which normative constraints on the representation of gay sex and HIV might be considered to be implicated in the proliferation of barebacking. It bears emphasizing at this point, however, that barebacking is only one of the descriptions that gay men give for unprotected sex; and individual 'intention' only one of the explanations. In Australia, for example, education has been conducted on how to ensure safe unprotected sex between HIV-negative gay men in regular relationships since 1994 (dubbed 'negotiated safety') in a move that many credit to have undermined much of the appeal of so-called 'barebacking'.[29] Apart from this and similar risk-reduction practices, gay men account for unsafe sex in a number of ways: erectile difficulty or frustration with condoms; getting carried away with the moment; slipping up; mistaken assumptions about one's partner's HIV status; desiring greater

bodies are not experienced without recourse to some ideality, some frame for experience itself, and that this is true for the experience of one's own body as it is for experiencing another, and if we accept that that ideality and frame are socially articulated, we can see how it is that embodiment is not thinkable without a relation to a norm, or set of norms' (28). The value of this approach is that it directs attention to the conditions in which subjecthood and identity are produced. It asks that we examine the interplay of practice and recognition, and see how social norms mediate and structure that process.

28 I thank Niamh Stephenson for pressing this point in her many discussions with me on this issue. See Stephenson and Papadopoulos 2006.
29 See Kippax 2002.

intimacy or intensity; particular relational dynamics (such as not wanting to compromise the encounter because of the partner's presumed superiority and/or desire for unprotected sex); not knowing how to introduce a condom; being drunk or out of it on drugs; forgetting; an accident; personal turmoil – and this is only the beginning of an interminable list, none of which are necessarily best understood as either 'barebacking' or 'intentional'.

Wanting greater precision in their documentation of the 'offending' practice, social scientists have come to define barebacking more strictly as 'intentional unsafe sex'. But as Gregory Tomso has observed, the move to define barebacking strictly as 'intentional unsafe sex' has had the effect of producing barebacking as a problem of volition and desire and generates an even greater scrutiny and policing of gay men's moral intentions (Tomso 2004). As it stands, even among self-identified barebackers the most common explanations given for their 'intentions' are wanting to experience greater physical stimulation and wanting to feel emotionally connected to their partner. Only 17 per cent of a sample of HIV-negative barebackers from San Francisco gave as their reasons wanting to 'do something taboo or racy' while 22 per cent cited as their motivation 'to take a major risk' (these items were not mutually exclusive) (Mansergh *et al* 2002).[30] Admittedly surveys are a blunt instrument when it comes to investigating the complexity of subjective meanings, but it would seem that on this definition the eroticization of risk counts for only a small portion of self-reported barebacking. The subject of my analysis, though, is not the actual incidence of eroticized risk in the gay population, which would seem to be limited, but *the processes through which unsafe sex materializes as a matter of defiant intention.* I want to approach eroticized risk as the mainly unrealized potential of normal processes of subjectivation and reification occurring at the intersection of familiar discourses of intimacy and risk.[31] These processes could be understood as disciplinary: they involve the recognition of some level of agency and desire among gay men in the vicinity of risk (e.g. the ordinary desire for sex without condoms); a normative confrontation or condemnation of that agency; and an individualized or aggravated response to that confrontation. Critically, then, my focus is on the refraction of individual desire through official discourse: the contrary effects of the mechanisms through which gay men are responsibilized.[32] I query the system that would erotically construct

---

30 Interestingly, these explanations were less pertinent for HIV-positive barebackers, of whom only 10 per cent and 7 per cent of cited them respectively.

31 See the discussion of how risk discourse intensifies intimacy in O'Hara's discourse above.

32 This can be theorized in Foucaultian terms as an operation of power that 'applies itself to immediate everyday life which categorizes the individual, marks him by his own individuality, attaches him to his own identity, imposes a law of truth on him which he must recognize and which others have to recognize in him', whereby barebackers identify the excitement of sex without condoms as the truth of their identity. Foucault 1982.

gay men as intentional deviates when it comes to HIV transmission.[33] As Tomso observes, one cannot separate out 'media representations' and 'scientific facts' here; the conflation of barebacking with other instances of unprotected sex takes place in both the media and the science (Tomso 2004). And since HIV is such a dense site of positivist social science, I want to turn now to a consideration of how social science participates in this process of risky responsibilization.

The study 'Barebacking Among Gay and Bisexual Men in New York City: Explanations for the Emergence of Intentional Unsafe Behaviour' sets out to assess 'the frequency with which gay and bisexual men in New York City engage in intentional unprotected sex, or "barebacking" ' (Halkitis, Parsons, and Wilton 2003). The authors set up their report with exemplary precision. They begin by noting that unprotected anal sex has 'gained momentum' in the last several years 'in part because of relapse from safer sex on the part of gay and bisexual men, but also to [sic] the increasingly popular behavioral phenomenon of intentional unsafe sex, referred to as "barebacking" '(2003: 351). They acknowledge that 'intentional unsafe anal acts may yield minimal or no risk' of HIV transmission in the context of seroconcordant partnerships: unprotected sex between two people known to be of the same HIV status poses no risk of HIV infection. And they discuss the need, by now registered in the science, to differentiate between 'unintentional' unsafe behaviour and 'the increasingly popular unsafe anal practices, which are "intentional" and/or premeditated', and have become 'colloquially known in the mainstream and academic press as "barebacking" '.

This initial meticulousness bears an ambiguous relation to the study's method, however, which the authors outline as follows:

> Participants were asked to respond to the following questions: I am familiar with the term 'barebacking' as it is used by gay men to describe their sexual behavior. No further definition of the 'barebacking' was provided to participants by the research team as we were interested in individual perceptions of the phenomenon; however, 'barebacking' was clearly identified by the survey as a term related to the sexual practices of gay men. Our previous work has shown that barebacking is typically understood by gay men in NYC to refer to intentional unprotected anal intercourse. If they reported familiarity with the term, participants were

33 As Tomso has written, 'bug chasing and barebacking exist as phenomena largely because of what Foucault would call the constitutive, disciplinary operation of scientific, activist, and popular discourses about them. That is to say that those who are currently investigating and writing about these phenomena, as much so if not more than the men whose sexual lives are the subjects of these investigations, are epistemologically accountable for the emergence of bug chasing and barebacking as social 'problems' (2004: 89). I would add ontologically.

then asked to report the number of men with whom they had engaged in bareback sex in the 3 months prior to assessment.

(2003: 353)

This method yields the result that 45.5 per cent of the 448 men familiar with the term barebacking reported engaging in bareback sex with at least one sexual partner in the previous three months[34] – a figure that is considerably higher than the 14 per cent reported in a 2002 San Francisco study that explicitly defined barebacking as 'intentional unprotected anal intercourse with a non-primary partner'(Mansergh *et al* 2002).[35] On the basis of these findings and documented increases in HIV seroconversion, the authors propose that 'intentional unprotected sex is increasing among gay and bisexual men' (Halkitis, Parsons and Wilton 2003).

To be fair, the meaning of the term 'barebacking' depends on its usage and circulation. It is not set in time, fixed once and for all. Indeed, the method of this study could be considered to be well attuned to the dynamics of the floating signifier: it is necessary and perhaps important for researchers to investigate everyday perceptions and usages of cultural terms, which, after all, may be much wider and more various than any 'original' definition. It's quite probable, in other words, that the term 'barebacking' has travelled well beyond any initial specification and that it is used loosely by many men by this time to refer to unprotected sex in general. (This might explain the fact that half the sample reported engaging in barebacking – a figure that is closer to the general incidence of unprotected sex among gay men in urban centres). That said; there is a tension here between what the study claims to be doing and what it actually does. In particular, it secretly narrows the definition of the term 'barebacking' even as it casts a wide net around the usage of the term among study participants. Through its prefatory definitional work, the study captures as 'intentional unprotected sex' what may in fact be a considerably more diverse range of practices and occasions. It misrecognizes the vernacular of participants as completely identifiable with the scientifically defined terms, and thus encourages the subject of its discourse to misrecognize them too. In this sense, the study does indeed offer a convincing 'Explanation for the Emergence of Intentional Unsafe Behavior', as it claims to in the title: The constitutive and normalizing work of HIV social science itself! The study is intimately involved in the misrecognition and materialization of unprotected gay sex as a matter of intention.

34 This figure represents 60.9 per cent of the HIV-positive respondents and 41.8 per cent of the HIV-negative respondents, and is inclusive of unprotected sex between men of the same HIV status (which in fact accounts for the majority of instances).
35 It should be noted that the latter study excludes instances of 'intentional unprotected sex' that have taken place within a primary partnership, which the Halkitis study may conceivably include.

In making this claim my aim is not to write off HIV social research in general, nor these researchers in particular, who certainly make a productive contribution to understandings of HIV risk. Rather, the concern is that this mode of inquiry actually promotes a subtle misrecognition of the contingencies of practice, such that gay men are encouraged to recognize, as a matter of 'intention', something that may in fact be much more variable. This is not to argue that gay men are not accountable for what happens in the various sexual contexts in which they find themselves; rather the point is that this mode of identification encourages a turning away from the material and contingent relations of risk, when what could otherwise be promoted is more careful consideration of them. What is being claimed, then, is that this mode of accountability, the crafting of an intentional individual subject of risk – which is as much a corollary of social scientific practice as it is of wider discourse – does not adequately address the circumstances, the matter at hand.

To explore this point further, let us turn to a valuable discussion of the talk of recently diagnosed HIV-positive gay men in Sydney. In a perceptive analysis, Sean Slavin and colleagues discuss the range of accounts of unprotected sex that the participants believe to put them at risk, including an account involving considered practices of risk reduction among serodiscordant partners; an account involving sex with an attractive partner while on the recreational drug ecstasy; an account involving 'not caring what happened' and intense feelings of passion and intimacy; and an account involving wanting to 'make things easy' in the context of a relationship with a positive partner (Slavin, Richters and Kippax 2004). As the authors discuss: 'These four men narrate their experience of risk not as a result of an accident or misinformation, but as individual choices, informed about risk. Informed, that is, about the technical principles and "objective" facts of viral transmission.'

> They all claim to have known what they were doing at the time of infection and had made a choice, freely and rationally. They all attempt to distinguish between these principles of choice and any emotional, social and cultural context in which they are situated . . . There is a sense in all these narratives that participants hold themselves solely responsible for having become infected, that they knew what they were doing. They do not consider that context or other factors beyond their control may have mediated the decisions they were making. Such an acknowledgement would seem to question their belief in themselves as 'in control' – of themselves and their circumstances.
>
> (2004: 45)

The authors treat these characteristics as a feature of the discourse or experience of this 'group' of individuals, but what if we were to approach these features as an effect of the disciplinary grid through which these subjects are encouraged to recognize themselves as subjects? These accounts are made in the context of open-ended interviews conducted a short time after seroconversion.[36] Participants are referred to the study by their HIV clinician and interviewed by a social researcher, either at home or at a community health centre. It is difficult to say whether the context of a private interview gives the participant more or less opportunity to explore their experience in tentative terms – most likely it differs from time to time. But it is interesting to consider what sort of subject is produced in this specific relational context. It is a subject who is rational and decisional and in control of their circumstances, whose choice with respect to risk exists outside any relational or temporal setting, as the authors discuss (2004: 48). Thus, while participants give fairly fluent accounts of the circumstances that they believe placed them at risk, they also insist, as the authors report, on a rational, choice-making self. In particular, they discount the effects of these circumstances on what they call their 'decisions about risk'. These accounts can be read as records of a process of subjectivation constrained by certain norms of intelligibility: they give clues to the sort of subject that emerges as a reflection of authorized discourse. Are these individuals participants in acts of 'intentional unsafe sex'? Only within a disciplinary frame that invites them to recognize themselves as such. While it would be possible to argue for the need for a subject even *more* in control of their circumstances given the event of HIV infection in these instances, it is worth considering that such an approach might actually promote further occlusion of the complex relations that make up sexual lives and sexual practices.

In his study of the discourses of HIV-positive men in Toronto who use the language of barebacking to refer to their practice, Barry Adam finds that 'interviews with self-professed barebackers reveal not so much rebellion or transgression as something more prosaic and more consistent with the discourses of government and capital. Not only does the responsibilization message resonate throughout their own accounts but the larger rhetoric of neoliberalism does as well, of which responsibility talk is a part' (Adam 2005). Adam's analysis deals only with HIV-positive barebackers, who can be expected to bear a mitigated relation to the erotics of risk.[37] He locates

---

36 Between two weeks and several months. Participants are asked to recount the event(s) they believe led to their infection. The accounts mentioned differ from other participants in the study who believed they had followed moral prescriptions regarding sexual morality and are taken by surprise (rather than experiencing themselves as 'in control' subjects).

37 See for example the findings from Mansergh *et al* discussed above in n 30. In barebacking fantasies on the internet, the HIV-positive role is usually constructed in terms of 'gift-giving' and 'seeding' – metaphors that have less to do with eroticized risk than with community initiation, belonging, and some version of a familiar mythology of intimacy, fertility and procreation.

barebacking as a personal policy found among some HIV-positive men within the urban gay community, embedded in a larger context of encountering men who are HIV-positive or 'in the know'. As is evident in O'Hara's accounts of his sexual practice, neither the practical morality nor the actual practices of the HIV-positive men interviewed 'overtly intend HIV transmission to happen' (2005: 341).[38] But, as Adam illustrates, their practice relies on extremely subtle negotiations that HIV-negative men are often unaware of and, perhaps more significantly, it does not allow for the complex 'vulnerabilities, emotions and tough dilemmas' that characterize everyday life and sexual interaction (2005: 344).

One of the values of Adam's study is the way it illustrates how the discourse of barebackers is consonant with wider, even dominant, discourses that structure social life and moral reasoning. If barebacking is an instance of gendered risk, it is so in this much more subtle sense; insofar as the terms through which the practice is rationalized appeal defensively to a masculine or normative subject of individualized rights, rationality and pure volition, and to the extent that that model is insufficient to account for sexual being and the social relations of HIV infection. 'In many ways,' Adam writes, 'these accounts for unsafe sex participate in the moral reasoning widely propagated by government and business today that constructs everyone as a self-interested individual who must take responsibility for himself in a marketplace of risks. It is perhaps also a particularly masculine discourse in its evocation of norms of competitive individualism' (2005: 340). However, unlike so many accounts of gay life circulating even in 'progressive' circles today, Adam does not hold gay men up as 'exemplars' of neoliberal ideology, but rather remains alive to the virtualities of subject formation. He suggests that 'neoliberal discourse is not totalising nor does it capture the subjectivity of these men in a fundamental way', pointing to competing discourses 'drawn from romance, masculine adventure, gay solidarity, communitarianism, and so on, that can come to the fore, according to circumstance' (2005: 345). By appealing to gay men to take care of other men '(instead of simply defending themselves against other men)', he locates his critique within a tradition of gendered counterpractice. 'It would be an appeal that would run against leading ideologies in circulation in our society today but one that would likely have considerable resonance among men whose sexual pursuits are often linked with the desire to love and be loved by other men' (2005: 345). Gregory Tomso has shown it is not so easy to exempt the practice of care from the possibility of violence (Tomso 2004), and indeed the moralized response to barebacking could be read as a certain demonstration of care (albeit a

---

38 Many participants speak of modifying their practice in the direction of safety upon learning of a partner's HIV-negative status, and the study includes accounts of the considerable lengths some men go to when they discover a mistake has been made.

particularly militant or ignorant one). Especially useful in this regard is the way Adam's methodology undercuts some of the epistemological and technical commitments of neoliberalism. He recognizes and documents the moral intentions of his subjects but also finds ways of suggesting that a mere focus on intentions is not the end of a practical response. In this sense, his analysis works in precisely the opposite direction to the discourses I have been discussing, which totalize the question of intention while ignoring the circumstances of prevention. Rather than debunking neoliberal ideologies in a familiar critical style, Adam recognizes their sedimentation in the embodied experience of those whom he engages and gestures towards other possibilities and tendencies. The ethical sensibilities of participants can thus become involved in a wider querying of normative terms. This provides a sound basis for an ethical engagement with barebacking.

LOCATING CRITIQUE

This chapter has used mainly North American texts and examples to conduct its inquiry. In Australia, the question of how to engage with barebacking has so far been treated as something of a non-question, which does not mean it has not been considered. Australian HIV policy has generally been much quicker to appreciate the prevention initiatives of gay and homosexually active men than elsewhere. While increases in 'risk practice' have been observed since 1996, the rate of new infections had remained relatively steady until 2002, prompting community educators and researchers to question whether our measures of risk practice had kept up with the practical initiatives of gay men 'on the ground'.[39] In place of the barebacker, the 'sophisticated gay man making complex decisions to reduce risk' was the identity that emerged from the constitutive work of social science and education at this point, and to some extent, this identity and the 'cultures of care' with which it was associated helped stave off the reactionary discourse of barebacking.[40] The nationalization of this policy difference was humorously captured (and perhaps even prompted) by an article that appeared in the Sydney gay press in 1999 which reframed the question 'Do you bareback?' to 'Do you jackaroot?' (Honnor 1999). Canvassing 'jackarooting' as seroconcordant unprotected sex, the article situated local sexual practice firmly within an Australian tradition of harm minimization, appealing to a national

---

39 A small increase was recorded in 2002 and more recent figures from Sydney and Melbourne suggest precarious stability in the rate of infection.
40 For an overview of this research see Race 2003. See generally Allan 2003; Honnor 1999; Hurley 2002; Kippax and Race 2003; Rosengarten, Race and Kippax 2000. These interventions have generally followed in the tradition of 'negotiated safety' as discussed in Kippax 2002; Kinder 1996.

image of outback masculinity to signal the possibility of a progressively provincial response to a gay Australian audience. It is interesting that this attempt to mark out a space of difference from the US context still found itself appealing to a national-masculine iconography.

Workers in the field sometimes infer a 'lag' between emerging phenomena overseas (whether this be a trend in risk practice or incidence of infections, the growing popularity of certain recreational drugs, or a cultural practice such as 'barebacking') and the local epidemic. Sometimes this lag tends to feature as a 'breathing space' in which Australia's 'splendid [cultural or epidemiological] isolation' affords practitioners some time to plan for impending threats in an attitude that typically positions the US as the pinnacle of gay development (or decadence?) and Australia, by implication, as 'a bit slow'. At other times, this temporality permits a more interesting and critical relation to certain events and developments overseas, whereby local formations take distance from what are understood to be dominant tendencies in the field and attempt to devise alternatives based on certain social or pragmatic commitments – sometimes informing and even pre-empting elements of international policy or popular discourse.[41] So, for example, in a certain genre of gay Australian journalism, which essentially consists in repackaging HIV stories that have appeared in US magazines for a local audience, journalists come up against some surprises and obstacles when they engage with the local field.

In April 2003 journalist Steve Dow wrote a piece for the *Sydney Star Observer* (Sydney's weekly gay newspaper) in which he argued 'the parlance of "barebacking" has entered the Australian gay lexicon, and AIDS organizations are not sufficiently addressing it. Their safe-sex materials and campaigns need to confront the Americanisation of the language and the misguided romantic notions of sexual outlawry that in this case go with it' (Dow 2003b). For Dow, the slight increase in HIV infections recorded in 2002 was a symptom of the dangerous aestheticisation of unprotected anal sex. What had initially been a North American gloss on unsafe sex had infiltrated Australian gay culture through international media and global technologies such as the internet, and was leading to unsafe behaviour. In a later piece in the *Sydney Morning Herald*, Dow pressed his point:

> That the dangerous has been made to sound exciting is one aspect to consider in the recent rise of HIV cases . . . What [AIDS organizations] haven't got their heads around is the use of language'.
>
> (Dow 2003a)

---

41 For example, the prohibitionist elements of US policy are frequently held up as a bad example and key policy voices speak peremptorily about the 'risk that America's solutions to HIV/AIDS will become our solutions' (Bowtell 2005). Progressive voices in the US often cite elements of Australian policy and research as an enlightened alternative. See, for example, Halperin (2007); Rofes 1998; Warner 1999; Wolitski 2005.

He called for a national campaign: 'The myth of barebacking needs to be confronted in community campaigns and educational material. Most often, the campaigns ignore the word'.

But the response of the Australian sector to the rise in HIV infections showed an awareness of the power of language to create, amplify, and intensify meanings and emotions in ways that can compromise bodies at risk. Their general media strategy could be paraphrased as 'let's all keep calm about this'. If anything, this strategy exposed the irony of Dow's position: despite his plea to address the machinations of language, Dow seemed unconscious of his own implication in the circuits of intrigue, interest, disgust and desire that work to encode unprotected anal sex and its meanings. This stems less from the information he delivers to an Australian audience than the power of the genre in which he participates – the tantalizing journalistic brew of excitement and disapproval – to amplify the very meanings he rails against. Through such media performances, barebacking is compounded as forbidden, exciting and utterly sensational.

As Dow's argument illustrates, the 'risk' of HIV prevention today is less a function of national boundaries and demarcations than a matter of forging a tactical relation to normative technologies. Certainly this can be enabled by different policy environments but it cannot depend (as I think Dow rightly argues) on a presumptive inoculation or quarantine of culture.[42] Moreover, while the 'de-dramatization of risk' pursued by the Australian sector is a far preferable policy to the North American response,[43] it has left us with a somewhat desexualized rational actor that is the staple of much harm reduction discourse.[44] As the studies by Adam and Slavin show, the model is highly consistent with neoliberal constructions of personhood (Adam 2005; Slavin, Richters and Kippax 2004). In the context of slight increases in HIV infections in Australia, one could say that the 'sophisticated gay man' runs into problems to the extent that his practices fail to account for the particular relations of gay sex, HIV risk, and responsiveness. Indeed, there is a sense in which the care taken to present this character in normatively intelligible terms hamstrings agencies from engaging with new risks, meanings, identities and pleasures as they emerge. A well-founded suspicion of the productive effects of moral panic creates a certain caution around communication and HIV education that is not always or inevitably in the best interests of those at risk of acquiring or even transmitting HIV. In this sense the barebacker and the sophisticated gay man are two sides of the same coin. There is no easy way out of this impasse, for as I have been arguing it is an

42 See generally Hardt and Negri 2000.
43 I borrow the phrase 'de-dramatization of risk' from Halperin (2007).
44 On the subject anticipated by harm reduction discourse see O'Malley 1999; O'Malley and Valverde; and Fraser 2004.

outcome of the sexed and gendered terms of public communication itself. Any attempt to constitute minority populations in normatively digestible terms forges a certain compromise that, in the effort to avoid sensationalization, entails a similarly risky occlusion of embodied practice. Addressing this problem requires not only care, but a commitment to querying and expanding the terms of care – a project that should run with positivist social and medical science in order to run against its risks.

REFERENCES

Adam, Barry D. (2005) 'Constructing the Neoliberal Sexual Actor: Responsibility and Care of the Self in the Discourse of Barebackers'. *Culture, Health & Sexuality* 7: 333–46.

Agamben, Giorgio (1995) *Homo Sacer: Sovereign Power and Bare Life*. Translated by D. Heller-Roazen. Stanford: Stanford University Press.

Allan, Brent (2003) 'Sex Strategies' p. 6 in *Positive Living*, August–September.

Anonymous (1997) 'Last Laughs', http://www.poz.com, October.

Berlant, Lauren (1997) *The Queen of America Goes to Washington City: Essays on Sex and Citizenship*, Durham and London: Duke University Press.

Berlant, Lauren and Michael Warner (1998) 'Sex in Public' *Critical Inquiry* 24: 547–66.

Bersani, L. (1988) 'Is the rectum a grave?' in D. Crimp (ed.) *AIDS: Cultural analysis, cultural activism*. Massachussetts: MIT Press.

Bowtell, Bill (2005) 'H.I.V. "Supervirus" Is a Warning to All' in *Sydney Morning Herald* 17 February.

Butler, Judith (1990) *Gender Trouble: Feminism and the Subversion of Identity*. New York: Routledge.

Butler, Judith (2004) *Undoing Gender*. New York: Routledge.

Crimp, D. (1992) 'Portraits of People with Aids' in L. Grossberg, C. Nelson and P. Triechler (eds) *Cultural Studies*, London & New York: Routledge.

Dean, Mitchell (1999) *Governmentality: Power and Rule in Modern Society*. London: Sage.

Dow, Steve (2003a) 'Denial Becomes the New Language of Casual Sex', p. 11 in *Sydney Morning Herald* 3 July.

Dow, Steve (2003b) 'Riding Bareback', p. 5 in *Sydney Star Observer* 10 April.

Eribon, Didier (2004) *Insult and the Making of the Gay Self*. Durham: Duke University Press.

Escoffier, J. (1999) 'The Invention of Safer Sex: Vernacular Knoweldge, Gay Politics and HIV Prevention' *Berkley Journal of Sociology* 43: 1–30.

Foucault, Michel (1977) *Discipline and Punish: The Birth of the Prison*, translated by A. Sheridan. London: Penguin.

Foucault, Michel (1982) 'The Subject and Power' pp. 208–226 in H. Dreyfus and P. Rabinow (eds) *Michel Foucault: Beyond Structuralism and Hermeneutics*. New York: Harvester Wheatsheaf.

Foucault, Michel (1984) *The Use of Pleasure: The History of Sexuality 2*, vol. 2, translated by R. Hurley. London: Penguin.

Fraser, Suzanne (2004) ' "It's Your Life!": Injecting Drug Users, Individual Responsibility and Hepatitis C Prevention' *Health* 8(2): 199–221.

Halkitis, Perry, J. Parsons, and L. Wilton (2003) 'Barebacking among Gay and Bisexual Men in New York City: Explanations for the Emergence of Intentional Unsafe Behavior' *Archives of Sexual Behaviour* 32: 351–57.

Halperin, David (1995) *Saint Foucault: Towards a Gay Hagiography*. Oxford and New York: Oxford University Press.

Halperin, David (2007) *What Do Gay Men Want? An Essay on Sex, Risk and Subjectivity*. Ann Arbour: University of Michigan Press.

Hardt, Michael and Antonio Negri (2000) *Empire*. Cambridge and London: Harvard University Press.

Heredia, Christopher (2006) 'The Same Sex Scene' *San Francisco Chronicle*, 12 February.

Honnor, Geoff (1999) 'Do You Jackaroot?' p. 12 in *Sydney Star Observer* 28 October.

Hurley, Michael (2002) 'Cultures of Care and Safe Sex Amongst HIV Positive Australians' Papers from the HIV Futures I and 2 Surveys and Interviews, Melbourne: Australian Research Centre in Sex, Health and Society, La Trobe University.

Kinder, P. (1996) 'A New Prevention Education Strategy for Gay Men: Responding to the Impact of A.I.D.S on Gay Men's Lives'. Paper presented at *XI International AIDS Conference*. Vancouver.

Kippax, S. (2002) 'Negotiated Safety Agreements among Gay Men' pp. 1–15 in A. O'Leary (ed.) *Beyond Condoms: Alternative Approaches to HIV Prevention*. New York: Kluwer/Plenum Press.

Kippax, Susan and Kane Race (2003) 'Sustaining Safe Practice: Twenty Years On' *Social Science and Medicine* 57: 1–12.

Mansergh, G., G. Marks, G. Colfax, R. Guzman, M. Rader, and S. Buchbinder (2002) ' "Barebacking" in a Diverse Sample of Men Who Have Sex with Men' *AIDS* 16: 653–59.

Morrison, Paul (2001) *The Explanation for Everything: Essays on Sexual Subjectivity*. New York University: New York University Press.

O'Hara, Scott (1993) 'Steam Gets Culture' *Steam*, Autumn, pp. 146.

O'Hara, Scott (1997a) *Autopornography: A Memoir of Life in the Lust Lane*. New York: Harrington Park Press.

O'Hara, Scott (1997b) 'Safety First? Risks of Sexual Intimacy' *The Advocate*, 8 July, p. 9.

O'Malley, Pat (1999) 'Consuming Risks: Harm Minimization and the Government of "Drug-Users" ' in R. Smandych (ed.) *Governable Places: Readings on Governmentality and Crime Control*. Aldershot: Dartmouth.

O'Malley, Pat and Mariana Valverde (2004) 'Pleasure, Freedom and Drugs: The Uses of "Pleasure" in Liberal Governance of Drug and Alcohol Consumption' *Sociology* 38: 25–42.

Patton, Cindy (1990) *Inventing AIDS* New York: Routledge.

Race, Kane (2003) 'Revaluation of Risk among Gay Men' *AIDS Education and Prevention* 15: 369–381.

Race, Kane (2005) 'Recreational States: Drugs and the Sovereignty of Consumption' *Culture Machine* 7 http://culturemachine.tees.ac.uk.

Race, Kane (forthcoming) *Pleasure Consuming Medicine*. Durham: Duke University Press.

Rofes, Eric (1998) *Dry Bones Breathe: Gay Men Creating Post-Aids Identities and Cultures*. Binghampton: Harrington Park Press.

Rosengarten, Marsha (forthcoming) *HIV: A Traffic in Information as Flesh*. Washington: University of Washington Press.

Rosengarten, Marsha, Kane Race and Susan Kippax (2000) 'Touch Wood, Everything Will Be Okay: Gay Men's Understandings of Clinical Markers in Sexual Practice' National Centre in HIV Social Research, University of New South Wales, Sydney.

Shearer, Tom (1990) 'Welcome to Our Brave New World' *Diseased Pariah News* 2.

Sheon, N and G Crosby (2004) 'Ambivalent Tales of HIV Disclosure in San Francisco' *Social Science and Medicine* 58: 2105–18.

Simon, J. (2002) 'Taking Risks: Extreme Sports and the Embrace of Risk in Advanced Liberal Societies', pp. 177–208 in T. Baker and J. Simon (eds) *Embracing Risk: The Changing Culture of Insurance and Responsibility*. Chicago: University of Chicago Press.

Slavin, S., J. Richters, and S. Kippax (2004) 'Understandings of Risk among HIV Seroconverters in Sydney' *Health, Risk & Society* 6: 39–52.

Stephenson, Niamh and D. Papadopoulos (2006) *Analysing Everyday Experience: Social Research and Political Change*. London: Palgrave.

Tomso, Gregory (2004) 'Bug Chasing, Barebacking, and the Risks of Care' *Literature and Medicine* 23: 88–111.

VanDeVen, Paul, P. Rawstorne, J. Crawford, and S. Kippax (2001) 'Facts and Figures: 2000 Male out Survey', National Centre in HIV Social Research.

Warner, Michael (1999) *The Trouble with Normal: Sex, Politics and the Ethics of Queer Life*. Cambridge, Massachusetts: Harvard University Press.

Warner, Michael (2002) *Publics and Counterpublics*. New York: Zone Books.

Wolitski, R. (2005) 'The Emergence of Barebacking among Gay and Bisexual Men in the United States: A Public Health Perspective' *Journal of Gay and Lesbian Psychotherapy* 9: 9–34.

Chapter 6

Criminal justice and 'risky' masculinities

Gaynor Bramhall and Barbara Hudson

INTRODUCTION

Our purpose in this chapter is to look at two aspects of the relationship between criminal justice risk assessment and 'risky masculinities'. The first aspect is the way in which criminalized identities are constructed in the processes of risk assessment; the second is the real risks to which the bearers of these identities may be exposed. Issues have been raised about correlation between factors used in risk assessment and race (Morris 1994), and the part played by the increased orientation of penal strategies towards risk control in rising rates of imprisonment of black Americans (Tonry 1995), but little attention has been given to the dynamic processes of risk assessment and construction of 'risky' identities. Exploring these questions means engaging with criminological themes which are not usually present in work on risk and criminal justice: masculinities, and the construction of criminalizing discourses of race and otherness.

   The chapter draws on research commissioned by an area probation service in North West England, an area which is one of the ten with the highest proportions of minority ethnic persons in the UK. We were asked by the service managers to look at pre-sentence reports written on ethnic minority offenders, following a Home Office thematic inspection which found reports on minority group offenders to be 'lower quality' than those written on white offenders (HMIP 2000). Because of our research interests in risk, in race and in gender, we persuaded the probation service to include risk assessment instruments in the remit, and in publishing findings from the research we have concentrated on these instruments and risk-related content in the pre-sentence reports (Hudson and Bramhall 2005).[1]

---

1 At the time of the study, the main risk assessment instrument used by the probation service in England and Wales was ACE (Assessment, Case-Management and Evaluation System). This was targeted on offenders' needs, but when combined with the earlier OGRS (Offender Group Reconviction Scale), produced a score which is treated as a risk score. OGRS contained

Research on gender and race issues in criminal justice – especially research on probation reports and similar decision-making processes – usually looks for bias or difference in the ways in which subjects are discussed. Racist/sexist language; childcare discussed in reports on females but not on males; questions about experiences of migration and cultural loss addressed to minority ethnic offenders, are examples of this bias and difference. Risk assessment schedules, however, are forms rather than discursive reports; probation officers tick boxes rather than composing descriptive paragraphs, and the information given in the boxes asking for evidence is often extremely brief. For example, a question concerning the defendant's personal skills provides a range of tick box answers that produce a 'problem' and 'offending related score'; an 'evidence box' in which comment, supporting material and explanation can be entered often has the brief comment 'this offence' entered. Even in the body of the pre-sentence reports, in the sections on risk the tick boxes replace the more discursive format of most of the report, and gradings of risk (high, medium, low) appear. So what we were exploring were not so much different descriptions of offenders and their circumstances, but absences, questions that weren't asked, and the ways in which similar circumstances appeared to result in different boxes being ticked, different recommendations made and different sentences imposed.

The first part of the chapter discusses two 'risky masculinities' that emerge from the risk assessments and pre-sentence reports. One is the Muslim Asian male closely entangled with family and community, where relatives and friends are implicated in the crimes committed by the offender. The other is the isolated, lonely white male with few social resources to help him resist pressures towards criminality. These emergent masculinities bear uncomfortably close resemblance to popular stereotypes. This section explores the construction of these masculinities through qualities and circumstances identified as risk factors. Discussion focuses principally on the construction of Muslim Asian masculinity, although the emergence of the counterpart white 'risky' masculinity is not overlooked.

Little research has been concerned with 'prisoners as men' (Sim 1994). Still less research has been devoted to relations between different constructions of masculinity and the vulnerabilities of prisoners. This is the concern of the second part of the chapter, prompted by a finding of both a preliminary review of the service's management information statistics, and the main study. This finding is that the rate of custodial sentences for the South Asian offenders was significantly higher than that for white offenders. For sentences

so-called 'static' risk factors (age, sex, criminal record etc.), while ACE introduced 'dynamic factors' in clusters concerned with attitudes and motivation; lifestyle and associates; personal and social skills. A further risk assessment tool, OASys (Offender Assessment System) which combines OGRS and ACE, has now been introduced.

of between 12 months and 5 years the rates were 15.8 per cent and 9 per cent respectively, and for sentences of less than 12 months they were 14 per cent and 7.6 per cent respectively. These are sentencing bands where there is considerable discretion for sentencers. With the less than 12 months sentence in particular, the prison/community decision is very much influenced by risk-of-reoffending assessment. The cases were matched for offence type, and study of the case-files found the South Asians to be a group with fewer previous convictions than the white offenders (proportionately more of the white offenders had six or more previous convictions; proportionately more of the South Asians had no previous convictions). There was nothing in the criminal histories or present offences to account for the differences in custody rates, suggesting the possibility that differences in the constructions of 'riskiness' for different ethnicities can have important differential consequences for penal outcomes.

Official statistics in the UK generally show that Afro-Caribbeans are overrepresented in prison populations, but that Asian imprisonment rates are the same or even slightly lower than those of whites.[2] However, the category 'South Asian'[3] aggregates Indians, Bangladeshis and Pakistanis, and thereby hides differences in imprisonment rates, and rises and falls in imprisonment rates, between these groups. In the last few years Indian and Bangladeshi imprisonment rates have had more or less average increases, while Pakistanis have had higher-than-average increases (Hudson and Bramhall 2005; Phillips and Bowling 2002). Moreover, Muslims are the largest growing religious group in UK prisons (Home Office 2003).

These trends in imprisonment suggest that Pakistani Muslim offenders are increasingly – and in our research disproportionately – vulnerable to the pains of imprisonment: they are not only 'risky', but also 'at risk'. They are at risk of suicide and self-harm; inadequate care for mental health problems; deterioration of family ties; racist attacks and bullying; and religious hatred. White prisoners are exposed to many of these risks of imprisonment of course; Pakistani Muslims are vulnerable to the same risks, and also to extra risks associated with their religion and ethnicity. Although all suicides in prison are, of course, cause of the gravest concern, it is noteworthy that during 2005, the proportion of suicides by black and minority ethnic prisoners was one in five of all prison suicides, rising from one in ten over the previous five years (Howard League 2006).

2 Race/ethnicity data has been collected in the UK since the Home Office conducted a census of the prison population including race/ethnicity information in 1985. The Criminal Justice Act 1991 placed a responsibility on the Home Secretary to publish data on race and criminal justice.
3 Official statistics used to use the category 'Asian' but this has now been split into two categories, one 'South Asian' and the other to include Chinese, Vietnamese and other east Asians.

'RISKY MASCULINITIES' IN CRIMINOLOGY AND CRIMINAL JUSTICE

The 'masculinity turn' taken by criminology in the 1990s produced a series of 'wild' (Campbell 1993), or 'exotic' masculinities. These adjectives express fascination; they combine repulsion and attraction, desire and rejection. Wild masculinities denote males who are in the tradition of the 'Orientalism' of Western thought (Said 1985): they may fascinate, but the constructs denote males who are intellectually inferior, uncivilized, barbarous, socially malfunctional (Walklate 1995). As Collier puts it, the masculinities constructed by criminology describe the fantasies of the white, male criminologist; they are 'his stories of class, of "dangerous" boys and underworld villains, his accounts of resistances, rituals and struggles' (Collier 1998: 52).

Criminology has looked to social science – sociology, psychology and psychoanalysis – to explain these masculinities and their links with crime (Connell 1995; Hood-Williams 2001; Jefferson 1997; Messerschmidt 1993, 2000; Seidler 2005). In doing so, criminology has veered towards essentialism, giving these masculinities a taken-for-grantedness that sees them as outcomes of social/political/historical cultures, but nevertheless as real, and as implicated in crime. Apart from work on policing, notably the work of Paul Gilroy and colleagues on police constructions of black muggers, robbers and other troublesome characters, there has been little criminological work on the construction of masculinities by the processes of criminal justice agencies (Gilroy 1982, 1987). Although work has been done on race relations in prisons (Genders and Player 1989) and on probation reports (Gelsthorpe and Raynor 1995), this work has concentrated on race-correlated differences in outcomes but not on the construction of racial/ethnic masculinities by the agencies themselves. Literature on risk assessment and criminal justice (at least in the UK) has paid almost no attention to race/ethnicity apart from in relation to policing (Kemshall 2003; Raynor *et al* 2000). When 'masculinity' is considered as a risk factor for criminality, it is again treated as an essential quality, concentrating on what is common to men regardless of race, ethnicity, religion etc., and little attention is paid to the role of the criminal justice system in constructing masculinities (Whitehead 2005).

Our study involved reading all pre-sentence reports and associated risk assessment schedules prepared on ethnic minority offenders by the probation service concerned between June and December 2000, together with an offence-matched sample of one-in-ten reports prepared on white offenders.[4] The sample was found to include only two female cases (one white and one South Asian), and only one case where the offender was identified as having

---

4 The time elapsed between reports being prepared and the research meant that cases had been completed and so sentencing data was available.

an ethnicity that was not white or South Asian; these were excluded as too few to be representative.[5] Those identified as South Asian, with three exceptions, were all Pakistanis. The study therefore became a comparison of the construction of Asian (Pakistani) and white 'risky masculinities': 201 cases, 144 white and 57 South Asians. Although this is obviously too small a study for us to be able to make any sweeping generalizations, the findings are nonetheless interesting and suggestive; moreover, comparison of the management statistics with national statistics showed that the service shared national sentencing and recommendation trends (Home Office 1999).

Analysing the static risk factors, the South Asians emerged as slightly less 'risky' than the white offenders. The cases were matched for offence type, and as already mentioned, fewer had previous convictions, and of those who did, fewer had convictions as juveniles. The proportions who were unemployed were identical (54 per cent), but of those who were unemployed, more of the South Asians were in full- or part-time education (6 per cent of whites; 14 per cent of South Asians).

Differences appeared in the attribution of dynamic risk factors. Proportionately more white offenders were recorded as having 'objective' behaviour problems (problems evidenced by treatment or diagnosis, or subject to calculation) such as alcohol or drug addiction, or financial difficulties. Proportionately more of the South Asians were assessed as having mental health problems, without supporting medical evidence. In the South Asian cases, the evidence most often quoted was 'this offence', although in some cases boxes were ticked without any evidence given at all.

In bringing the items checked on the OGRS and ACE tools together with the comments made in the pre-sentence reports, what struck us was the different treatment of the 'same' items. Most striking of all was the way in which employment, family and lifestyles were interpreted. For the white offenders, problems to do with employment, family and residence were problems of *absence*, whereas for the South Asians they were problems of *presence*.

With employment, for example, lack of employment or its part-time and/or temporary nature was perceived as the problem with the white offenders, and was associated in the reports with low self-esteem, and with financial pressures. The employment/family nexus most often mentioned was that of lack of employment putting pressure on family relationships through the offender not being able to support partner and children financially, not being able to socialise with family and friends, not being able to afford stable accommodation. Lack of employment was depicted as one of the factors most closely associated with offending.

For the South Asians, on the other hand, it was employment, rather than

5 'South Asian' is a classification used in Home Office statistics. It denotes persons from the Indian sub-continent, predominantly Indians, Bangladeshis and Pakistanis.

Table 1 Offending related problems

	White		South Asian	
	No.	%	No.	%
Dangerous	1	0.7		
Reckless/irresponsible	22	15.3	10	17.5
Addictions/alcohol	79	54.9	15	26.3
Financial difficulties	11	7.6	2	3.5
Relationship difficulties	2	1.4	1	1.8
Anti-social attitudes	2	1.4		
Psychiatric problems	2	8.3	7	12.3
Other	4	2.8	5	8.8
Nothing recorded	11	7.6	17	29.8
Total	144	100.0	57	100.0

its lack, that was associated with offending. The work/family nexus in many of these cases was that the employment was in association with family members, and that pressures were put on the offender to engage in illegal activity during the course of work. This was the case in most of the driving whilst disqualified and/or without insurance cases, but work/family was also mentioned in connection with a range of run-of-the-mill property crimes.

Lack of family contact and support were frequently mentioned in cases of white young men committing assault, drugs offences, and a range of other street crimes. On the other hand, it was family dynamics and other family members that were associated with similar crimes for young South Asian men. Identification of offending-related factors in employment, family and community associates reflected popular stereotypes of controlling Asian families, and of violence or public order offences arising from defence of 'community' territories or to prevent young South Asian women from associating with white men. However, families and communities were constructed as the solution rather than the problem for the white offenders: finding a job, re-establishing contact with family, and building ties to the local community were suggested as support frameworks to reduce offending for white young men. For South Asians, offending is linked to a web of family and community pressures; for white young men offending is linked to a life of isolation and rootlessness.

Although these links of risk factors to white and South Asian masculinities were very clear in the research findings, there was often very little on which to base constructions made by the report writers and risk-assessors. In particular, the construction of risk factors for the South Asian offenders was based on very little evidence. In Table 1 above, it is noteworthy that the 'nothing recorded' category has the highest percentage score for the South Asians, and it is the one category where there are more South Asian cases absolutely as well as proportionately. It was common to refer to individual family members in the South Asian cases – often a cousin or uncle – who was pressuring the offender into illegality. Again, this seems to be based on very little, if any, evidence. The offenders discussed in the reports are often the first members of their families to be in trouble with the law, so there is no criminal record or other official contact being given as evidence for these constructions of pressure coming from 'dodgy' family members. In the body of the pre-sentence reports, the circumstances of the subject's employment or unemployment were described straightforwardly; the difference was that in the tick-box sections of the risk-assessment sheets, 'employment' was often checked for the South Asians, whereas this was extremely rare for the white offenders; and in the box requesting evidence, 'this offence' was usually all that was put. The 'lifestyle and associates' box was often checked for both groups, but in the boxes for evidence, 'uncles' and/or 'cousins' was entered for South Asians but 'friends' or 'peers' for the white offenders.

Recording of attitudes to offending places proportionately more of the South Asians in the 'nothing recorded' category and in the 'risky' category of denying responsibility for the offence, while white offenders are recorded as more often expressing remorse and not understanding the seriousness of the offence. (See Table 2 below.)

The 'nothing recorded' figure is noteworthy, but perhaps even more significantly, the cases where the 'denies responsibility' box was checked often had no actual comment in the body of the pre-sentence report. These figures suggest a lack of exploration of attitudes of South Asian offenders by interviewing officers, and a greater readiness to assign them to a risky/ blameworthy category 'denial', rather than the less intransigent categories of remorseful or lacking understanding.

Table 2 Attitudes to offending

	White		South Asian	
	No.	%	No.	%
Expresses remorse/regret	89	61.8	26	45.6
Denies responsibility for offence	8	5.6	11	19.3
Does not understand seriousness of offence	30	20.8	9	15.8
Nothing recorded	13	9.0	11	19.3
Total	144	100.0	57	100.0

RISKY MASCULINITIES AND POPULAR STEREOTYPES

[handwritten marginal note: Crisis of white masculinities]

The two risky masculinities constructed in these probation reports and assessments were very close to current popular stereotypes. The workless, rootless white male fits the 'crisis of masculinity' thesis that emerged in the early 1990s. According to this thesis the rise of unemployment in the 1980s had been a rise in unskilled or minimally skilled male unemployment. Decline of traditional employments in manufacturing and in other industries such as coal mining had led to a generation of young men who could not join the traditional working-class culture of their families and communities. The most effective barriers to crime (and the most effective factors in bringing about desistence in those who committed offences as juveniles) – a job and a steady relationship – were denied to countless young men. They could not find gainful employment, and so were not good prospects as providers for girl-friends and their children. As right-wing politicians and press endlessly repeated, young women preferred to be 'married to the state' than married to the helpless and hopeless young men available as partners. Although employment has expanded in recent years, the recovery has largely been in jobs seen as feminine (notably call-centres and retail). The 'crisis of masculin-ity' explanation has been criticized as over-simplified and over-generalized (Collier 1998), but it nonetheless retains considerable resonance, particularly with liberal criminal justice professionals such as probation officers.

While the same phenomenon – the rise of an underclass of impoverished males – has occurred in the USA, this has especially affected African and Hispanic Americans. In the UK, apart from some areas of London and other major cities, the affected groups are largely white. Pakistani immigrants, however, suffered more than other South Asian groups from the economic downtown of the 1980s. A greater proportion of them than of Indians and Bangladeshis came after the Second World War to work in the traditional industries (mainly textiles) of the Midlands and Northern England. Along-side the white working-class of those areas, they shared the loss of jobs, and while some opened small businesses (for example, small corner convenience stores), the impoverishment of white and Pakistani areas meant that this alternative economy is no longer able to supply a significant number of jobs for its younger generation (Webster 1997: 84, n. 21). As one commentator has said, 'If a racial underclass exists in Britain, here it is' (Modood 1992: 261). This analysis is consistent with the equal proportions of unemployed white and South Asian offenders found in the present research.

When the different South Asian ethnicities are aggregated, however, as they are in most official statistics, their crime rates have generally been lower than those of comparable white groups, and so what has seemed to need explan-ation is Asian conformity, rather than Asian criminality. The explanation is generally located in the strength of Asian family and community bonds and controls. Asian youth are held to be embedded in a strong system of informal social control, with firm commitments to close family, extended family and to community. They are, it is argued, strongly committed to protection of 'izzat', family prestige, and refrain from crime so as not to bring dishonour on family or community (Mawby and Batta 1980). Recently various factors, including common economic pressures, appear to have led to the behaviour of young Pakistani men becoming more like that of young white men living in similar circumstances: in impoverished, segregated areas, groups of young Pakistani men have become more likely than previously to retaliate against white racism, to defend their 'territory' against incursions by white youth, and to engage in violence, criminal damage and public order offences. These young men have been termed 'resisters': resisting racism and economic marginalization, and also resisting the traditional cultural constraints on criminality (Desai 1999).

The idea of young Pakistani males reacting actively and violently to white racism and to general social-economic disadvantage has certainly entered the discourse of Asian 'otherness', challenging the stereotype of Asians as passive, more likely to be victims than offenders (Webster 1997). This emergent image of Asian resisters and perpetrators of violence has been reinforced by disorders in three northern cities in the summer of 2001, but it had already entered criminological and popular discourse (Goodey 2001). Media stories about the emergence of Asian gangs appeared intermittently throughout the 1990s. In our research, many of the assessments of South Asians as denying responsibility for their offences were in cases of inter-racial violence and disorder. Asians in the pre-sentence reports were regarded unproblematically as perpetrators rather than victims, with their accounts of racial motivation not endorsed by the probation officers but transposed into denial of responsibility. These professional judgements are consistent with a changing discourse of Asian otherness, an emergent discourse of Asian male criminality.

Stereotypes of Asians were double-edged, even before post-disturbance and post-September 11 deteriorations in white British attitudes towards Muslims. They had been regarded as tightly knit, ordered by tradition, self-regulating (Bowling and Phillips 2002): but expressions such as 'tightly-knit' have negative as well as positive connotations, such as disregarding the concerns of 'outsiders', or being uncooperative towards authorities. Connotations of Muslim Asianness include deviousness, secrecy, duplicity – scarcely surprising, then, that their accounts are not readily accepted. Asians are seen as strange, and since September 11, and even more since the London transport bombings and attempted bombings in July 2005, their adherence to religion and tradition is seen far more as a negative than as a positive feature of Muslim communities. As well as the link in the popular mind between Islam and terrorism, stories about 'honour killings', forced marriages and 'street cleaning' to remove prostitution and to circumscribe the dress and behaviour of young women, have furthered the recasting of close family ties, strong informal social control, self-regulation and conformity from positive to negative constructions of Asianness.

Jefferson (1993) suggests that Asians are even more 'other' in English culture than African/Caribbeans. Their dress is different; their music is unfamiliar and discordant; their deference, religiosity and enterprise are unappealing. Although, however, their 'otherness' might be that of the absolutely strange, Jefferson explains that the characteristics ascribed to them do not feed so readily into a criminalizing discourse as do those of African/ Caribbeans. Writing in 1993, however, he included the caveat that constructions of Asianness were of strangeness and conformity but not of criminality 'for the moment' (1993: 37). Other commentators have predicted that because of the combination of socio-economic and demographic pressures, together with changing perceptions of Muslim Asians, 'this group may well face similar processes of criminalization as black ethnic groups in the coming years' (Phillips and Bowling 2002: 613). Our research suggests that as well as this happening in public/political discourse, criminal justice risk assessment is playing a role in constructing and reinforcing this discourse of Asian criminality.

These offenders are classified as South Asian in official statistics and recorded as Pakistani in the probation files, but Pakistanis are predominantly Muslim. Whilst there are many degrees of adherence and fervency, and different streams of Islam among Pakistanis, Muslim Asians are now regarded with suspicion generally, and religion has come together with race/ethnicity in the emergence of this criminalized discourse.

What emerged from the reports and risk assessments were two contrasting discourses of 'risky masculinity' which had divergent implications for the penal treatment of white and South Asian offenders. We noted that white and South Asian offenders with the same risk scores received different sentencing recommendations: probation officers were generally more willing to recommend community penalties for white offenders assessed as of medium risk of reoffending than for South Asians with the same numerical risk assessment. The implications of the constructions of riskiness for the two groups were clearly different: the problems associated with the white offenders – lack of employment, lack of stable relationships and accommodation – are problems that probation officers tend to identify as problems with which they can work. They are the needs/risk factors which are the prime targets of community penalties. On the other hand, the problem factors attributed to the South Asians – their families, their employment, their characters and attitudes – are taken to indicate the need for distancing from community and lifestyle.

RISKY MASCULINITIES AND THE RISKS
OF IMPRISONMENT

This section discusses relations between the differing constructions of 'risky' masculinities and their vulnerabilities to the pains and deprivations of imprisonment. Whilst some existing research considers the vulnerability of men as prisoners, there has been little work that addresses what Connell (1987) in his conceptual framework for analysing state institutions argues is needed: an examination of the relationships between different masculinities (Sim 1994). Both white offenders and South Asians who were sentenced to imprisonment in our research are not only constructed as 'risky', but are also 'at risk' from the range of well documented pains of imprisonment. As our research indicated that the custodial rate for South Asians was significantly higher than for white offenders, we consider that South Asian offenders constructed as 'risky' males, and thus more likely to receive a custodial penalty, are thereby made disproportionately vulnerable to the pains of imprisonment and further exposed to risks associated with ethnicity and religion. The discussion that follows examines some of the pains of imprisonment and considers their relationship with the differing 'risky' masculinities of white and South Asian offenders.

Suicide and self-harm in prison are extreme responses to the pains of imprisonment. Study of these phenomena is beset with difficulties for researchers due to methodological difficulties, accuracy of recording, varying interpretations of self-inflicted and non self-inflicted deaths, and differing interpretations of what is classified as self-harm (Crighton 2002; Liebling 1995). Despite such methodological and interpretive difficulties existing, research effectively demonstrates that the rate of suicide and self-harm in prisons is higher than in the community. A thematic review of suicides and self-harm in prisons by the Chief Inspector of Prisons acknowledges and confirms this finding (HMCIP 1999). Much of the knowledge and information gained from the growth of interest in and research on self-harm in prisons over the last 30 years is statistical, with its inherent flaws and difficulties, giving data on the rising suicide rates of men and women. Headline figures of two people a week taking their own lives inside prisons (Wilson 2005) attempt to bring more attention to the high rates of suicide, but few studies separate out significant minority ethnic groups, with recent data referring to black prisoners generally subsuming South Asians within this umbrella category. The production of 'at risk' data based on traditional prediction approaches led Liebling (1995) to argue for a move towards a more ethnographic approach to understanding the real life world of suicide and self-harm in prisons. In her comprehensive research, which included qualitative work by interviewing prisoners who were classified as having attempted or not attempted suicide in prisons, Liebling drew up a list of variables of significance in the accounts of prisoners' lives that offers a framework from which the relationship between different 'risky' masculinities and this particular pain of imprisonment can be explored.

Of particular relevance here is Liebling's argument that there is a range of situational factors in prison that contribute to the suicide and attempted suicide of those prisoners she identified as 'poor copers' or vulnerable prisoners, and that 'successful coping in prison reflected, in part, prisoner's lives in the community' (1995: 178). She argues that those prisoners who attempted suicide had fewer personal resources on which they could call to enable them to cope with imprisonment. Some of the situational factors that she noted as significant were: the presence or absence of family; violence; an upbringing in local authority care; offending histories; education; and employment. For Liebling (1995) it was the degree of their absence or presence that was the significant difference between those prisoners who attempted suicide and those who did not. The significant situational factors bear a close resemblance to the features identified in the construction of 'risky' masculinities in this chapter, and the emphasis placed upon their presence or absence resonates with our research.

Looking at the risky masculinities we identified in the light of Liebling's framework, the South Asians appear to be more likely to be 'copers' and the white males the 'non-copers'. The lonely white male with few social resources is likely to have many of the factors identified with suicide and self-harm. If unemployed, he is less likely than his South Asian counterpart to be involved in education; he is more likely to have identifiable alcohol, drug or financial difficulties; he is more likely to have six or more previous convictions, and he is more likely to be living alone in unstable accommodation, estranged from family and community. The presence of employment, education, family and community ties in the risk assessments on the South Asians who received short custodial sentences, suggests that this group of 'risky' males take with them into custody more resources to call on as 'copers' and would thus be less likely to feature in suicide attempts and self-harm statistics. As noted, most suicide data do not identify significant minority ethnic groups, but what has been shown by existing research that would support this contention is that white prisoners tend to be over-represented in prison suicide figures, although the increase in the proportion of minority ethnic prisoners in prison suicides noted earlier means that this now needs to be treated with caution (Crighton 2002).

Caution is required in considering the differences between the 'risky' masculinities of white offenders and Asians, as one interpretation of the suggestion that they may possess to varying degrees differing abilities as 'copers' is that exposure to the pains of imprisonment is not as 'risky' for South Asians as it is for white offenders and thus is not an area of concern. This interpretation misses two extremely important points. First, the factors identified by Liebling as 'coping' factors in prison are also those associated in most prediction studies with lower re-offending rates as well as lower risks of suicide and self-harm: employment, education, family ties were identified as 'present' in the risk assessments on South Asians. Our study suggests that 'risky' Asian males possess, to a greater degree than white 'risky' males, the very factors that would indicate that a community penalty would be more likely to be successful by enabling supervision to build on existing family, community, educational and work ties. The ways in which the South Asian offenders were constructed as 'risky' males denies them the most appropriate penalty for their personal attributes and relative lack of criminal histories.

The second point is the damage to these coping resources risked by imprisonment. A clear theme that emerges from existing research on the pains of imprisonment is the significant impact of the fracturing of family and community ties, often made worse by the distances from home that inmates may experience:

> The fracturing of family bonds is so sudden and overwhelming that dislocation, shock, insensibility, grief and the ability or inability to deal with all these means that prisoners feel a degree of powerlessness and apathy in the face of a disaster that is highly personal – as do their families.
>
> (Reuss 2003: 427)

South Asian males in our research were more likely to be closely involved with family and community, to have found work through family connections, and to be undergoing full or part-time education: their involvement with family and community is a highly significant source of identity and self-esteem. The sudden and immediate impact of fracturing family and community bonds is likely to be more strongly felt by those who have such family and community bonds that could be broken, thus rendering South Asians more likely to be vulnerable to this difficulty of imprisonment.

Again this does not mean that other males such as the white offenders considered here do not experience this deprivation, but rather that they experience it in a different way. For white 'risky' males the fracturing of their already tenuous bonds with family and community poses very significant difficulties for their rehabilitation and may confirm their low sense of self-esteem and self-worth. This lack of sense of individual worth comes clearly through the discussions Liebling (1995) reports where prisoners vocalize their feelings of isolation, despair and worthlessness. For South Asians there is an emerging popular discourse on the shame brought to families by their offending and imprisonment which is not yet fully addressed in the research literature, raising the possibility of rehabilitation difficulties of a different kind for these 'risky' males that might lead to similarly high reconviction rates – 59 per cent – as the rest of the prison population (Councell 2003).

For white males sentenced to short periods of imprisonment the early stages have already been identified as a period of vulnerability to suicide and self-harm (Crighton 2002; HMCIP 1999) and this is reflected in a range of prison initiatives throughout the prison estate. On the other hand, assessments of South Asians as lacking remorse, criminally risk taking, and their families and lifestyles being implicated in their offending, seem to justify their imprisonment without full consideration of the impact of imprisonment as opposed to the potential benefits of a community disposal. Again, we see the white risky male having needs reflecting social deprivation, while the South Asian male has risks reflecting character and culture. Moreover, construing these family, community and employment 'coping' factors as risk-of-reoffending factors, as is done in these probation risk assessments, transforms them from something to be worked *with* to something to be worked *on*.

The criminal justice correlative of the recasting of strong family and community ties from positive to negative in popular discourses is their recasting from resources and supports to dynamic risk factors in risk assessment. As such, they become targets for change in the cognitive-behavioural approaches of reduction of reoffending programmes in prisons. Such programmes risk eroding the very circumstances that have long been associated with low Asian crime rates, and, rather than reversing the harm of fracturing family and community ties that is so often an outcome of imprisonment, seeing these ties as risks to be worked on may amplify the role of the prison in 'manufacturing handicaps' (Gallo and Ruggiero 1991) and so may play a part in a rise in recidivism among South Asian offenders.

If suicide and self-harm statistics reveal white offenders as more likely than South Asians to be at risk from themselves, South Asians feel themselves to be more at risk from other prisoners. The Chief Inspector of Prisons in England and Wales, Anne Owers, in a recent review of race relations in prisons stated that Asian inmates were more likely to say they felt unsafe in prison than black inmates were (52 per cent and 32 per cent respectively), and more likely to face racist bullying and abuse from other inmates (HMIP 2005). Incidents such as the killing of Zahid Mubarek, a young South Asian offender, in Feltham Young Offenders Institution, in west London, in March 2000 by a self-proclaimed racist white young man with whom he shared a cell, add to this fear of violence from other inmates, and also prove that it is not unfounded.

Comments from this recent review raise a number of issues concerning differing masculinities and their relations to the risks of imprisonment. Black prisoners have formed, and remain, the largest and most significant minority group in the prison population of England and Wales, constituting 10 per cent of the prison population in 1992 and rising to 15 per cent in 2002 (Home Office 2003: 121). Whilst some of this increase has been attributed to the rise in foreign nationals in the prison population (Councell 2003), black males have remained the most significant minority group in both percentage terms and actual numbers, enabling black prisoners to draw on some support from within their own cultural group in response to racist abuse and bullying. For South Asians, whilst there has been a rise in actual numbers imprisoned from

1,363 in 1992 to 2,160 in 2002, their percentage presence as a minority ethnic group has remained the same at 3 per cent (Home Office 2003: 121). This group are arguably less able to call on support from within their own culture where they form a smaller minority ethnic group, in percentage and absolute numbers, to ameliorate their exposure to racist abuse and bullying; their vulnerability is increasing whilst support from within their own culture remains marginalized.

Apart from prisoners from minority ethnic groups being able to draw or not on support from within their own cultural group, the review on race relations within prisons by the Chief Inspector of Prisons comments on the low level of understanding within prisons on cultural differences, identifying lack of choice of food and a general lack of respect for different religious beliefs (Travis 2005). This is an issue of some significance for the group of South Asian males we are considering. Whilst South Asians have remained a static proportion of the prison population, the pattern for religious beliefs within prison is not so straightforward. Official statistics show that the largest growth of actual numbers related to religious views in the years 1992–2002 has been that of 'no religion', which seems reasonably to be located within the growth of white prisoners, reflecting the change from a religious to a more secular society in the population in general. Within prisons, of those declaring religious affiliation, South Asians are overwhelmingly Muslim and whilst they may form only 3 per cent of the prison population, their significance in terms of religion is greater, forming a minority religious group of 8 per cent (Home Office 2003).

Given the rise of anti-Muslim feeling in society referred to earlier, South Asians in prisons are increasingly vulnerable to risks brought about by racial and religious intolerance, including violence and abuse by other inmates, and cultural disrespect and neglect by officers. For South Asians in prison the rise of anti-Muslim sentiments in recent years may begin to decrease the degree to which they could be seen as 'copers'. This would reflect the concerns of Asians in the general population who are voicing their disquiet about increased hostility towards them – demonstrated clearly in the dramatic rise in stop and searches of them recorded by the police. In London stop and searches increased by 8 per cent for whites, 30 per cent for blacks and 40 per cent for Asians in 2001–2002; figures elsewhere in England and Wales are lower but reflect the same proportional increases (IRR News 2002). The increasing involvement of South Asians in the general population with the criminal justice system may herald an increase in the numbers processed, charged, convicted and sentenced to custody given the way 'risky' South Asian males are constructed as blameworthy and unremorseful, reflecting popular discourse and apparently confirming as 'reality' the 'risky' nature of Muslim Asians.

CONCLUSIONS

In exploring relations between differing masculinities and the risks of imprisonment during report/sentencing stages and in prison regimes, we are forcefully reminded of the need to reflect that we 'seem to be moving ever nearer to human warehousing and containment based on risk assessment rather than on offending' (Reuss 2003: 429).

Risk assessment in criminal justice proceeds as though what are being evaluated are *real* risk factors which can be identified through objective, non-discriminatory schedules and techniques. Although management of the risk of crime is clearly a legitimate – and indeed foundational – aim of penal systems, its stance of scientificity and moral neutrality cannot go unquestioned. Risk assessment is an ordering mechanism, and new approaches and technologies in criminology and criminal justice are the latest in a long line of classificatory mechanisms producing orders of criminal sheep and goats, assigning offenders to groups who are deemed worth taking the chance of inclusionary, rehabilitative sanctions, or in need of exclusionary penalties marking them and their families and associates as blameworthy, untrustworthy, and permanently risky. Risk taking is one of the crime-related attitudes most often ticked for South Asians; being 'risky' is always a condemnatory judgement in criminal justice. This contrasts with the approval of risk taking in other spheres: the entrepreneur, the emergency services, for example.

What we have sought to argue is that criminal justice risk assessment is not an objective measure of a real, existing state: it is itself part of a process of construction of gendered risky identities. The cultural resources for this construction are the popular stereotypes of the time and place in which the assessment is carried out. Risk assessment, however, constructs identities which are treated as real, and which have real consequences, such as exposure to the risks of imprisonment. The attempt to explore and consider different relations between 'risky' males and the risks of imprisonment demonstrates how having once been assessed as 'risky', differing groups of males are exposed in varying degrees to the pains of imprisonment. For the 'risky' South Asian those pains of imprisonment are aggravated by racial and religious intolerance, fracture of the family and community bonds that are vital for rehabilitation and for identity and feelings of self-worth. Risk assessment in criminal justice processes reinforces rather than challenges popular discourses of masculinity, and plays its part in constructing the increasing criminalization of these discourses.

REFERENCES

Bowling, B. and Phillips, C. (2002) *Racism, Crime and Justice*, Harlow: Pearson/Longman.
Campbell, B. (1993) *Goliath: Britain's Dangerous Places*, London: Methuen.

Collier, R. (1998) *Masculinities, crime and criminology*, London: Sage.

Connell, R. (1987) *Gender and Power*, Cambridge: Polity.

Connell, R.W. (1995) *Masculinities*, Cambridge: Polity.

Councell, R. (2003) 'The Prison population in 2002: a statistical review' *Findings: 228*, London: The Home Office.

Crighton, D. (2002) 'Suicide in prisons: a critique of UK research', in G. Towl, L. Snow and M. McHugh (eds), *Suicide in Prisons*, Oxford: Blackwell.

Desai, P. (1999) *Spaces of Identity: Cultures of Conflict: The Development of New British Asian Identities*, PhD Thesis, University of London, Goldsmiths College.

Gallo, E. and Ruggiero, V. (1991) 'The "Immaterial" Prison: Custody as a Factory for the Manufacture of Handicaps', *International Journal of the Sociology of Law*, 19: 273–291.

Gelsthorpe, L. and Raynor, P. (1995) 'Quality and Effectiveness in Probation Officers' Reports to Sentencers', *British Journal of Criminology* 35: 188–200.

Genders, E. and Player, E. (1989) *Race Relations in Prison*, Oxford: Clarendon Press.

Gilroy, P. (1982) 'Police and Thieves' in Centre for Contemporary Cultural Studies, *The Empire Strikes Back*, London: Hutchinson.

Gilroy, P. (1987) 'The Myth of Black Criminality', in P. Scraton (ed.) *Law, Order and the Authoritarian State*, Milton Keynes: Open University Press.

Goodey, J. (2001) 'The criminalisation of British Asian youth: Research from Bradford and Sheffield', *Journal of Youth Studies* 4(4): 429–450.

Her Majesty's Chief Inspector of Prisons for England and Wales (1999) *Suicide is Everyone's Concern: A Thematic Review*, London: The Stationery Office.

Her Majesty's Inspectorate of Prisons (2005) *Parallel Worlds: A thematic review of race relations in prisons*, London: Home Office.

Her Majesty's Inspectorate of Probation (2000) *Towards Race Equality, Thematic Inspection Summary*, London: Home Office.

Home Office (1999) *Statistics on Race and the Criminal Justice System*, London: Home Office.

Home Office (2003) *Prison Statistics for England and Wales, 2002*, London: Home Office.

Hood-Williams, J. (2001) 'Gender, masculinities and crime: From structures to psyches', *Theoretical Criminology*, 5(1): 37–60.

Howard League (2006) *Howard League Magazine* 24(1): 3, London: The Howard League for Penal Reform.

Hudson, B. and Bramhall, G. (2005) 'Assessing the "Other": Constructions of "Asianness" in Risk Assessments by Probation Officers', *British Journal of Criminology*, 45, 5: 721–740.

IRR (Independent Race and Refugee News Network) (2002) 'The Criminal Justice System', *Factfile*, November 2002 (downloaded from: http://www.irr.org.uk/2002/november/).

Jefferson, T. (1993) 'The Racism of Criminalization: Policing and the Reproduction of the Criminal Other' in L.R. Gelsthorpe (ed.) *Minority Ethnic Groups in the Criminal Justice System*, Cropwood Conference Series no. 21, Cambridge: Institute of Criminology.

Jefferson, T. (1997) 'Masculinities and crimes' in M. Maguire, R. Morgan and R. Reiner (eds) *The Oxford Handbook of Criminology*, 2nd edn, 535–558, Oxford: Oxford University Press.

Kemshall, H. (2003) *Understanding Risk in Criminal Justice*, Maidenhead: Open University Press.

Liebling, A. (1995) 'Vulnerability and Prison Suicide' *British Journal of Criminology*, 35, 2: 173–187.

Mawby, B.I. and Batta, I.D. (1980) 'Asians and Crime: The Bradford Experience', Middlesex: Scope Communication.

Messerschmidt, J. (1993) *Masculinities and Crime*, Lanham, Mld: Rowman and Littlefield.

Messerschmidt, J. (2000) *Nine Lives: Adolescent Masculinities, the Body and Violence*, Boulder, Colorado: Westview Press.

Modood, T. (1992) 'British Asian Muslims and the Rushdie Affair', in J. Donald and A. Rattansi (eds) *Race, Culture and 'Difference'*, London: Sage.

Morris, N. (1994) 'Dangerousness and Incapacitation' in R.A. Duff and D. Garland (eds) *A Reader in Punishment*, Oxford: Oxford University Press.

Phillips, C. and Bowling, B. (2002) 'Racism, Ethnicity, Crime and Criminal Justice' in M. Maguire, R. Morgan and R. Reiner (eds) *The Oxford Handbook of Criminology*, 3rd edn, 579–619, Oxford: Oxford University Press.

Raynor, P., Kynch, J., Roberts, C. and Merrington, S. (2000) *Risk and need assessment in probation services: an evaluation*, Home Office Research Study 211, London: Home Office.

Reuss, A. (2003) 'Taking a Long Hard Look at Imprisonment' *The Howard Journal*, 42, 5: 426–36.

Said, E. (1985) *Orientalism*, Harmondsworth; Penguin.

Seidler, V. (2005) *Transforming Masculinities*, London: Routledge.

Sim, J. (1994) 'Tougher than the rest? Men in prison' in T. Newburn and E.A. Stanko (eds) *Just Boys Doing Business? Men, masculinities and crime*, London: Routledge.

Tonry, M. (1995) *Malign Neglect – Race, Crime and Punishment in America*, New York: Oxford University Press.

Travis, A. (2005) 'Asian inmates feel most unsafe in prison system' *The Guardian*, 20 Dec 2005 (downloaded from: http://www.guardian.co.uk/prisons/).

Walklate, S. (1995) *Gender and Crime: An introduction*, Hemel Hempstead: Prentice Hall/Harvester Wheatsheaf.

Webster, C. (1997) 'The Construction of British "Asian" Criminality', *International Journal of the Sociology of Law*, 25: 65–86.

Whitehead, A. (2005) 'Man to Man Violence: How Masculinity May Work as a Dynamic Risk Factor', *Howard Journal of Criminal Justice*, 44, 4: 411–422.

Wilson, D. (2005) *Death at the Hands of the State*, London: Howard League for Penal Reform.

Chapter 7

Gendered risks of retirement

The legal governance of defined contribution pensions in Canada

Mary Condon *

INTRODUCTION

This chapter examines how the governance of new employer-sponsored pension arrangements in Canada mediates the relationship between gender and discourses of economic risk. It considers the role played by these pension regimes in maintaining gendered forms of financial self-governance and economic insecurity. It asks whether evolving precepts of pension regulation assist or hinder women who wish to resist the disciplinary reach of policy restructurings in the employer-based pension sector.

The argument will be made in this chapter that legal governance of defined contribution (DC) pensions is an example of a shift away from 'command and control' forms of regulation, and that one of its effects is to redistribute economic risks away from employer pension sponsors and towards employees, particularly lower-paid women. The central objective is to examine, from a feminist point of view, several specifically legal devices for the management of employee financial risk in a DC context. A core feature of a DC pension is that it typically allows workers to make decisions about where pension contributions should be invested. At one level, the ability to make choices, and a governance regime facilitating this, is broadly consistent with feminist emancipatory goals. Choice making in this context replaces older-established, more paternalistic notions of fiduciary duties[1] owed to workers by employers or pension trustees. Indeed fiduciary duties employed as legal responsibility devices in various contexts have been critiqued from a feminist perspective (Gabaldon 1995; Nedelsky 1989). However, I argue that the detail of how this shift to facilitating choice making might play out in the pension context needs to be interrogated closely, particularly with regard to the push to embrace risk in order to self-provide financial sustainability.

* Osgoode Hall Law School. The author acknowledges the research support of SSHRC as well as the hospitality of the Centre of Criminology, University of Toronto.
1 A fiduciary duty is usually taken to mean the requirement to act with loyalty, good faith and in the best interests of the person. or group to whom the duty is owed

In particular, feminist legal analysis of evolving pension governance may need to take more seriously research findings from disciplines such as social psychology and feminist economics, to the effect that structures of rationality and decision making may themselves be gendered, particularly with respect to the advantages and disadvantages of risk taking (Finucane *et al* 2000; Strauss 2006b). The argument is that perceptions of degrees of risk are correlated with the levels of vulnerability and control experienced by those assessing the risk (Finucane *et al* 2000). As Slovic (1999: 693) expresses it:

> . . . race and gender differences in perceptions and attitudes point toward the role of power, status, alienation, trust, perceived government responsiveness, and other sociopolitical factors in determining perception and acceptance of risk. To the extent that these sociopolitical factors shape public perception of risks, we can see why traditional attempts to make people see the world as White males do, by showing them statistics and risk assessments, are often unsuccessful . . .

The claims made in this chapter will be addressed by first placing the evolving legal regime for DC pensions in Canada in larger political economy perspective. Here the argument is that this macro perspective betrays gendered underpinnings. Then the chapter will focus in on the legal regime for DC pensions in Canada, in order to demonstrate how it is likely to reinforce gender disadvantage, and how it is based on a valorization of forms of choice making that is not sensitive to gendered rationalities about risk.

THE POLITICAL ECONOMY OF DEFINED CONTRIBUTION PENSIONS

It is widely accepted in the pension and labour studies literatures that there has been a shift in the employer-based retirement income sector away from 'defined benefit' (DB) forms of pension provision and towards DC plans.[2]

---

2 This shift has been occurring at varying paces in different countries. In the US, 'more than four-fifths of all workers covered by employer-sponsored pension plans are participants in DC plans' (US Department of Labor). In the UK, 'over 60% of defined-benefit schemes have been closed or replaced by defined-contribution schemes' (Ring 2003: 67). However, in Canada, 'the vast majority of DC plans are with small or medium-sized employers, representing less than $10 million in assets each' (Sharratt 2003: 31, 36). In 2004, the Joint Forum of Financial Market Regulators noted that over three million Canadians belong to Capital Accumulation Plans (CAPs), which have approximately $60 billion in assets, and over 80 per cent of which allow members to make investment choices (Joint Forum 2004 Backgrounder). Figures from the same year indicate that there are slightly more DC plans in Canada than there are DB plans (7,507 of the first type and 7,014 of the second), though more than

In the first type, employers remain liable for funding a calculable 'pension promise' to workers, while in the second, employers undertake only to make specific contributions, with the ultimate financial outcome for the worker being largely dictated by how well the employers' and/or employees' contributions perform when invested in various financial products. In a DC pension, individual employees usually make the decisions about where to invest the contributions. In contrast, investment decision making in the traditional DB format is centralized in the hands of pension trustees who make decisions for the fund collectively. A vigorous debate exists in the political economy literature as to whether the genesis of this policy shift is in the 'shareholder primacy' thesis of corporate organization (i.e. that corporations are more interested in providing short-term returns to shareholders than benefits to employees), or alternatively in the moral economy of state-sponsored neo-liberalism (which valorizes autonomous, individualized choice making and market-based service provision) (Cutler and Waine 2001).

In earlier work I have argued that the political economy of the shift to DC pensions is gendered at many levels.[3] Gendered features of this shift include foundational understandings of the relationship between periods of productive work and 'non-productive' work (in retirement or for childcare) in individuals' life cycles. The idea that provision for retirement is based on a model of continuous full-time employment for a 30- or 40-year period followed by a shorter period of retirement does not tend to capture the complicated nature of the relationship between 'productive' labour and caring work in women's lives (Bezanson and Luxton 2006). Meanwhile, considering the situation of women in labour markets only, there remains ample data demonstrating that women remain more likely to have lower incomes and to engage in non-standard employment[4] than men, with adverse consequences for avoiding poverty in old age (Vosko 2000). Such economic disadvantage in employment situations has a knock-on effect for financial well-being in retirement, once it is assumed that labour market involvement is meant to provide the bulk of that financial provision. This empirical data about the gendered nature of the labour market remains relevant despite the need now to be cognisant of the fact that a new gender order has been evolving over the last several decades (Cossman and Fudge 2002). This new gender order requires that the category of gender be disaggregated, according to the extent to which women interact with the labour market.[5] The conclusion to be drawn from this material is

80 per cent of all pension plan members remain in DB plans (Kaplan 2006: 3). The preponderance of employees still covered by DB plans are in the public sector, with less than 25 per cent of private sector workers in Canada being members of DB plans (SEI Canada 2006: 2).

3 Condon (2006).
4 That is, not full-time, full-year.
5 In other words, those women who are streaming into professionalized, full-time, high-paying jobs are not necessarily economically disadvantaged compared to men.

that turning to pension structures that reduce responsibilities on employers and heighten the need for workers to interact directly with investment markets has the capacity to create 'new forms of gender inequality, new forms of discursive discipline, and new forms of gendered insecurity' (Condon 2006).

THE ROLE OF THE STATE IN PENSION PROVISION

Pension policy restructuring in the employer sector is itself embedded in a broader institutional and policy context concerning how to provide adequate levels of retirement income for all citizens. In earlier work I and others have canvassed how the discourses undergirding entitlements to retirement income have changed from being centred around norms of collective citizenship rights to being premised on neoliberal individualized responsibility (Miller and Rose 1990; Condon 2002). Specifically, I have argued that in the current era of neoliberalism, the role of the state with respect to retirement income has shifted away from a focus on the direct provision of economic benefits and towards developing the institutionalized and regulatory structures within which privatized retirement takes place. In that sense, the role of the state has become increasingly focused on strategies of risk management, often by way of reshaping regulatory norms (O'Malley 1998; Moss 2002; Braithwaite 2000). More specifically, Strauss has recently argued that various welfare states may be plotted along a continuum, according to the extent to which they seek to ameliorate what she calls 'gender inequality risk' (Strauss 2006a). Examples of welfare state policies that address gender equality risks include 'sex discrimination and equal pay legislation, individual and household systems of taxation, affirmative action programmes . . . and the treatment of unpaid caring work by pension regimes' (Strauss 2006a: 11). It is notable that many of these risk management strategies do not involve the direct payment of benefits. Specifically in relation to pensions, Strauss argues that there are 'four interrelated risk dimensions associated with gender'. These are 'the public/private mix and commitment to redistribution, basis of entitlement, treatment of unpaid work and caring, and access to income' (ibid: 13). While the preoccupation of this chapter is more directly with the role of the 'private' employment sector rather than the state in ameliorating pension risk based on gender, it is clear that issues of the basis of pension entitlement and the mix of public and private provision of retirement income are central to the analysis of the legal governance of gender-based pension risk in Canadian labour markets.

Yet, it is true that Canada's uptake of Keynesianism after the Second World War was still organized around the idea that direct public provision of individual benefits would be supplemented significantly by retirement benefits payable by employers (Deaton 1989). In this sense, Canada is more closely aligned with the UK than any other European country plotted on Strauss's continuum of national pension regimes (Strauss 2006a). There is a universal state-provided retirement benefit (Old Age Security) as well as a further retirement amount payable to all who participated in the paid labour force on the basis of contributions made by employers and workers (Canada Pension Plan). However, these two benefits taken together are expected to provide only 35 per cent of pre-retirement income for those earning the Canadian average wage or less. Any retirement income beyond this must come from a third tier of benefits payable by individual employers or personal investment resources.

Importantly, this third tier has always been assumed to be voluntary on the part of employers. Thus, individual employers will provide employer-specific pension benefits (either DB or DC) only if they consider it beneficial to retaining or attracting a qualified labour force. Nonetheless, the state has attempted to provide incentives to employers to provide these benefits, by according favourable taxation status to money accumulated in so-called registered pension plans (RPPs).

HOW IS LEGAL GOVERNANCE OF DEFINED CONTRIBUTION PLANS ACCOMPLISHED?

As noted above, the underlying premise from which the regulation of employer-sponsored pension plans springs is one whereby there is no legal requirement on employers to provide them at all. If the financial or legal obligations attendant on maintaining a plan become too onerous, employers may terminate them, though detailed procedures must be followed to do so (Kaplan 2006: Chapter 9). It is no surprise then that the legal discourse surrounding the development of a regulatory framework for DC plans in Canada emphasises so-called 'decentred' or voluntary forms of governance such as codes of conduct, best practices, contractual arrangements and the like.[6] This is most obvious in the recent Guidelines for Capital Accumulation Plans (CAPs), promulgated in Canada by the Joint Forum of Financial Market Regulators (Joint Forum) in May 2004. These guidelines open with

6 The same philosophy underlies the recommendations of the 2001 Myners report in the UK, (Institutional Investment in the UK: A Review) advocating codes of practice and robust disclosure requirements (see Chap 11). An important feature of the evolving regulatory landscape is the way in which the growth of DC pensions provide a case study of global political economic influences on law. Thus, '[G]lobally the DC pension plan industry is moving towards more common regulatory standards and practices ... global harmonization of DC governance practices assists multinational companies in introducing a common global DC risk management approach, which is appropriate in each local jurisdiction' (Felix 2005: 11). But differences which persist in governance requirements as between different countries, such as Australia and the UK, illustrate the continuing importance of local variation here (DC Forum December 2005 at 10 and 11).

the sentiment that they are 'intended to support the continuous improvement and development of industry practices (s.1)'. Indeed, one of the stated revisions to the final version of the CAP guidelines was that 'any language suggesting mandatory requirements has been eliminated to reduce confusion regarding the voluntary nature of the Guidelines'.[7]

In terms of the background to these guidelines, the Joint Forum worked between April 2001 and May 2004 to develop a final version. While it invited written comments and held focus group sessions across the country, it is notable that almost no workers provided input into the content of the guidelines.[8] The difficulties for individuals in penetrating regulatory discourses monopolised by repeat players and 'experts' has been well documented in the literature, and is a particular difficulty for advocacy groups supporting marginalized interests. As Condon and Philipps argue with respect to various arenas of economic governance, 'a particular challenge is to increase the participation of women in market governance and to problematize the use of gender-blind analytic frameworks by economic policymakers' (Condon and Philipps 2005: 128).

The focus of the remaining sections of this chapter, then, is to unpack further the legal and conceptual underpinnings of the Guidelines for Capital Accumulation Plans (CAP guidelines), as the primary source of regulatory structure for the operation of DC plans in Canada. In undertaking this examination, we should be alert to whether this legal regime – designed to facilitate choice making – is sensitive to the possibility of gendered consciousness with respect to risk.

HOW DO THE GUIDELINES WORK?

The players and their risks

The primary goal of these guidelines is to create a division of labour among the roles and responsibilities of the plan sponsor (the employer), the service

7 Joint Forum of Financial Market Regulators, Summary of Stakeholder Comments and Regulators Responses From Consultations on Proposed Guidelines for Capital Accumulation Plans, May 28 2004, at 2.
8 Twenty-six written responses were received to the Joint Forum's request for comments, all except one from organizations. While two comments were received from an organization called Canada's Association for the Fifty-Plus (CARP) and a third from a similar organization based in Quebec, the rest came from institutions and organizations such as insurance companies, investment funds, consulting firms and industry lobby groups. The Joint Forum held 12 focus group sessions across the country, which were attended by plan sponsors, service providers and pension plan members. It also met with 'representatives of industry associations throughout the consultation period' (Backgrounder: 2).

provider (typically, an insurance company) and the members (the employees). Service providers are defined as 'any provider of services or advice required by the CAP sponsor in the design, establishment and operation of a CAP (s.1.1.3)'. Although sponsors may delegate their responsibilities to service providers, they are initially responsible for setting up and maintaining the pension plan, and 'providing investment information and decision-making tools to CAP members (s.1.3.1)'. Meanwhile, the guidelines make clear that plan members are 'responsible for making investment decisions within the plan and for using the information and decision-making tools made available to assist them in making those decisions'. Thus, in contrast to typical DB pension plans, where investment allocation decisions for the plan are made by fund trustees or delegated by them to investment managers, the regulatory scheme for DC plans responsibilizes individual workers to engage in the investment enterprise. Pension fund trustees, with their attendant legal fiduciary responsibilities to beneficiaries, are thereby removed from the equation in a DC context (Davis 2004).

The guidelines further indicate that CAP members should 'also consider obtaining investment advice from an appropriately qualified individual in addition to using any information or tools the CAP sponsor may provide'. Not only is the obtaining of investment advice also downloaded to individual employees, but the guidelines contain an explicit acceptance of the idea that the information to be provided by the sponsor may be inadequate or subject to a conflict of interest (s.1.3.3). In distributing to workers the risk of making inadequate or inappropriate contribution investment decisions, and thereby ending up with an inadequate pension, the guidelines take no account of variation in the willingness or ability of individual workers to assume these risks. No account is taken of the possibility that the willingness to assume risk is itself gendered or racialized. We have noted above Slovic's contention that risk perceptions and attitudes reflect race and gender differences. This gender-variable acceptance of risk occurs in a context in which there is no enforcement mechanism provided by the guidelines themselves to assist with the actual carrying out of the various responsibilities assigned to the relevant parties.

According to the guidelines, responsibility to employees in a DC context is satisfied if various disclosures are made to them. While this issue is discussed in more detail below, one stakeholder comment made in the process of discussing these guidelines before they were implemented was that '[T]he Guidelines underplay the aspect of risk. CAP sponsors should be required to sensitise members to risk factors'. The Joint Forum's response to this submission was that this issue was already adequately addressed in the guidelines, pointing as an example to the disclosure to be provided to workers about the characteristics of specific investment funds and the risks associated with investing in them. This response is limited to issues of the risks associated with specific investments, as opposed to more global risks of this form of pension provision or those that flow from interaction with financial markets more generally. Revealingly, a participant in a 2005 discussion among sponsors of CAPs across Canada noted that

> My focus is very much on the employee group. From a DC perspective, getting them to clearly recognize what their role is vs. what their employer's role is. I think too many of them still have the DB mindset that the organization is going to look after them. We have to make sure they know it might not be a happy ending.
>
> (Richards 2005: 22)

These guidelines participate in and facilitate the assignment of a more intense form of pension risk to workers. At the same time, they rely on assumptions about the enthusiasm and competence with which employees will process information about the relative risks of various investment vehicles, to enable them to manage the possibility of increased financial insecurity. No distinctions among workers in terms of how variables such as gender, race or class impact on dispositions towards risk are contemplated in the overall legal governance framework.

Constructing the universe of choice making: employer selection of investment options

The idea of making investment choices is built into the very definition of a CAP; we turn now to look in more detail at the parameters established by the guidelines for making those choices. The first significant issue is that they provide that it is the role of the *sponsor* to select the investment options to be made available in the plan. While the guidelines indicate that the sponsor should 'ensure a range of investment options is made available', it is clear that from the perspective of the worker, the much-vaunted autonomy being accorded to them is not unlimited, but constrained by prior choices made by the sponsor. The guidelines further provide that some considerations that should factor into the resulting menu of choices provided by the sponsor include the fees[9] associated with the various options, as well as the liquidity,[10] degree of diversification, and level of risk associated with them, and the sponsor's ability to review them. There is no encouragement provided to sponsors to assess the levels of investment risk that employees would be comfortable with assuming. The risk characteristics intrinsic to the investment *options* are given much more prominence than the risk characteristics of

---

9 Such as transaction or management fees.
10 The degree of liquidity of an investment refers to the ease with which it may be resold. An investment that will be hard to resell is described as illiquid.

the ultimate *consumers* of the options. Although reference is made to an additional factor to be considered, which is described as 'the diversity and demographics of CAP members', there is little attempt to explicitly acknowledge the worker's gender or race as a relevant factor in decisions about the menu of investment options to be made available (e.g. low risk versus high risk) that will have the effect of structuring individualized choice.[11]

As noted in the introduction, the psychological and behavioural economic literature suggests that gender and race are significant constructs for choice making. In particular, feminist and behavioural economists have begun to point to the masculinity of rational utility-maximizing decision paradigms (Fineman 2005; Barber and Odean 2001). From the perspective of feminist economics, England distinguishes between the 'separative' and the 'soluble' self. She argues that the 'separative self, for whom relations are fundamentally irrelevant, is the assumed *homo economicus* of the Market model' (Nelson and England 2002). For 'economic man', rationality is equated with the maximization of wealth and the pursuit of self-interest. In contrast, 'soluble' selves – generally female or of a subordinate class or race – are those whose 'individual identity is effaced in the service of dependents and . . . allegedly autonomous actors' (Nelson and England 2002). While feminist economists are interested in the way these stereotypes influence the methodologies and value systems of economics as a discipline, as opposed to a claim that this is an accurate description of how actual men and women behave, it suggests that economically acceptable forms of rationality (especially in an investment choice-making context) tend to be coded masculine rather than feminine.

Finally, the menu of investment options available in a DC plan may be considerably circumscribed by the decision of the plan sponsor about involving a service provider. The guidelines make clear that in some cases, the choice of a service provider will 'define or limit' the type of investment options available to a plan. Again the discourse of choice is constrained by the prior decisions of employer-sponsors, which may be made on utilitarian, cost-effectiveness grounds, or because of a pre-existing relationship with the service provider. Workers may ultimately have some legal remedies to counteract the disadvantage of being provided with inadequate investment choices. However, these will likely be mobilized only after financial losses have been sustained, and may do little to destabilize the prevailing ideology of the benefits of rational choice making in the mould of the masculinized 'heroic financial risk-taker' (de Goede 2004).

---

11 An earlier version of the guidelines had contained a reference to sponsors taking into account 'any preferences voluntarily indicated by members' in designing overall investment options. The final version removed this reference to member preferences, substituting a request to sponsors that they consider member complaints in subsequent monitoring of the investment options provided (Stakeholder comments: 11).

What forms of regulatory support for choice making are provided?

It is generally acknowledged among pensions academics and industry parti-cipants that there is considerable resistance among large numbers of workers to the alleged opportunities being provided via DC plans to make pension-related investment decisions (Mitchell and Utkus 2004; Blake 2003). The suggestion has also been made that the appetite for engaging in this form of decision making may vary culturally. David O'Brien, a vice president with McCain Foods Ltd in New Brunswick, who oversees 34 pension plans in 56 countries, points out that 'employees in many countries in which he has set up DC plans are simply not interested in a vast array of investment options' (Davis 2005: 9). He elaborates; 'This live free or die mentality in the U.S. isn't replicated in a lot of countries around the world and employees don't want choice ... In Brazil, for example, we had an awful time trying to get employees to make decisions. They simply didn't want to' (ibid). As I have argued elsewhere, the repeated finding in the burgeoning 'personal finance' literature as well as academic research about the greater 'risk aver-sion' of women as compared to men may obscure the possibility that the unwillingness to enter into the financialized risk discourses required of indi-vidual workers is in fact an exercise of gendered agency rather than a sign of lack of agency. In other words, this systemic unwillingness should be taken seriously on its own terms as opposed to being considered a 'problem' to be overcome.[12] It is against this background that we should return to the question of how the legal governance of CAP choice making is presently accomplished.

Information disclosure

The CAP guidelines place a heavy emphasis on disclosure of information as the predominant form of support to workers faced with investment choice making. As Kaplan points out, the focus of the CAP guidelines is 'to ensure that employees in a defined contribution plan have adequate and informed access to investments. This is because the adequacy of that access can neces-sarily affect the quality of the employee's pension' (2006: 107). The approach taken here is quite consistent with the demise of traditional command and control forms of regulation that might be more prescriptive in terms of the menu of choices to be offered to employees or that would require the provi-sion of impartial advice. We have already noted the limitations of an approach to information disclosure that focuses on disclosing the risks of specific investments to workers, as opposed to a more global definition of

12 Condon (2006).

pension risks as they relate to workers' situations. Such a more holistic approach to disclosure might emphasize the vulnerability of pension results to the state of the financial markets, or the relative inefficiency of disaggregating pension funds into individual plans as opposed to large collective arrangements, or the emerging evidence that large groups of people, including many women, exhibit systematic tendencies to make decisions (or to refuse to make them) that deviate from what the norms of rational utility-maximizing would predict (Mitchell and Utkus 2004; Nofsinger 2005).

In the evolving regulatory regime of DC pensions constructed by these guidelines, one of the primary responsibilities of sponsors to employees is that of providing them with investment information and decision-making tools. The guidelines indicate that the documentation provided should be prepared using 'plain language and in a format that assists in readability and comprehension'. Section 3 elaborates that in deciding what types of information and decision-making tools sponsors should provide – a decision for them to ultimately make – they should consider issues such as access to the internet and the 'location, diversity and demographics of the members'. Again there might have been an opportunity here to consider whether information retrieval and processing might be gendered, but the guidelines do not specifically advert to this. For example, do interactions and comfort levels with technological tools for obtaining information about investment options vary by gender? Do women employees systematically prefer specific types of information about investments (for example, the labour practices of a multinational firm)? Should women with fewer financial resources to invest in retirement vehicles (as a result of lower wages) choose different investment strategies than more affluent women or men? The issue of whether the information people want to make investment decisions or the ways in which they use that information varies by gender is not raised.

Instead the guidelines suggest that examples of appropriate investment information include glossaries explaining investment terms, information about investing in different types of securities (stocks and bonds), information about the 'relative level of expected risk and return associated with different investment options' and performance reports for any investment funds offered in the CAP. Meanwhile, examples of decision-making tools include asset allocation models,[13] retirement planning tools, projection tools to help members determine contribution levels and project future balances, and investor profile questionnaires.

It is clear that the information considered relevant to members is considerably technocratic, despite the fact that empirical evidence suggests that even professionalized pension trustees, to whom responsibility is delegated to make centralized investment decisions for much larger pools of money in

---

13 Such as, for example, the allocation of contributions as between shares and bonds.

a DB context, do not always have the expertise required to make those investment decisions (Clark 2000). Again these forms of support for investment choice making seem of ambiguous value, when viewed through a feminist lens. While some feminists may applaud the apparent move away from reliance on 'expert knowledges' inherent in the decline of centralized decision making by trustees, it is unclear just how preferable it is for women who are members of CAP plans to now be required to familiarize themselves with similar technocratic information in order to make individualized pension investment choices (Condon and Philipps 2005).

Nor do the guidelines address the issue of whether employers need to take additional steps to encourage members to access these choice-making tools at all. In this sense, employees are required to be self-motivated to take advantage of the information and assistance provided. Indeed, a frequently expressed concern among sponsors is that they not be perceived by their employees as providing them with pension *advice*. This is because the provision of advice might legally be considered to place the employer in a fiduciary relationship with the employee, opening up the possibility that the sponsor could be sued by plan members for inadequate advice giving. This fear is argued by some commentators to have a chilling effect on interactions between sponsors and employees, and is a major source of the alleged 'legal risk' faced by sponsors of DC plans (Kaplan 2006). It should be reiterated that the broader context here is that one of the central effects of a shift from DB forms of pension provision to DC forms is the *removal* of traditional fiduciary responsibilities formerly imposed on pension trustees, who have traditionally exercised centralized investment decision making on behalf of worker-beneficiaries as a group.

In the U.S., the damaging effects on the pensions of Enron employees of over-investment in Enron securities in their 401(k) plans, following the corporation's bankruptcy has been documented (Blackburn 2002). In this context, it is not surprising that the Canadian guidelines provide that additional information must be provided to members of a plan where securities of the employer itself or a related party are included as an investment option. This additional information includes 'the risks associated with investing in a single security'. Again the influence of the Enron debacle may possibly be discerned in the regulation of the process of making transfers among investment options in section 4.3.[14] This process requires that sponsors should provide members with information about 'any restrictions on the number of transfers among options a member is permitted to make within a given period,

---

14 As Blackburn describes it, part of the damage to Enron employees' retirement portfolios occurred because they were prevented by a company-imposed transfer freeze from selling the Enron stock in their 401(k) plans, at the same time as Enron management were able to dispose of their stock options. See Blackburn (2002).

including any maximum limit after which a fee would be applied'. The sponsor should also provide 'a description of possible situations where transfer options may be suspended'. The possibility for sponsors to download expenses associated with operating the pension plan is signalled by the guideline that the sponsor should indicate 'all fees, expenses and penalties relating to the plan that are borne by members' including any costs that must be paid when investments are bought and sold. By s.5.3 of the guidelines, sponsors are required to provide performance reports for each investment fund to members at least annually. This requirement for ongoing performance reports, as well as periodic review by sponsors of the investment options offered (s.6.3), is taken by some commentators as an incentive to sponsors to provide 'more limited' investment options in the future (Austin 2004). This systematic effect of how the guidelines are framed runs counter to the express goal of introducing DC pensions, which is to expand the universe of pension choice making available to workers.

Again, the question raised by the foregoing discussion is whether these disclosure norms adequately respond to the insights from various academic disciplines about actual decision-making practices. There is considerable empirical data emerging from the field of behavioural economics examining the ways in which individual decision making is 'skewed' by phenomena like framing, anticipatory regret, pride, endowment effects,[15] mental accounting, decision paralysis and herd behaviour (Barber and Odean 2001; Nofsinger 2005). For example, Mitchell and Utkus argue that there are framing effects that result from the very detail of how a menu of options is superficially presented to employees, even beyond the design of the underlying investment alternatives (Mitchell and Utkus 2004: 16). Mitchell and Utkus also report in detail on research dealing with the importance of plan design in driving participant decision making (ibid: 31). The findings of these types of investigations by cognitive psychologists all bear on the question of the extent to which behaviour, such as investing behaviour, deviates from a rational profit-maximizing model.

Meanwhile, from an economic geography perspective, Strauss has argued that 'the fact remains that people make decisions about their pensions in the context of a web of social relations, networks, institutions, and structures of power that for them constitute the "real world" of everyday life' (Strauss 2006b). Thus she argues that the model of 'assisted rationality' that grounds the provision of the type of technocratic information enumerated above will not be enough to produce useful choice making for many workers. More empirically, Greenwich Associates in the US report that 'only a small

---

15 This is the idea that people often 'demand much more to sell an object than they would be willing to pay to buy it' (Nofsinger 2005). Cognitive psychologists have run a number of experiments designed to find out why this is. One theory is that people are affected by the 'pain associated with giving up' an object (ibid).

fraction of participants [in 401(k) plans] use the Internet advice tools available to them' (March 2005). The limits of education as a response to the need to make DC choices are well articulated by Mitchell and Utkus (ibid: 32), who point to endemic problems of inertia and lack of 'rationality'.[16] We have noted above that the apparently applicable norms of rationality may themselves be gendered and racialized. Thus, for example, feminist critiques of corporate and securities law have argued that the elevation of norms of corporate profit maximizing over other plausible goals of business activity or organizational decision making (for example, social responsibility) is gendered (Sparkes 2002; Gabaldon 1992; Condon 2000). This empirical information casts doubt on the usefulness of regulating information disclosure as a risk management strategy for workers in a pension context. The question from a feminist perspective is whether there are might be more gender-aware forms of information disclosure that could be effective to mitigate the gender-based risk of economic insecurity in this area. A first step would be an openness to the possibility that the unwillingness to engage in risk-based decision making is not because of a lack of education about the positive features of risk, but rather a rejection of the premises of this discourse.

Advice provision

The CAP guidelines explicitly acknowledge the possibility that employees may need to access the 'expertise' of investment advisors in addition to utilizing the investment information provided by their employer. This decision is presented as one for the individual employee to make, in a context in which there is 'no requirement that the plan sponsor test the investment knowledge of its members' (Austin 2004). Indeed, one of the effects of the deployment of DC plans is to produce an 'increasing involvement of third-party vendors of protection, investment and savings instruments' (Shuey and O'Rand 2004: 464; Miller and Rose 1990).

The CAP guidelines exhort sponsors to periodically review service providers to whom they have referred members to help them make their investment decisions (s.6.2). Possible criteria to be used to frame such reviews include any complaints arising from members about the service provider or from the sponsor itself. However, the guidelines caution that 'Because the primary relationship of a service provider who provides investment advice is with each member, it will not be possible or practical for the CAP sponsor to directly review the quality of the advice being provided'. This creates an accountability gap with respect to the practices of service providers in a

---

16 See also Stabile (2002).

pension context, with employer sponsors assuming little oversight responsibility for providers' interactions with employees.[17]

That the provision of advice by service providers may itself be gendered is suggested by the following excerpt from the financial planning literature. Yao and Hanna state (2005: 75):

> Although clients should ultimately decide whether they would like to take a certain level of financial risk, as a fiduciary of the client, a financial planner has the duty to act in the client's best interest – to evaluate the client's situation and make appropriate recommendations. It is the job of financial planners to educate clients (especially unmarried females) who choose inappropriate investments with low financial risk about their need to take more risk; and to educate male clients who have inappropriate investments with high risk about the importance of preserving wealth.

The reference to the 'education' of clients about 'appropriate' risk levels based on gender and wealth suggests that advice givers do not take seriously the possibility that refusing to interact with risk discourses is a reasonable exercise of investment rationality. Significantly for the role of legal governance in the process of valorizing financial risk taking, the gender-based disciplining of investors outlined in the above quote is justified by invoking a fiduciary duty imposed on financial planners with respect to their clients. In a DC world the fiduciary duty of financial planners operating within the financial services industry is substituted for a similar duty that used to govern employers themselves in their pension dealings with workers.

Sponsor monitoring

An important aspect of the Canadian CAP guidelines is the exhortation to plan sponsors to engage in periodic review of their service providers, their investment options, their records maintenance and the decision-making tools provided to members. It is clear, however, that, for example, with respect to reviews of the adequacy of service providers, it is for the sponsor to decide what action to take in the event that a provider fails to meet the sponsor's expectations. Thus, the accountability of service providers is downloaded to employers rather than being regulated centrally, in a context of an ongoing business relationship that is more consensual and contractually oriented than the traditional regulatory command and control model would be. We have seen already that this decentred monitoring of service providers is considered

---

17 Kaplan takes a somewhat different view of the employers' exposure to claims for negligent misrepresentation here. See Kaplan 2006: 368–370.

particularly important where the employer has engaged the service provider to provide investment advice to employees. Meanwhile, the guidelines suggest that reviews of investment options provided by the plan should be undertaken at least annually, though again no further guidance is provided to sponsors as to whether or what action to take if particular investment options are no longer considered maintainable. This model creates incentives to streamline the investment choices being offered, since fewer choices mean less employer resources devoted to monitoring; nor is any direction provided as to the consequences of inadequate monitoring.

Whither fiduciary duties?

A noteworthy issue in the contemporary legal regulation of DC pensions in Canada is the ambiguity associated with the treatment of fiduciary responsibilities towards employees. Traditionally, in a DB form of pension plan, it is clear that the trustees of a pension fund have a fiduciary responsibility to maximize the interests of the employee-beneficiaries.[18] Where employees make investment decisions pertaining to their own pension account, the trustees' fiduciary responsibility to make appropriate investment decisions on behalf of employees is removed. It may even be speculated that the removal of the legal liability risks associated with being a pension fund trustee is one of the subsidiary purposes of the shift from DB forms of pension provision to DC forms. Yet, as Kaplan notes in his contemporary treatment of Canadian pension law, it is possible that legal decision makers may find there to be residual fiduciary responsibilities expected of employer sponsors in a DC context. This concern on the part of Canadian employers is heightened by the contrast with the legal construction of DC plans in the US, where the Employee Retirement Income Security Act of 1974 (ERISA) specifically provides that no fiduciaries have any liability for any losses incurred in plans that permit participants to exercise control over the assets in their individual accounts. No such 'safe harbour' removing participant-directed pension plans from the fiduciary realm exists in Canadian pension law, nor is it adverted to in the CAP guidelines.

Thus, Kaplan locates the sources of continuing legal risk for employers in the uncertainty surrounding fiduciary liability for both inadequate plan communication and inadequate investment choice. Similarly, Ahing argues that 'DC plan sponsors may continue to face risks arising in at least 4 primary areas (1) insufficient plan information provided to members (2) incorrect plan

18 Though the extent of that responsibility in the context of a DB plan, and in particular whether it may facilitate the making of fund investment decisions so as to achieve corporate social responsibility goals is currently the subject of intense academic and legal debate. See Davis (2004); Yaron (2001); *Cowan v. Scargill* [1985] 1 Ch D 270, [1984] 2 All ER 750.

information provided to members (3) improper choice of service provider in delegating responsibilities (4) insufficient monitoring of those service providers'.[19] Even more specifically, does having a default investment option for employees who do not exercise their own choices create the possibility of liability for the sponsor who selected it? The argument would be that having a default option (e.g. a low risk, low return money market fund) presumes that the investor is not making her or his own choices, and opens up for legal scrutiny the adequacy of the option created by the sponsor (Benney 2004). The format this legal scrutiny would take is likely to flow from litigation engaged in by a group of employees as a class, alleging that the employer had breached a fiduciary duty to them.

In this apparent atmosphere of uncertainty as to the application of residual fiduciary responsibility norms to employer sponsors, the question that might be raised from a feminist perspective is whether the legal device of creating a fiduciary relationship to mitigate worker pension risk is one to be supported or rejected for its gender-based consequences. Is fiduciary responsibility (either of employers in a DC context or trustees in a DB context), as a legal device for the management of risk, to be preferred over more enlightened forms of information disclosure? The argument of this chapter has been that women and minorities are more likely to be economically disadvantaged by the ideology of individualized, technocratic choice making that underlies the shift to DC pensions. Yet some problems from a feminist perspective with the invocation of protective fiduciary norms should also be flagged. These include the dangers of paternalism, centralization of power, excessive reliance on expert knowledge, the privileging of some interests over others, as well as the possibility that fiduciaries' conflicts of interest will in fact influence their decision making (Gabaldon 1995: 19–20; Davis 2004).[20] We have also noted above the way in which fiduciary duties may be invoked as a reason for 'educating' women to accept more risk in pension decision making. This issue of which legal risk management strategy is preferable for women is one that should be taken seriously by feminists engaging in gender-based advocacy in the retirement context.

CONCLUSION

At a material level, the gendered risks of pensions are ultimately deeply connected to persistent inequalities in labour markets. The shift to DC pensions is gendered in that it removes economic security from vulnerable, lower-paid

19 Ahing (2004).
20 For a detailed non-feminist case in favour of paternalism in the context of DC plans, see Stabile (2002).

workers, and lauds individualized and masculinized risk taking, while at the same time reducing the financial risk exposure of employers. Emerging legal norms – as exemplified by the CAP guidelines – that govern the allocation of material risks among employers, service providers and employees, can be seen to promote flexibility and choice for employers rather than workers. They are light on substantive regulatory requirements to be fulfilled by employers, and backstopped mainly by the possibility of workers launching suits for damages as a result of negligence or breach of fiduciary duty.

At the discursive level, the prevailing legal conceptual universe tends to support the idea of the individual heroic risk taker, by attempting to situate risk taking in the context of partial and decontextualized information disclosure, rather than to offer alternatives to those employees, especially women, who do not wish to participate in the discourse of risk taking (Peggs 2000; Strauss 2006b). But not participating in decision making means that the locus of decision making shifts elsewhere, either back to trustees, or to employers. Presented with the option of the capacity to choose or paternalistic choice making on her behalf by others, many feminists would be likely to support choice over paternalism. The question being raised in this chapter is whether this approach is still the right answer in the contemporary world of pension provision. Thus, alternative approaches for feminist advocacy could include either agitating for more effective gender-aware support for choice making and expanding the categories of 'rational' decision making, cautiously reopening the debate about the merits of creating fiduciary relationships among employers or trustees and employees, or, more radically, problematizing the foundational and deeply gendered link between labour market participation and adequate retirement security.

REFERENCES

Ahing, D. (2004) 'Drivers Wanted', 2004 DC Plan Summit http://www.benefitscanada.com 77.
Austin, B. (2004) 'Update on Pension Case Law and Regulatory Trends', Blakes Bulletin on Pension and Employee Benefits http://www.blakes.com.
Barber, B.M. and Odean, T. (2001) 'Boys will be boys: gender, overconfidence, and common stock investment' *Quarterly Journal of Economics* 261–292.
Benney, B. (2004) 'Legal issues for defined contribution schemes when selecting investments' *Pensions* 10(1): 50.
Bezanson, K. and Luxton, M. (eds) (2006) *Social Reproduction: Feminist Political Economy Challenges Neo-Liberalism*, Montreal and Kingston: McGill-Queens University Press.
Blackburn, R. (2002) 'The Enron Debacle and the Pension Crisis' *New Left Review* 14: 26.
Blake, D. (2003) 'The UK pension system: Key issues', *Pensions* 8(4): 330.
Braithwaite, J. (2000) 'The new regulatory state and the transformation of criminology' *British Journal of Criminology* 40: 222.

Clark, G.L. (2000) *Pension Fund Capitalism*, Oxford: Oxford University Press.

Condon, M. (2006) 'The feminization of pensions? Gender, political economy and defined contribution pensions' in L. Assessi, D. Wigan and A. Nesvetailova (eds) *Global Finance in the new century: beyond deregulation*, Basingstoke, UK: Palgrave MacMillan.

Condon M. and Philipps, L. (2005) 'Transnational Market Governance and Economic Citizenship: New Frontiers for Feminist Legal Theory' *Thomas Jefferson Law Review* 28(2): 1.

Condon, M. (2002) 'Privatizing Pension Risk: Gender, Law, and Financial Markets', in B. Cossman and J. Fudge (eds) *Privatization, Law, and the Challenge to Feminism*, Toronto: University of Toronto Press.

Condon, M. (2000) 'Limited by Law? Gender, Corporate Law and the Family Firm', in D. Lacombe and C. Chunn (eds) *Law as a Gendering Practice* Toronto: Oxford University Press.

Cossman B. and Fudge J. (eds) (2002) *Privatization, Law, and the Challenge to Feminism*, Toronto: University of Toronto Press.

Cutler T. and Waine B. (2001) 'Social Insecurity and the Retreat from Social Democracy: Occupational Welfare in the Long Boom and Financialization', *Review of International Political Economy* 8: 96.

Davis, A. (2005) 'Global Trends in DC Plans', DC Forum http://www.benefitscanada.com 8.

Davis, R.B. (2004) 'Democracy and Accountability in Pension Funds' Corporate Governance Activity' S.J.D. thesis, Faculty of Law, University of Toronto.

Deaton, R. (1989) *Political Economy of Pensions*, Vancouver: UBC Press.

de Goede, M. (2004) 'Repoliticizing Financial Risk', *Economy and Society* 33: 197.

England, P. (2005) 'Separative and Soluble Selves: Dichotomous Thinking in Economics', in M. Fineman (ed.) *Feminism Confronts Homo Economicus: Gender, Law, and Society*, New York: Cornell University Press.

Felix, S. (2005) 'Back Stretch: How do CAP Guidelines measure up globally?', DC Forum http://www.benefitscanada.com 11.

Fineman M. (ed.) (2005) *Feminism Confronts Homo Economicus: Gender, Law, and Society*, New York: Cornell University Press.

Finucane M.L., Slovic P., Mertz, C.K., Flynn, J., Satterfield, T.A. (2000) 'Gender, race and perceived risk: the "white male" effect' *Health, Risk and Society* 2(2): 159–72.

Gabaldon, T.A. (1995) 'Feminism, fairness, and fiduciary duty in corporate and securities law' *Texas Journal of Women and the Law* 5: 1–36.

Joint Forum of Financial Market Regulators (2004) 'Guidelines for Capital Accumulation Plans' http://www.jointforum-forumjoint.ca.

Kaplan, A.N. (2006) *Pension Law*, Toronto: Irwin Law.

Miller P. and Rose, N. (1990) 'Governing Economic Life' *Economy and Society* 19 (1): 1–31.

Mitchell O.S. and Utkus, S.P. (2004) *Pension Design and Structure: New Lessons from Behavioral Finance*, Oxford: Oxford University Press.

Moss, D. (2002) *When all else fails: government as the ultimate risk manager*, Cambridge: Harvard University Press.

Myners P. (2001) 'Institutional Investment in the United Kingdom: A Review', http://www.hm-treasury.gov.uk/mediastore/otherfiles/31.pdf.

Nedelsky, J. (1989) 'Reconceiving autonomy: sources, thoughts and possibilities' *Yale Journal of Law and Feminism* 1: 7–36.

Nelson J. and England P. (2002) 'Feminist Philosophies of Love and Work' *Hypatia* 17(2): 1–18.

Nofsinger, J.R. (2005) *The Psychology of Investing*, 2nd edn, New York: Pearson Prentice Hall.

O'Malley, P. (1998) *Crime and the Risk Society*, London: Ashgate.

Peggs, K. (2000) 'Which Pension?: Women, Risk and Pension Choice', *The Sociological Review* 48(3): 249.

Richards, B. (2005) 'Seeing Beyond', 2005 Capital Accumulation Report http://www.benefitscanada.com 15.

Ring, P. (2003) ' "Risk" and UK Pension Reform', *Social Policy & Administration* 37:65.

SEI Canada (2006) 'Canada's DEC Forum: The Voice of Canadian Plan Sponsors', DC Forum http://www.benefitscanada.com 2.

Sharratt, A. (2003) 2003 defined contribution plan report http://www.benefitscanada.com 28.

Shuey, K.M. and O'Rand, A.M. (2004) 'New Risks for Workers: Pensions, Labor Markets, and Gender', *Annual Review of Sociology* 30: 453.

Slovic, P. (1999) 'Trust, Emotion, Sex, Politics, and Science: Surveying the Risk-Assessment Battlefield', *Risk Analysis* 19: 689–701.

Sparkes, R. (2002) *Socially Responsible Investment: a global revolution*, New York: Wiley.

Stabile, S.J. (2002) 'The Behavior of Defined Contribution Plan Participants' *New York University Law Review* 77: 71.

Strauss, K. (2006a) 'Gender inequality, Risk and European Pensions' http://www.ouce.ox.ac.uk/research/spaces/wpapers/wpg06–13.pdf.

Strauss, K. (2006b) 'Rational idealism, uncertain reality: the context of choice and UK pension welfare' http://www.ouce.ox.ac.uk/research/spaces/wpapers/wpg06–09.pdf.

Vosko, L.F. (2000) *Temporary Work: The Gendered Rise of a Precarious Employment Relationship*, Toronto: University of Toronto Press.

Yao R. and Hanna, S.D. (2005) 'The Effect of Gender and Marital Status on Financial Risk Tolerance' *Journal of Personal Finance* 4(1):66.

Yaron, G. (2001) 'The Responsible Pension Trustee: Reinterpreting the Principles of Prudence and Loyalty in the Context of Socially Responsible Institutional Investing' *Estates, Trusts and Pensions Journal* 20: 305.

Chapter 8

Risk and criminal victimization

Exploring the fear of crime

Sandra Walklate

> Gender is an expression of risk because, at its core, it represents the opposition of 'women' and 'men' both as analytic categories and social constructs as well as actors in a universe of potential harms.
>
> (Chan and Rigakos 2002: 757)

INTRODUCTION: CRIMINOLOGY, GENDER AND RISK

The relationship between risk and macro social change has been a focal concern for the social sciences over the last two decades (see Beck 1992; Lupton 1999; Strydom 2002), with some commentators now of the view that given the prevailing 'culture of fear' (Furedi 2002) a meaningful adage might be 'I am a victim therefore I am'. Given recent social and political pre-occupations with such issues as international terrorism, the threat of bio-terrorism, and other global natural disasters like the 2004 tsunami, there is undoubtedly some sympathy to be had with Furedi's view. In addition to these global concerns, however, there is clearly still something to be under-stood concerning people's continued expressed fears in relation to more local issues like crime, as reported by national and international criminal victimiza-tion surveys, despite (reported) declining rates of recorded crime. It may be that these global and local pre-occupations are in some way connected. Therefore exploring the fear of crime and how that has been understood and mediated by structural variables might be a useful vehicle for untangling some of the wider conceptual problems in understanding the relationship between risk, gender and the fear of crime.

Traditionally, criminology has, in line with other social science disciplines, embraced the actuarial approach to risk (see Kemshall 2003) and as we shall see this approach is evident in mainstream analyses of the fear of crime. Indeed, there is some justification for this, given that statistical models based on considerable samples have enabled criminologists to quantify various prob-lems and issues (see Loader and Sparks 2002: 93). Much of the critique of this embrace of risk has focused on concerns about the potential of actuarial justice following on from the work of Feeley and Simon (1994). Much less of this critique has concerned itself with the gendered presumptions embedded within it (though for an insight into some aspects of this see Walklate 1997; Weaver *et al* 2000; and Chan and Rigakos 2002). O'Malley (2006) offers a thorough assessment of the general criminological current state of play in relation to risk so there is no intention to replicate that coverage here. However, in focusing on the fear of crime here the intention is to explore the extent to which the criminological embrace of a unitary and unifying concept of risk (O'Malley 2004) has resulted in the perpetuation of a rather circum-scribed understanding of risk in which the question of gender (as opposed to sex or women) has been mobilized in particular ways that has resulted in a limited appreciation of both risk and gender.

In order to engage in this exploration this chapter falls into three parts. The first will review the different efforts that have been made to explore the fear of crime with a view to outlining the way in which a gendered concept of risk has been mobilized. The second will consider the extent to which crimi-nology's persistent commitment to positivism frames these debates and as a consequence structures this gendered understanding of risk. In conclusion I shall make some observations on the extent to which current social condi-tions might lead us to think more critically and constructively not only about the fear of crime but also about the concept of risk.

RISK THEORY, CRIMINOLOGY AND THE FEAR OF CRIME

Chan and Rigakos (2002: 748) identify two theoretical approaches to risk that have influenced the criminological agenda: the ontological (largely emanating from the work of Beck); and the institutional (largely emanating from the work of Foucault). In their analysis of each of these approaches they conclude that 'these notions of risk stunt our understanding of women in late capitalism'. So, from their point of view, these approaches presumed women as risk avoiders rather than risk seekers (Miller 1991) and adopted the converse position in relation to men with the resulting effect of assuming that the concept of risk is itself gender neutral (see also Stanko 1997; Walklate 1997). These resulting effects may be attributable, as O'Malley (2006) observes, to the fact that, 'while there is general agreement that risk has moved into a central issue for criminology, there is not always consistency either about what exactly this means, or how it should be understood'. He also identifies two forms to the appearance of risk in criminology; the statistical use of predictive techniques and what he calls an understanding of 'subjective risk'. Under this second heading he places both concerns about victimization (especially the fear of crime and the mobilization of policies designed to address this) and concerns about the motivation for criminal behaviour (as risk- or thrill-seeking behaviour). In some respects each of these analyses of risk within criminology reflect the partial and eclectic way in which criminology has thought about risk, so it will be useful to capture how that partial understanding is embedded in approaches taken to risk, gender and the fear of crime.

Farrall *et al* (2000: 399) observe that 'fear of crime is now one of the most researched topics in contemporary criminology', going on to state that 'it appears that the fear of crime is a social phenomenon of truly striking dimensions'. The question remains, however, as to how well this has been researched and what shape and form these 'striking dimensions' take. This is not just an empirical question it is also a conceptual one. Fears about crime are located within a wider tapestry of risk biographies (for example, lifetime experiences, structural and geographical location, cognitive abilities). This may also include fears about employment, the family, finances, consumption and so on (see also Tulloch and Lupton 2003). Furthermore, in the context of macro-social transformations, crime, disorder and incivilities can provide portals for a range of wider (potentially) sublimated concerns about and challenges to the certainty, order and security of everyday life (see Ewald 2000; Caldeira 2000; Kearon and Leach 2000).

Walklate (1998a) has offered a review of the development of the fear of crime debate from the early 1970s' concern with fear of the 'other' through to the 1990s' focus on fear as anxiety (*qua* Taylor 1996; 1997 and Hollway and Jefferson 1997; 2000). The appraisal offered by Walklate (1998a) identified four conceptual shifts in the 'fear of crime' debate: from rationality/irrationality; safety; anxiety; to trust. It is of value to say a few words about each of these and their relationship with risk and the mobilization of gendered understandings of the fear of crime, in order to obtain a fuller picture of the shape and form to its 'striking dimensions'.

The debate as to whether the fear of crime was rational or irrational was one largely conducted in the 1980s between those who were referred to as 'administrative' criminologists and those who called themselves 'left realist' criminologists. This approach linked criminal victimization survey data on people's expressed fear of crime to their reported statistical risk from criminal victimization. That research concluded that both women and the elderly were particularly 'irrational' given the disparity between their (high) levels of expressed fear and their (low) levels of actual risk. Presented in this way, this expressed fear of crime by women (and the elderly) lent weight to the view that women were indeed irrational creatures and by implication not capable of making 'proper', that is 'rational', sense of the 'real' risks they faced, as opposed to their perception of the risks that they faced. Linking expressed fears and actual risk in this way exemplifies the actuarial approach to the concept of risk and risk assessment embraced by much criminological work commented upon earlier. This approach failed to unlock what such expressed fears might be a reflection of, or be connected to, as well as presuming that risk itself was an unproblematic concept.

Yet, connecting fear and risk in this way has become a perpetual and consistent feature of the criminal victimization survey industry. For example, it has become commonplace on the annual publication of crime statistics to spotlight the disparity between falling crime rates and rising public fears about crime. However, whether or not the 'fear of crime' is rational or irrational is a debate that was not – and arguably could not be – fully resolved. As Sparks (1992) asked some time ago, what would a rational fear look like anyway? Nevertheless, the perpetuation of this view, especially as articulated within international criminal victimization survey work and the standardized approach to the questions that that survey process asks, renders this understanding and approach to fear very powerful in denying the importance of local structural and cultural differences (see Walklate, 2003).

The academic debate on the rationality/irrationality of the fear of crime was enhanced by a conceptual sidestep that emanated from feminist work. That conceptual sidestep introduced the concept of safety, or as Stanko (1990) would prefer 'climates of unsafety'. The introduction of this concept endeavoured to do three things: first, to challenge the view of women's expressed fears as irrational; second, to locate those fears within the lived reality of women's everyday lives; third, given the empirical evidence from feminist work that fear was a normal condition for women (demonstrably connected to their experience of male violence and fear of sexual danger both in public and in private; see for example, Warr 1985; Stanko 1990; Crawford et al 1990), it might make better sense, for both men and women, to ask questions about the conditions under which people felt safe. This concept placed a gendered understanding of fear (and by implication risk) at the centre of exploring the fear of crime by asking questions about whose standards are used as a marker of what might count as a rational or reasonable fear.

Talking about safety rather than fear, then, constituted a deep-rooted challenge to the production of empirical findings that presumed women as fearful (and thereby risk avoiders) and men as fearless (and thereby risk seekers) (Goodey 1997). Walklate (1997) argued that such presumptions were the result of the processes that had become embedded in the fear of crime debate that reduced both fear and risk to a measurable, calculable entity. Yet if the fear of crime (read 'fear of sexual danger' for women) is a normal condition for women, a 'governing of the soul' (Stanko 1997; Campbell 2005), exploring the everyday lives of women (and men) through the lens of safety would offer a better understanding of this. Indeed, in the light of this feminist incursion in this debate, the criminal victimization survey industry made important efforts to take account of the differently structured relationship that women have with the experience of crime especially within the questions asked (efforts were made to consider the question of domestic violence, for example) and the sample design (efforts have been made in exploring some issues with women-only samples). As a result, discussions of how, where, and when people (women) feel safe are contemporarily much better informed, though still embedded in a calculable approach.

The third academic shift in the fear of crime debate deployed the concept of anxiety. This addressed the relationship between fear and risk in two quite distinct ways. The work of Taylor *et al* (1996) and Taylor (1996; 1997) explored anxiety as an expression that was rooted in locally constructed and locally understood 'structures of feeling'. This approach argued that such structures of feeling were/are fuelled by perceptions, myths and folklore about what is known locally about crimes. These feelings act in a meta-phorical capacity for concerns not just about crime in a locality but about other things going on in local areas, such as rising or falling house prices, or the efficacy of the local job market, for example (see Girling, Loader and Sparks 2000). This approach situated people in the context of the 'risk positions' in which they find themselves in which questions of gender will be differently expressed (*qua* Tulloch and Lupton 2003 referenced earlier). Hollway and Jefferson (1997), on the other hand, adopted an explicitly psychoanalytical approach to the concept of anxiety. Using anxiety as the universal human condition, their concern was to map the extent to which people's expressed fear of crime (dis)connects with their mobilization of defence mechanisms against anxiety. They too situated this process of mobil-ization within the risk society thesis in which individuals seek biographical solutions to systemic problems (Bauman 2000) but very much as a process that demands the harnessing and embellishing of individual defence mechan-isms that again may or may not be differently expressed according to gender and/or other structural variables, like, for example, age, ethnicity, faith or any combination of these.

The implication from each of these different uses of the concept of anxiety, given their differently constituted relationship with the risk society thesis, was to downplay the importance of understanding the fear of crime as a gendered experience. This downplaying was in line with the risk society thesis as a whole (see Stanko 2000) and thus lends support to the analysis offered by Chan and Rigakos (2002) with which this section began. Moreover, the embrace of the risk society thesis, with its implied presumption of the uni-versal victim (Mythen, forthcoming), by the fear of crime debate, arguably contributed to the marginalization of more fully gendered analyses of the relationship between risk and fear, as a result of that same presumption. Contemporaneous with this work, other researchers were adopting more subtly and situationally nuanced understandings of the fear of crime that would also put gender in its place. This work drew on the concept of trust.

From a point of view work emanating from the feminist movement, especially radical feminism had always been, both implicitly and explicitly, concerned to problematize the question of trust in relation to women's

experiences of criminal victimization. That work rendered clearly problematic the notion of the safe haven of the home. Work on rape in marriage
(Russell 1990), 'domestic' violence (see, for example, Dobash and Dobash
1980; 1992), sexual harassment (Stanley and Wise 1987) challenged the view
that women need not fear men that they know: work colleagues, boyfriends,
partners and relatives. The recognition of the familiar and the familial as not
being necessarily any more trustworthy than the stranger put a very different
picture on the screen of who is and who is not to be trusted, a picture which
feminist research demonstrated routinely informs women's sense of 'ontological security', their sense of well-being, their fears (see Stanko 1997). This
matters, since risk and trust are two sides of the same coin. This coin can
carry a masculine or a feminine image but this image does not necessarily
correlate with being male and female.

The argument presented by Walklate and Evans (1999) also supported the
usefulness of exploring the mechanisms of trust that underpin people's sense
of ontological security especially in high crime areas. They suggested conceptualizing the fear of crime through an understanding of relationships of
trust in which:

> '. . . your place in relation to crime places you in a community of belong-
> ing and exclusion . . . It is consequently important to recognise who is
> seen to be protecting you and how: for many people it is not the police or
> the council but local families and/or the Salford Firm. Moreover it is the
> absence of confidence in the formal agencies which creates the space for
> those other forces to come into play.
>
> (Evans et al 1996: 379; see also Walklate 1998b)

This work placed the gendered nature of criminal gang (that is, male-
dominated) activity, and its role in community relationships, at the centre of
people's sense of 'ontological security' in one of the communities they
investigated but not in the other. Their data suggested that actual manifestation of trust relationships may be differently mediated by the nature of
community relationships, age, gender, ethnicity etc., thus suggestive of quite a
complex relationship between crime, fear, trust, community and gender. The
complex ways in which interaction community networks fuel people's perceptions of their locality in relation to crime and their fear of it is one that has
been similarly articulated in the concept of collective efficacy in the work of
Sampson et al (1997) and Dekeseredy et al (2003), the latter of which was also
concerned to reflect upon how such community processes facilitate (or
otherwise) responses to violence against women.

This work on the role of trust and trusting relationships, along with the
work around questions of safety, clearly centred not only women's variable,
problematic relationship with men, but also men's relationship with their
sense of themselves as men. As a result the fear of crime debate reached a

particular turning point under the influence of the developments of theoretical work on masculinity. Feminist work had already placed the problematic behaviour of men's violence towards women on the criminological
agenda, and this precursor brought to the fore, for academics working in this
area, the consistent finding of the criminal victimization survey data that
whilst young males were the most at risk from crime, they expressed the least
fear or concern about it (Stanko and Hobdell 1993; Goodey 1997).
Indeed some of the work conducted by Hollway and Jefferson (1997; 2000)
also tried to address this conundrum. As Stanko and Hobdell stated:
'Criminology's failure to explore men's experience of violence is often
attributed to men's reluctance to report "weakness". This silence is, we are led
to believe, a product of men's hesitation to disclose vulnerability.' (Stanko
and Hobdell 1993: 400). As a result of such observations there was a brief
moment in which awareness of the gendered nature of the fear of crime
debate became possible through exploring the value and applicability of
concepts derived from masculinity theory.

How men experience, understand, and then articulate their relationship with risk, 'fear' and danger is relatively under-explored in the context
of criminology. In a more general context Lyng (1990: 872–3) had suggested
that:

> Males are more likely to have an illusory sense of control over fateful
> endeavours because of the socialisation pressures on males to develop
> a skill orientation towards their environment. In so far as males are
> encouraged to use their skills to affect the outcome of all situations, even
> those that are almost entirely chance determined, they are likely to
> develop a distorted sense of their ability to control fateful circumstances.

These images emphasize a positive relationship between men and risk-taking
behaviours. The interviews with men reported in Stanko and Hobdell's (1993)
work offered a somewhat different emphasis. Whilst it is possible that Lyng's
skydivers might have been asserting control over the uncontrollable in a very
positive and ego-enhancing way, Stanko and Hobdell's work might be viewed
as illustrating how men lost control in an ego-damaging way. Taken together,
they both articulate aspects of 'hegemonic masculinity' as developed by
Connell (1987). The question of the motivation for, and experience of, each
of these different types of behaviour is, of course, a highly individual one.
However, each response captures some sense of what it is that is culturally
expected of a man, and how the variable responses of individual men in
the light of those cultural expectations may be rendered silent in the discourses that claim to speak about them, especially in relation to risk and the
fear of crime.

Hegemonic masculinity promotes certain expressions of masculinity, for
example, that of provider, procreator and protector (Kersten 1996) in

preference to others such as that of the unemployed, homosexual and vulnerable. In so doing they can provide a framework in which to understand both the inhibition of and the expression of fear, and of risk-taking behaviour in (young) men. The powerful presence and influence of hegemonic masculinity not only silences women's experiences (especially those that challenge the vulnerable, weak, fearful image of femininity) but also silences the experiences of some men too (especially those that also express weakness, vulnerability and fearfulness). Awareness of this sets quite a complex agenda for those interested in the fear of crime. For example, whilst women may not fear all men, they do have considerable knowledge about men that they know, places they deem dangerous, and the potential for sexual danger from men that they know and do not know. They might also be afraid of some women (as evidenced by work on bullying in schools, for example), though this does not mean necessarily that there is a symmetrical relationship between 'women's' fears of men and their fears of other women. The same, of course, might also be said of men in relation to men and women that they know. So a truly gendered understanding of risk would be an understanding that was detached from stereotypical assumptions associated with the biological categories of male and female.

This discussion returns us to the way in which the criminological discourse on the fear of crime reflects the wider criminological adoption of the concept of risk as a unitary and unifying concept (O'Malley 2004). This discourse hides both the risk-seeking behaviour of women (Miller 2002) and the vulnerability of men. When female risk-seeking behaviour has been explored, it has more often than not been pathologized, situating women in this way as 'The Other' (Walklate 1997); it casts them outside of this discourse, though not necessarily outside the experience of risk seeking. Simultaneously that discourse arguably fails to capture the lived reality for some men, especially those who are not comfortable with the risk-seeking (and other) expectations associated with hegemonic masculinity. This discourse reflects the cultural imperatives of what counts as the more legitimate behaviour for men and women, and in part explains why women who choose to engage in risk-taking activities, whether that be mountaineering, motorcycling or crime, receive such a bad press (see also Lois 2005). As Chan and Rigakos (2002: 756) state:

> A recognition of risk as gendered relies on acknowledging that there can be no essential notion of risk; that risk is variable; risk itself is more than one type ... Risk is gendered on a continuum both in the sense of empirical potential harm and the recognition and the definition of that harm. Women, it may be argued, are required to engage in instrumental risk in order to interact socially, work, cohabitate with a man etc. However, this does not signal women's victimhood but rather their agency in flouting potential dangers in the general pursuit of material subsistence.

This view is supported evidentially in the work of Sanders (2005) on the way in which prostitutes work to maintain their personal safety. Her work illustrates a 'continuum of risk', a highly subtle and active process of making choices about where to work, how to work, along with emotional, identity, health and relationship management work, that the material demands of prostitution entail. However, such a gendered view of risk, that is a view that questions presumptions of victimhood for women and agency for men, is still largely absent from the fear of crime debate. Some of this absence is clearly attributable to the way in which this issue has been investigated and the presumptions with which that investigative process has operated.

INVESTIGATING THE FEAR OF CRIME

The fear of crime debate has been dominated by the data generated by criminal victimization surveys. Generally criminal victimization surveys still operationalize the 'fear of crime' in relation to perceptions of 'risk from crime'. For example, respondents are asked how long they have lived in their area, their levels of satisfaction with their neighbourhood, and their views of the kind of neighbourhood they live in. These questions are then followed by others which focus on how safe they feel walking alone at night in their area, how safe they feel when they are alone in their own home, and how much they worry about different kinds of crime happening to them. The respondent is then moved on from discussing these 'fears' to their estimation of the chance of different crimes happening to them and the extent to which they think certain crimes in their area are common or uncommon. These are followed by questions which ask the respondents to recall their actual experience of criminal victimization during a given time period. Despite the increasing sophistication of the criminal victimization survey methodology with respect to these issues (see, for example, Sutton and Farrall 2005; Farrall and Gadd 2004; Gabriel and Greve 2003) there remains a commitment to operationalizing the 'fear of crime' in this way and this raises a number of issues some of which are discussed below.

As Maxfield (1984) pointed out some time ago in his analysis of the fear of crime based on British Crime Survey data, operationalizing the concept of fear is fraught with difficulties. From the summary offered above it is possible to see that in this process some effort is made to distinguish 'fears' from 'worries'; indeed the questions asked in fact display an interesting preference for 'how *safe* do you feel?' Individual levels of expressed safety are therefore used as indicators of levels of fear. Without entering into questions of semantics here, this does appear to be a little odd. The conceptual transformation from fear to safety is neither an easy nor a straightforward one to make, as the conceptual incursion of feminist work discussed above suggests. At a minimum it raises questions concerning what is actually being measured here. A number of issues associated with this are worthy of further comment.

Whilst making the distinction between 'fears' and 'worries' might be useful, this distinction is often pursued with the respondent in the vacuum of criminal victimization. In other words, these data provide us with little sense of how these 'fears' and 'worries' measured in this way compare with other 'fears' and 'worries' that people might have and how those situational experiences might be a reflection of structural and/or material inequalities (an issue that is addressed in relation to other impacts of criminal victimization; see, for example, Mawby and Walklate 1994, but not in relation to the fear of crime). This observation becomes more acute in the context of the international criminal victimization survey process rendering that process subject to the criticism of occidentalism (Cain 2000; Walklate 2003); that is, assuming that the presumed Western models of relationships between men and women are legitimately and viably defensible in other socio-cultural locations.

Moreover, the way in which fear has been operationalized traditionally within the criminal victimization survey reflects a narrow behavioural focus. For example, questions focus on when an individual is alone, reflecting an assumption that this is the behavioural condition in which fear is most likely to be experienced (returning us to the presumptions of the protector embedded in hegemonic masculinity). The questions also make a distinction between outside the home and inside the home, as though in terms of fear these constitute separate and separable experiences. This is particularly problematic for understanding women's expressed fear of crime as Pain (1991) and Valentine (1992) have clearly demonstrated. Despite women's expressed fearfulness of the stranger, the footsteps behind her (Morgan 1989), of being in public, the context of fear for many women is also the domain of the private, the safe haven of the home, when she is with her partner. Some of these dilemmas, especially the transgressive nature of the public and the private, in understanding the role of the familiar in generating fear, are increasingly coming to light in relation to questions of homophobia and hate crime (see, for example, Brooks Gardner 1995; Mason 2005a, 2005b).

Finally, though by no means least in importance, these are questions that are subsequently analysed in relation to both actual and perceived risk from crime. Importantly, what this process of operationalization does is to link fear, risk and behaviour together. Formulating an equation between expressed worries and reported behavioural strategies of dealing with such worries assumes a risk management view of human behaviour. This view sees individual behaviour as being constructed as a rational response to perceived situations of worry, threat or danger. Behavioural responses, however, can be constructed in response to a number of different processes, that may or may not be articulated (that is spoken about), that may or may not be intuitive (he makes her 'feel' uncomfortable), or can be the result of a combination of factors. In other words, the risk management view is one that, empirically, and in relation to explanation, is only one possibility amongst several (see, for example, Skogan 1986). However, this risk management view is the favoured view because it proffers the opportunity for both prediction and control. In other words, it can offer practical policy advice (see, for example, Haggerty 2003; Campbell 2005) and presumes the primacy of a motivational world of risk avoidance that Douglas observed (1992) some time ago and, as Walklate (1997) argued, genders both risk-seeking and risk-avoiding behaviours as well as permitting gendered presumptions of responsibility.

To summarize, the pre-eminent position that the actuarial approach to risk occupies within criminology, at the expense of other ways of thinking about risk, have resulted in a measurable and calculative operationalization of the concept of fear. The dominance of this interpretation of the relationship between risk and fear has persisted despite significant alternative conceptual incursions into the fear of crime debate that have been documented elsewhere in this chapter, and despite the work that clearly demonstrates that both fear and risk are gendered. The persistence of this way of thinking is well articulated by the recent work of Sutton and Farrall (2005) who discuss the social desirability effect that can be linked with women's survey responses in relation to the fear of crime. They argue that women's responses to survey questions can be understood, in part, as a result of them offering answers seen to be the socially acceptable answers, and that this needs to be taken into account when making sense of data generated in this way, especially when compared with men's responses. They go to suggest that 'they (men) are suppressed by the perception that it is not socially acceptable to express ones' fears' (Sutton and Farrall 2005: 222). Now there is a surprise! So the question remains as to why this approach persists. One part of the answer to this question lies within criminology's persistent embrace of positivism to which we shall now turn.

RISK, GENDER AND SCIENCE

The belief that science could transform and control nature has its origins in the 17th century and the implicit, endemic adherence of criminology to this modernist project has been well documented (see, for example, Taylor *et al* 1973; Roshier 1989, amongst others). Indeed it is the commitment to this modernist project that can be discerned in the drive for prediction, control and policy evidenced by the study of the fear of crime. There is, however, another structural agenda in this project. Bacon, for example, believed that the 'man of science' could make 'nature a slave to man's needs and desires' (Sydie 1989: 205). In seeking this control, nature was characterized as female and the association of women with nature, as being that to be controlled, was perpetuated. As Eagle-Russett (1989: 63) has pointed out 'Women and savages, together with idiots, criminals, and pathological monstrosities, were a constant source of anxiety to male intellectuals in the late nineteenth century'. This anxiety centred men as rational and women as emotional, expressed by Smith (1987: 74) in the following way: 'the knower turns out after all not to be an abstract knower perching on an Archimedean point but a member of a definite social category occupying definite positions in society.' In this 'regime of rationality' (Smith 1987) women became the dangerous other (those to be controlled), not possessors of that which could be known. In this way scientific ideology equated male knowledge with reason and female knowledge (almost a contradiction in terms) became equated with the emotional and/or intuition. In this way the emergence of science as a foundation of knowledge was implicated in the emergence of the dualism of 'natural woman'/'cultural man'; that privileges a masculine view of the world (Seidler 1994: 429).

So science, (and by implication social science) as a social practice articulates a particular view of the world; through it male knowledge became equated with reason and what counted as knowledge in the process called science. Unfortunately the failure to transcend such dualistic thinking has taken its toll on both men and women in different ways and is demonstrated in the criminological exploration of risk and the fear of crime discussed here. So an apparent outcome of the end of tradition and the end of nature, as articulated in the risk society thesis, appears to have resulted in the social search for a situation of zero risk, of risk avoidance: the ultimate control by Man, the scientific criminologist (as we can now see) of crime. Yet, how accurate a view is this? Is there another way of thinking about the question of what counts as knowledge? Or put another way, how accurate is it to think of science, whether natural or social, as a social practice that is rooted in reason? Moreover, in this particular discussion, how well does this view of knowledge resonate with how human beings experience risk and fear?

Intuition, another form of knowing, is variously interpreted as meaning an absence of reason, *a priori* knowledge, a hunch, and feminine logic (Roget's Thesaurus). In the formative processes from which science and scientific practices emerged, the notion of intuitive knowledge certainly found itself on the feminine side of the knowledge dichotomy and was subsequently seen to be less reliable and consequently less valuable. I am using the notion of intuition here somewhat metaphorically for all kinds of knowledge/ experience that might equally be deemed lacking in reason (in the scientific sense, i.e. not universally applicable) and thereby not so valued. There are different ways of illustrating the impact of the downgrading of this kind of knowledge, but one of the most graphic I have read is to be found in Pirsig (1976) *Zen and the Art of Motorcycle Maintenance*.

In discussing motorcycle repair Pirsig makes the following observations:

A screw sticks for example, on a side cover assembly. You check the manual to see if there might be any special cause for this screw to come off so hard but all it says is 'Remove side cover plate' in that wonderful terse technical style that never tells you what you want to know . . . This isn't a rare scene in science or technology. This is the commonest scene of all. Just plain stuck . . . What you're up against is the great unknown, the void of all Western thought. You need some ideas, some hypotheses. Traditional scientific method has always been at the very best 20–20 hindsight. It's good for seeing where you've been. It's good for testing the truth of what you think you know, but it can't tell you where you ought to go, unless where you ought to go is a continuation of where you were going in the past. Creativity, originality, inventiveness, intuition, imagination – 'unstuckness' in other words – are completely outside its domain.

This example captures the clear tensions between what it is that can and cannot be delivered by the cultural adhesion to science: when a specific problem emerges under specific circumstances the universalism of science does not necessarily equip anyone (the scientist and scientific criminologist included) with either the knowledge or the ability to solve it. In these circumstances people reach for other forms of knowing.

As was suggested earlier, intuition is assigned to the feminine side of the knowledge dichotomy and is seen in opposition to rationality. In the hierarchy of knowing it is a form of knowledge which is downgraded partly because of its feminine connotations and partly because it is not measurable and thereby not objective. Yet intuition is not only a source of knowledge for becoming 'unstuck' in practical circumstances; it is also a form of knowledge that contributes to the way in which importance (value) is assigned to 'facts'. Women's knowledge of men to be feared can be known intuitively as much as it can be a reflection of actual experience. This is what is felt. However, what is felt does not necessarily lend itself to a rational risk management model of understanding behaviour. However, it does return us to the question of whether or not fear, which is a feeling, can be measured at all (Garofalo 1981).

CONCLUSION: RISK, REASON AND FEELING

As was suggested above, Garofalo (1981) observed the difficulties inherent in talking about the 'fear' of crime. Fear is a feeling. It has immediacy. It is associated with acute sensory and physical reactions. In this sense, taking account of what women feel about particular men in a very real sense captures some aspects of 'fear'. This is not just about articulating socially desirable responses; this is about their lived experience in their relationships with men whom they know (the familial and familiar) and men whom they do not know (stranger-danger). However, this does not and will not apply to all men. So, how women engage in risk negotiation, how they maintain their sense of well-being, will take their experiences into account. In everyday practices this reflects a sense of agency (Sanders 2005) that sits very uneasily with the criminological discourse on the fear of crime. By the same token men's fears in relation to crime (or anything else) should not be presumed to be a contradiction in terms. Hence, the nature/culture divide between reason and emotion embedded in criminology takes its toll on us all; men and women.

As Wootton (1959) suggested some time ago, criminology was good at seeing sex, but as Cain (1990) commented, it could not see gender. Little has changed. Yet in the contemporary world there is surely an imperative to challenge criminology's continued and persistent commitment to understanding risk and fear in the way that it does. It is clear that risk and fear, in a world in which it appears that people believe has changed forever (Worcester 2001), need to be unpacked much more carefully, thoughtfully, and through a structured lens if we are to keep pace with, resonate with, and genuinely understand how the fear of crime impacts on all of us, whether that be in the local conditions of our own home or the global condition of a post-terrorist world society (Beck 2002). Of course, in order to do this, it may be necessary to reconsider what counts as scientific knowledge and embrace a more subjective appreciation of risk and less of an actuarial one.

ACKNOWLEDGEMENT

I would like to thank the editors of this volume and my partner Ron Wardale for their very helpful comments on earlier drafts of this chapter.

REFERENCES

Bauman, Z. (2000) *Liquid Modernity*, Oxford: Polity Press.
Beck, U. (1992) *The Risk Society*, London: Sage.
Beck, U. (2002) 'The Terrorist Threat: World Risk Society Revisited', *Theory, Culture and Society* 19 (4): 39–55.
Brooks Gardner, C. (1995) 'Men of steel: gay men and the management of public harassment' in S. Edgell, S. Walklate and G. Williams (eds) *Debating the Future of the Public Sphere*, Aldershot: Avebury.
Cain, M. (1990) 'Towards transgression: new directions in feminist criminology' *International Journal of the Sociology of Law* 18: 1–18.
Cain, M. (2000) 'Orientalism, Occidentalism and the Sociology of Crime' *British Journal of Criminology* 40 (2): 239–260.
Caldeira, T. (2000) *City of Walls: Segregation and Citizenship in Sao Paulo*, Berkeley, Ca.: University of California Press.

Campbell, A. (2005) 'Keeping the "lady" safe: the regulation of femininity through crime prevention literature' *Critical Criminology* 13: 119–140.

Chan, W. and Rikagos, G. (2002) 'Risk, Crime and Gender' *British Journal of Criminology* 42 (4): 743–761.

Connell, R.W. (1987) *Gender and Power*, Oxford: Polity.

Crawford, A., Jones, T., Woodhouse, T., Young, J. (1990) 'The Second Islington Crime Survey', Middlesex University: Centre of Criminology.

Dekeseredy, W.S., Schwartz, M., Alvi, S., and Tomaszewski, A. (2003) 'Perceived collective efficacy and women's victimization in public housing' *Criminal Justice 3/* 1: 5–27.

Dobash, R. and Dobash R. (1980) *Violence Against Wives*, Shepton Mallett: Open Books.

Dobash, R. and Dobash, R. (1992) *Women, Violence and Social Change*, London: Routledge.

Douglas, M. (1992) *Risk and Blame: Essays in Cultural Theory*, London: Routledge.

Eagle-Russett, C. (1989) *Sexual Science*, Cambridge, Mass.: Harvard University Press.

Evans, K., Fraser, P., and Walklate, S. (1996) 'Whom do you trust? The politics of grassing on an inner city housing estate', *Sociological Review* August: 361–380.

Ewald, U. (2000) 'Criminal victimization and social adaptation in modernity' in T. Hope and R. Sparks (eds) *Crime, Risk and Insecurity*, London: Routledge.

Farrell, S., Bannister, J., Ditton, J. and Gilchrist, E. (2000) 'Social psychology and the fear of crime' *British Journal of Criminology* 40(3): 376–399.

Farrall, S. and Gadd, D. (2004) 'Research Note: The Frequency of the fear of crime' *British Journal of Criminology* 44/1: 127–133.

Feeley, M. and Simon, J. (1994) 'Actuarial justice; the emerging new criminal law' in D. Nelken (ed.) *The Futures of Criminology*, London: Sage.

Furedi, F. (2002) *The Culture of Fear*, London: Continuum.

Gabriel, U. and Greve, W. (2003) 'The psychology of fear of crime; conceptual and methodological perspectives' *British Journal of Criminology* 43/3: 600–615.

Garofalo, J. (1981) 'The fear of crime: causes and consequences' *Journal of Criminal Law and Criminal Policy* 72: 839–957.

Girling, E., Loader, I., and Sparks, R. (2000) *Crime and Social Change in Middle England*, London: Routledge.

Goodey, J. (1997) 'Boys Don't Cry: masculinities, fear of crime and fearlessness' *British Journal of Criminology* 37 (3): 401–418.

Haggerty, K. (2003) 'From risk to precaution: the rationalities of personal crime prevention' in R. Ericson and A. Doyle (eds) *Risk and Morality*, Toronto: University of Toronto Press.

Hollway, W. and Jefferson, T. (1997) 'The risk society in an age of anxiety' *British Journal of Sociology* 48: 255–266.

Hollway, W. and Jefferson, T. (2000) 'The role of anxiety in the fear of crime' in T. Hope, and R. Sparks (eds) *Crime, Risk and Insecurity*, London: Routledge.

Kearon, T. and Leach, R. (2000) 'Invasion of the body snatchers: burglary reconsidered' *Theoretical Criminology* 4 (4): 451–473.

Kemshall, H. (2003) *Risk and Criminal Justice Policy*, Buckingham: Open University Press.

Kersten, J. (1996) 'Culture, masculinities and violence against women' *British Journal of Criminology* 36(3): 381–395.

Loader, I. and Sparks, R. (2002) 'Contemporary Landscapes of Crime, Order and Control: Governance, Globalisation and Risk' in M. Maguire, R. Morgan and R. Reiner (eds) *The Oxford Handbook of Criminology*, Oxford: Oxford University Press.

Lois, J. (2005) 'Gender and emotion management in edgework' in S. Lyng (ed.) *Edgework: The Sociology of Risk Taking*, London: Routledge.

Lupton, D. (1999) *Risk*, London: Routledge.

Lyng, S. (1990) 'Edgework: a social psychology of voluntary risk taking' *American Journal of Sociology* 95: 4.

Mason, G. (2005a) 'Hate crime and the image of the stranger' *British Journal of Criminology* 45(6): 837–860.

Mason, G. (2005b) 'Being hated: stranger or familiar?' *Social and Legal Studies* 14(4): 585–605.

Mawby, R. and Walklate, S. (1994) *Critical Victimology*, London: Sage.

Maxfield, M. (1984) 'Fear of Crime in England and Wales' HORS 78, London: Home Office.

Miller, E. (1991) 'Assessing the risk of inattention class, race/ethnicity, and gender: comment on Lyng', *American Journal of Sociology* 96(6): 1530–4.

Miller, J. (2002) 'The strengths and limits of "doing gender" for an understanding of street crime' *Theoretical Criminology* 6: 433–460.

Morgan, R. (1989) *The Demon Lover*, London: Mandarin.

Mythen, G. (forthcoming) 'Cultural Victimology' in S. Walklate (ed.) *The Handbook of Victims and Victimology*, Cullompton: Willan.

O'Malley, P. (2004) 'The uncertain promise of risk' *Australia and New Zealand Journal of Criminology* 37/3: 323–343.

O'Malley, P. (2006) 'Criminology and risk' in G. Mythen and S. Walklate (eds) *Beyond the Risk Society: Critical Reflections on Risk and Human Security*, Maidenhead: Open University Press.

Pain, R. (1991) 'Space, sexual violence and social control: integrating geographical and feminist analyses of women's fear of crime' *Progress in Human Geography* 15 (4): 415–431.

Pirsig, R.M. (1976) *Zen and the Art of Motorcylce Maintenance*, London: Corgi.

Roshier, B. (1989) *Controlling Crime*, Milton Keynes: Open University Press.

Russell, D. (1990) *Rape in Marriage*, Bloomington, Ind: Indiana University Press.

Sampson, Richard. J., Raudenbush, W and Felton, E. (1997) 'Neighbourhoods and violent crime: a multilevel study of collective efficacy' *Science* 77 15 August.

Sanders, T. (2005) *Sex Work; A Risky Business*, Cullompton, Devon: Willan Publishing.

Seidler, V. (1994) *Unreasonable Men: Masculinity and Social Theory*, London: Routledge.

Skogan, W. (1986) 'The fear of crime and its behavioural implications' in E.A. Fattah (ed.) *From Crime Policy to Victim Policy*, London: Macmillan.

Smith, D. (1987) *The Everyday World as Problematic*, Milton Keynes: Open University Press.

Sparks, R. (1992) 'Reason and unreason in left realism; some problems in the constitution of the fear of crime' in R. Matthews and J. Young (eds) *Issues in Realist Criminology*, London: Sage.

Stanko, E.A. (1990) *Everyday Violence*, London: Virago.

Stanko, E. A. (1997) 'Safety talk; conceptualising women's risk assessment as a technology of the soul' *Theoretical Criminology* 1/4: 479–499.

Stanko, E.A. and Hobdell, K. (1993) 'Assaults on men; masculinity and male victimization' *British Journal of Criminology* 33/3: 400–415.

Stanko, E. A. (2000) 'Victims R Us: the life history of "fear of crime" and the politicisation of violence' in T. Hope and R. Sparks (eds) *Crime, Risk and Insecurity*, London: Routledge.

Stanley, L. and Wise, S. (1987) *Georgie, Porgie: Sexual Harassment in Everyday Life*, London: Macmillan.

Strydom, P. (2002) *Risk, Environment and Modernity*, Buckingham: Open University Press.

Sutton, R. and Farrall, S. (2005) 'Gender, social desirable responding and the fear of crime: are women really more anxious about crime?' *British Journal of Criminology* 45/2: 212–224.

Sydie, R. (1989) *Natural Women, Cultured Men*, Milton Keynes: Open University Press.

Taylor, I., Walton, P. and Young, J. (1973) *The New Criminology*, London: Routledge.

Taylor, I. (1996) 'Fear of crime, urban fortunes and suburban social movements: some reflections on Manchester' *Sociology* 30: 317–337.

Taylor, I. (1997) 'Crime, anxiety and locality: responding to the condition of England at the end of the century' *Theoretical Criminology* 1(1): 53–76.

Taylor, I., Evans, K. and Fraser, P. (1996) *A Tale of Two Cities*, London: Routledge.

Tulloch, J. and Lupton, D. (2003) *Risk and Everyday Life*, London: Sage.

Valentine, G.(1992) 'Images of danger: women's sources of information about the spatial distribution of male violence' *Area* 24: 23–29.

Walklate, S. (1997) 'Risk and criminal victimization: a modernist dilemma?' *British Journal of Criminology* 37: 35–45.

Walklate, S. (1998a) 'Excavating the fear of crime: fear, anxiety or trust?' *Theoretical Criminology* 2(4): 403–418.

Walklate, S. (1998b) 'Crime and community: fear or trust?' *British Journal of Sociology* 49(4): 550–570.

Walklate, S. (2003) 'Local contexts and globalised knowledges: what can international criminal victimization surveys tell us about women's diverse lives?' Paper presented to the Women, Crime and Globalisation Workshop, Onati, Spain, September, 2003.

Walklate, S. and Evans, K. (1999) *Zero Tolerance or Community Tolerance? Managing Crime in High Crime Areas*, Aldershot: Ashgate.

Warr, M. (1985) 'Fear of rape among urban women' *Social Problems* 32: 3.

Weaver, K., Carter, C., and Stanko, E.A. (2000) 'The female body at risk' in S. Allan, B. Adam and C. Carter (eds) *Environmental Risks and the Media*, London: Routledge.

Wootton, B. (1959) *Social Science and Social Pathology*, London: George, Allen and Unwin.

Worcester, R. (2001) 'The world will never be the same: British hopes and fear after September 11th 2001' *International Journal of Public Opinion Research* http://www.mori.com.

Chapter 9

Sentenced to treatment/ sentenced to harm

Women, risk and the drug treatment courts

Dawn Moore and Tara Lyons

INTRODUCTION

Rehabilitative endeavours that wed psy knowledges and legal sanctions promise to lower the risk an offender poses of recidivism by offering change oriented practices designed to render her less criminogenic. Such legally ensconced therapeutic practices are often packaged in the language of risk management. Under this rubric, treating particular pathologies is not only of benefit to the individual but also is intended to lessen the potential harm an individual might inflict on the public. These governing schemes appeal to contemporary neoliberal regimes as they promise objectivity and serve to responsibilize the individual, eschewing social and structural understandings of criminality. At the same time, the advent of risk management and psy-based programming are touted as humanizing forces designed to counter the alleged 'punitive turn' by drawing on welfarist practices intended to rehabilitate (Meyer and O'Malley 2004; Moore and Hannah-Moffat 2004). The intersection of risk, law and psy is not, contrary to the prevailing dis- course, inherently benevolent and progressive. Working to reduce the risk of harm to the public paradoxically involves the constitution of particular risks of harm to the individual caught up in such schemes. That is, initiatives designed to both treat AND punish through the same acts rely on placing people in conflict with the law in risky situations. This constitution of risks is particularly acute for women. Women's statuses as both women and mothers (would be and actual) form the bases of particular, gendered harms. In this chapter we explore the experiences of women enrolled in Canadian drug treatment courts (DTC). We discover that, in facing the harms constituted for them in risk management schemes, women deploy their own forms of counter risk management. Responding to gendered risks, these practices are themselves gendered and designed to assist women in navigating their criminal justice involvement.

FIRST AND SECOND ORDER RISK MANAGEMENT

Contemporary research has done a great deal to reveal the troubling nature of what we call 'first order' criminal justice based risk management (Ericson *et al* 2003; Ericson and Haggerty 1997; O'Malley 2004; Feeley and Simon 1992). These are initiatives that fit broadly into the neoliberal, managerial framework. In the realm of punishment these mentalities manifest as a rather narrow but pervasive range of interventions that rely on actuarial risk assessments, the identification of 'criminogenic factors' and targeted interventions through standardized programmes (Andrews *et al* 2006). At the heart of these initiatives is the core belief that criminality and the risk of recidivism are individualized problems that can be managed by altering specific aspects of the person through generic treatment modalities. The risks to be managed, then, are those posed by the individual to the community (in the form of crime) or to herself (through self-injury, suicide and drug use). These practices have been roundly critiqued in critical criminological scholarship, not least of which by feminist criminologists who flag their gendered and exclusionary bases.

Gendered practices impact women in specific ways (Hannah-Moffat 2004; Bosworth 2006; Chunn and Lacombe 2000; Smart 1995). In Hannah-Moffat's (2004) study of gender-responsive interventions by Canada's Parole Board she highlights how Parole Board members use gendered understandings of risk to manage women. Specifically Hannah-Moffat (ibid: 373) notes, '[r]isk is gendered in that for women (but not for men) victimization and relationships become central to general and violent recidivism'. Women's histories of victimization and their relationships are considered a central risk factor for managing women on parole, factors rarely considered in men's parole applications.

These same observations were born out in a recent human rights complaint launched by the Canadian Human Rights Commission (CHRC) at the request of the Canadian Association of Elizabeth Fry Societies (CAEFS). CHRC (2003) claimed, among other things, that the use of actuarial risk assessment tools on women prisoners constituted a form of discrimination because it resulted in the amplified punishment of women engaged in practices such as self-injury. For example, reading self-injury as an indicator of the need to place a woman in a higher security environment, according to CAEFS, ignores the context of women's lives and the reasons for which they engage in self-injurious behaviours (which, according to CAEFS, are regarded largely as a means of coping with the pains of imprisonment). CHRC (2003) also found that racialized women were both forced into segregation more often than other women, and spent more time in segregation than other women who engaged in the same behaviour.

These first order risk management strategies are aptly unpacked and challenged through the use of analytic tools like governmentality that allow for a top-down view of governance revealing the translation of mentalities of rule into the 'messy actualities' of lived experiences (Rose, Valverde and O'Malley, 2006). Such critiques explore the ways in which governing strategies act on the individual or direct the individual to act on herself (Cruickshank 1999; Rose 1996). The result of such an approach is solid critique of such initiatives that reveals their moralistic and political nature. Emerging feminist critiques deploy this top-down analysis to declare these initiatives as gendered, racist and marginalizing (see Hannah-Moffat in this volume).

From a different but complementary perspective, feminist scholars like Mary Bosworth, Sylvie Frigon, Nagaire Naffine, Carol Smart and Elizabeth Stanko remind us of the importance of paying careful attention to the lived experiences and social contexts of women in conflict with the law. Commenting on the lived reality of women's economic marginalization, Comack (2006: 39) notes, 'as more and more women are confronted with the task of making ends meet under dire circumstances, the link between poverty and women's lawbreaking becomes more obvious'. In her study of women's acts of resistance in prison, Bosworth (1999, 2001) draws on women's accounts of their incarceration to show the gendered nature of the prison environment. Bosworth's focus on women's experiences in this context reveals the ways in which women are subjected to gendered programming such as sewing and cooking, designed to 'rehabilitate' by teaching them to embrace traditional notions of femininity. Importantly, Bosworth is not only able to reveal these practices but also to show how women deploy their own notions of femininity as tools of resistance within these gendering regimes. For example, women contested the low quality, abrasive toilet paper they were given in prison. They tried various tactics, including stealing the staff's better quality toilet paper. Higher quality toilet paper was only received after the women filed complaints that the toilet paper they were forced to use was inappropriate for women who were menstruating and women with haemorrhoids (Bosworth 1999). The lack of privacy in prison is no doubt demoralizing; in this instance, however, women re-deployed private issues and feminine identities as an act of resistance. Stereotypes of women as beings who suffer from biological, female ailments were used to successfully challenge the prison administration. Because of their physical needs (menstruation and haemorrhoids), the women contended that they needed special consideration in the form of softer toilet paper. This strategy was also used by some women in advocating better food in prison when they argued that women needed food rich in iron because of their menstruation (ibid).

Chan and Rigakos (2002) extend this methodology into attempts to understand the ways in which women experience risk. Considering women's risk of criminal victimization, Chan and Rigakos argue that women's risk calculation and management is qualitatively different from that of men. In deciding how she will respond to the gendered crime of domestic assault, for

Postmodern guns   Risk = non-risk

cognitive mapping

example, a woman must calculate not only the risks she faces of further victimization but also the risks constituted for her in attempting to access criminal justice as a means of extracting herself from a violent situation. If the justice system is able to make good on its promises to protect women, the woman who calls the police may alleviate her immediate risks of further physical violence but, in so doing, constitutes other risks she must manage, risks that are not necessarily recognized as such by justice institutions. Specifically, when a woman reports domestic assault she loses the ability to control the process of responding to her victimization. The incarceration of her partner can place her at risk of economic and social marginalization and in some cases jeopardize immigration status (Wachholz and Miedema 2000). These risks are gendered, not only because of the nature of the crime but also because, reflecting the gendered imbalance of social structure, women routinely face economic and social hardships in the wake of losing a partner. Where the justice system only sees risk in terms of further victimization, the lived reality of women's lives indicates a much more complicated matrix of risk to be calculated and negotiated by these women.

In this instance, then, risk management is not solely the domain of governing bodies. Rather, as Chan and Rigakos suggest, in dealing with victimization, women must manage risks that are constituted on different levels. To do so women deploy a range of risk management techniques including 'cognitive mapping' where women establish the areas and people that put them at risk of facing violence. Based on this map, women make decisions about where to go and who to interact with on a daily basis (Chan and Rigakos 2002). Women manage their behaviour to both prevent violent encounters and to prevent being seen as responsible for violence if it occurs (ibid). Chan and Rigakos suggest that to understand risk through a feminist lens that emphasizes both its gendered and experiential nature also allows for a more politicized understanding, one that locates risk discourses in the context of a patriarchal justice system that does little to actually alleviate the dangers women face, often having the opposite effects of creating more harms for women than it relieves.

Harms are not only constituted for those caught up in the criminal justice system as victims. The status of being in conflict with the law is a status that inherently places people at risk of experiencing a wide array of harms at the hands of governing bodies. Any person on probation is all too familiar with these second order risks. Derived directly from the status of probationer, those serving community sentences are at risk of being incarcerated for things such as missing a curfew or drinking alcohol, events for which an otherwise non-criminalized person would not face sanction. At the same time, the increased surveillance that characterizes probation can place the probationer at risk of experiencing further state intervention into her home life from the likes of welfare officers and public health and child protection workers in addition to her probation officer. Left to manage the risks she poses to society in terms of recidivism, the probationer is also negotiating these second order risks, the risks the system poses for her.

Such risks are also present in the drug treatment court (DTC). Under amplified surveillance and control born of a combination of therapeutic and legal actors and processes (Moore 2007), women in the DTCs must negotiate risks of incarceration, eroding self-determinacy, especially around housing issues, and losing custody of children. While the courts fail to acknowledge that these risks exist, understanding them instead as benevolent incentives to help women overcome their drug addictions, the women in the courts clearly experience court actions as harmful and work to manage them as such. Women deploy a range of tactics as a means of managing the risks they face in DTC.

RISK AND HARM

In attempting to understand these risks, it is helpful to locate the discussion in relation to the notion of harm. This is particularly important in the context of initiatives targeting drug users because harm reduction is now central to almost any attempt to govern drug use.[1] As O'Malley (2004) notes, harm reduction eschews the classic notion of the addict as an individual suffering from a diseased will (Valverde 1998). Instead, harm reduction imagines the addict as a rational and free actor, cobbling together a project of normalization that, in many instances, aims to erase the notion of addiction altogether, opting instead to use descriptors such as 'drug user'. Of course, there is no one version of harm reduction, and practices shaded under the umbrella term sit on a continuum that can range from prescribing heroin to mandating abstinence (Ericson and Haggerty 1997). Following this amorphous definition, harm reduction in the context of punitive schemes is fraught with strains. O'Malley (2004: 155) points to these, noting that '. . . treatment comes into tension with punishment, for while the addict suffers from a disease or pathology that should be treated as a medical problem, this condition was contracted voluntarily through an illegal act and thus is subject to penalty'. We argue that it is this same tension that makes addiction treatment alluring to criminal justice. As Moore (2007) shows in her work on criminal justice-based addiction treatment, the 'addict' offers criminal justice the ultimate liberalized subject. Her criminality is explained by her own individual choices (rather than structural considerations) and, as a result, she is imagined to be eminently curable of both her addiction and her law breaking.

---

1 Although the same clearly cannot be said about drug dealing. In Canada, for example, the new Conservative government is introducing legislation that will 'get tough' on the drug trade through the implementation of mandatory minimum sentences for drug dealing and cultivation.

The fact that the criminal justice system is already so heavily laced with risk discourses is all the better for the seamless integration of harm reduction initiatives targeting drugs because, through this wedding, it becomes possible to erase the punitive elements of risk management, constituting a regime whose only goal is the surely benevolent one of reducing harm. This becomes important in our considerations of risk management because the effect of the schemes we study is to erase coercion in favour of free choice. In such a context, it is difficult if not impossible for those who are subjects of such interventions first to read the things done to them as anything other than helpful and, second, to resist initiatives which are, after all, only meant to ameliorate their lives.

THE DRUG TREATMENT COURTS

Mangasat

DTCs are examples of how therapeutic knowledge and legal endeavours are meshed with the goals of reducing recidivism and reforming 'criminals'. There are now five operating DTCs in Canada with more on the way. DTCs are such a burgeoning movement that the courts are now forming their own national association and have a yearly conference. To be eligible for DTC, an individual must be a non-violent offender who can prove an addiction of at least six months to heroin, crack/cocaine or, more recently, crystal methamphetamine. The likely sanction for the current offence must be custodial and of considerable duration (three months appears to be the minimum).[2] Those meeting these qualifications and accepted into the court undergo an intensive, court-supervised treatment programme lasting anywhere from one to two years (usually more time than the individual would have spent in custody). The programme directs court 'clients'[3] to attend court twice weekly, as well as attending regular (typically daily) treatment sessions. Clients are also subject to a random urinalysis regime. The courts function on a system of sanctions and rewards designed to help people stay engaged with treatment. Thus, court clients doing well in the programme (attending groups and court, slowing down or stopping drug use, actively 'engaging' with treatment) can be rewarded through lessening court appearances, extending curfews, receiving bus passes, and coupons for coffee. Likewise, those who fail to engage in treatment, continue to use drugs or fail to show up in treatment

---

2 There are not official guidelines determining how much jail time people should be facing in order to be accepted into the DTCs. The Ottawa drug treatment court admitted a person who had served all of their time and someone who is facing 45 days less time served.

3 We wish to flag the deployment of the term 'client' here as a point of concern. While it is beyond the scope of our present project, the notion that people facing criminal sanction are somehow voluntary consumers of a court-mandated programme is deeply troubling and the subject of further study.

face a range of sanctions including increased court appearances, community service hours, stricter bail conditions and/or therapeutic remands either to prison or to treatment centres.

To date, DTCs do not have exceptional graduation/completion rates. Current data exist for the Vancouver and Toronto courts.[4] As of March 2005, there have been 322 people admitted to the Vancouver DTC (VDTC). Only 10.6 per cent of those graduated (34 people) (VDTC Evaluation Report: xx), Of those who did not graduate, 13.7 per cent withdrew of their own accord and were sentenced and 43.8 per cent were removed from the programme at the request of the Crown and/or treatment team and transferred to sentencing (ibid). Approximately 20 per cent of treatment court participants are still enrolled in the programme. An even smaller number have died or have not been officially expelled from the programme. In Toronto, 15.6 per cent of people admitted to the Toronto DTC (TDTC) have graduated, three-quarters of which graduated after 9 to 12 months (Gliksman et al 2004: 84). Of the 365 people admitted, 308 people (84 per cent) were expelled, with close to half (46.8 per cent) of people are expelled in the first two months (ibid). Each year, there have been decreases in the number of people graduating from the TDTC (ibid: 85).

Rates of enrolment and successful completion are considerably lower for the women in the DTCs (ibid: 29). Women make up 42 per cent of people admitted into the VDTC (VDTC Evaluation Report: xix), and 24 per cent of those admitted to the Toronto DTC (ibid: 89). In Vancouver, less than 10 per cent of women admitted to the VDTC have graduated compared with 16 per cent of men. Likewise in Toronto, women have low rates of graduation and are less likely to apply to the TDTC (ibid: 29). Women who do apply and are admitted to the TDTC are less likely than men to attend their first court appearance after their clinical assessment (ibid: 88). Similar experiences of women dropping out of the DTC at high rates are seen in the VDTC. In Vancouver, women finished fewer treatment hours and were less likely to complete the initial assessment (VDTC Evaluation Report: xxi). Women, however, were more likely to enrol in the VDTC than men, in contrast to the experiences in Toronto (ibid: 4–18).

At the time of wording evaluations of the Ottawa DTC (ODTC) were not available. Currently, out of a total court population of 16, there are five women. Of the five women admitted, four continue to be enrolled in the ODTC. One did not come to her second court appearance, but has since re-entered the court. Another woman was removed from the ODTC for being charged with crimes when she relapsed. We know of two other women who declined to participate in the court.

4 The Toronto DTC began operation in 1998 and the Vancouver DTC has been in operation since 2001, making them the longest running DTCs in Canada.

While all the operating courts are aware of the problem of keeping women in the court programmes, to date, none of the courts have a clear sense of why the attrition rate for women is so high. In part the low enrolment of women can be explained by the relatively low population of women caught up in the criminal justice system overall. Standard estimates place the population of women in conflict with the law as approximately 10 per cent of the total offender population. Still, the low numbers of women in the system does not account for the high rates at which women leave the programme. This is especially true in considering the fact that, proportionally, the Toronto and Vancouver courts have been relatively successful at recruiting women and in fact have an over-representation of women introduced to their programmes. We suggest that it is the gendered, second order risks women face in DTC that serve as deterrents to their continued participation.

RISK AND THE HARMS OF DRUG TREATMENT COURT INVOLVEMENT

The courts pose risks to both male and female court participants. As in the example given above regarding probation, DTC participation places people on strict bail conditions that also increase the risk of incarceration. DTC participants can be remanded for drinking, not providing a urine screen, or being found in their area restrictions.[5] They face a system of sanctions and rewards that places them at risk of remand if they do not perform well in treatment (i.e. through adequately processing a relapse), change their housing arrangements without permission from the court, or continue to relapse into drug use[6] (Moore 2007).

One bail condition is living at an address approved by the treatment provider. Housing is carefully controlled in all the courts as a risk management practice designed to lessen an individual's exposure to triggering substances (especially their drug of choice) and also so-called 'risky' situations such as parties or drug dealing. Binding of court participants to particular housing

---

5 All the DTCs place a great deal of emphasis on the geography of drug use. On intake into the court clients are given area restrictions intended to keep them out of 'triggering' areas of the city. In Toronto and Ottawa the restrictions are specific to each individual whereas in Vancouver clients are universally restricted from the downtown eastside.

6 None of the courts automatically sanction clients for drug use. Especially in the early days of the programme, relapses are expected and allowed for as long as the client is upfront about them. However, the court expects that, approximately by the six-month marker, clients will stop relapsing. After six months of enrolment in the programme it is quite common to see clients being sanctioned for continuing to use. There are higher expectations in Ottawa. People are expected to stop using drugs and alcohol immediately and to stop relapsing after around two months. People have their bail revoked if they continue to relapse after the first month.

situations creates second order risks that require management by DTC participants because the places people are ordered to live are not always safe in the eyes of the court participants. When Bill[7] relapsed he was evicted from his housing. He was informed at his subsequent court appearance that he would have to go to a shelter. Bill resisted this direction, citing the elevated levels of violence and drug use associated with shelters. In Bill's own words, '. . . shelters are not conducive to healthy living with addiction'. The court, however, rejected Bill's assessment of the risks posed by shelter involvement, directing him to a shelter despite his concerns.

People in the DTC are refused the permission to make decisions, particularly snap decisions, about where to live. Presented as a risk management strategy, the practice of putting housing restrictions on bail conditions serves to place court participants at risk by removing their ability to leave a situation they find problematic. Such an arrangement speaks to particular iterations of the notion of choice within the DTCs.

In another example, Angela explained to the court that she relapsed because she was living in a house where people were using crack cocaine. Immediately after her relapse she moved out of this house. At the following court appearance the treatment liaison officer[8] conveyed her concern about Angela's decision to move: 'There was also a decision that you moved locations without notifying your counselor ahead of time. This is also very concerning.' The Crown emphasized that one of her bail conditions was to live at an address approved by the treatment provider and told the court: 'We're getting close to the edge here', the edge being the revocation of her bail. Angela's choice, in this example, is to stay in an environment in which drug use is taking place or leave and face the consequences of breaching her bail (including possible imprisonment).

In these examples, the court demonstrates first order risk management strategies. By controlling Angela's housing situation, the court is trying to limit her exposure to so called 'high risk' situations, such as living in an apartment or neighbourhood where drug use is taking place or, in the case of women in the court, with a former pimp or abusive partner. Flagging the second order risks in this same strategy, for Angela the court's directions place her at risk not only because she was living in an environment in which there was drug use but also, because of the nature of her bail conditions, she lost the ability to make her own decisions regarding her living arrangements.

---

7 All the examples we use come from our research notes. In the interest of protecting the anonymity of court clients we use pseudonyms and do not identify the court in which the client is enrolled.

8 Liaison officers are addiction counsellors who appear before the court and represent the treatment side of the DTC. They give reports on how the participant is doing in group and individual counselling and report any concerns about people's motivation, willingness and participation in treatment.

As a result, in order to manage the risks she felt she faced by being exposed to drug use, Angela must face the risk of being sanctioned by the court for taking action to change her living arrangements without court approval. Forcing people to have any decision regarding housing pre-approved puts them at risk of being, and staying, in situations that they consider harmful. In this case, Angela managed this second order risk by breaching her bail conditions.

Gendered risks

Similar to broader experiences of women in the criminal justice system, women in the DTC must negotiate the kinds of second order risks detailed above alongside additional, gendered, risks. As others have found in the contexts of prisons and parole, women in the DTC are enrolled in a gendering system that relies on traditional notions of femininity and sexuality as a means of managing women in conflict with the law. In the DTCs, pregnancy, motherhood and involvement in the sex trade all become fields of risk management.

Men in the court who are parents do not face the same scrutiny as women. The court is aware that certain men have children because this information is included on their intake forms and assessments. The court's response, however, is qualitatively different than when responding to women who have children. The court shows more interest in the women's children and the relationships women have with their children. The judges and Crown ask the names and ages of a woman's children, they inquire about the last time she saw them, and follow up with questions about how visits went. Men with children, on the other hand, are not asked about their children, even when they bring them up in court. Men's visits with their children do not face the same scrutiny because these relationships and visits are not considered risk factors that will lead men to relapse. When a man reports having visited with his children it is typically given a nod of approval from the court. There is rarely a discussion of whether or not the man will regain custody of the children (or even whether he wants to). Of male parents the courts only expect a display of interest in their children, not a desire to parent full time. Children cannot be a threat to men's sobriety because they simply do not play a central enough role in men's lives or place as taxing demands on men's emotional and physical resources as they do on women.

For example, when Carl was called before the judge he told of his visit with his son on the weekend. The judge asked if it was a good visit and queried the nature of the child's living arrangements. When Carl explained that his son lives with his ex-wife (the child's mother) the judge nodded and said 'that's fine then, we like to see you stay involved in your kid's lives'. Staying involved is clearly different from the expectations placed on women in the court regarding their children.

In another example, when Sheena told the judge about her visit with her two children the judge immediately asked her about her plans to get the children back. The judge explained to Sheena 'this [regaining custody] is a great long term plan we want to work on with you. We just need to take it slowly'. Comments are routinely made to women regarding how they need to consider their children as motivation for not using drugs. For example, when Stacey reported using marijuana, the Crown commented, 'what happened, you had been doing so well. You have your daughter to consider'. In another instance the judge said to a woman: 'try to have a clean weekend, keep thinking about your daughter'. In contrast, we have never seen a male DTC participant urged to motivate himself to stay clean by thinking of his children.

In the DTC women who have children and use drugs are assumed to put their children at risk by having continued access to them, and also jeopardize their treatment by having to divide attention between parenting and recovery. The women are expected to give up their children to relatives or the Children's Aid Society at least for the first six months of their treatment court involvement, if they have not lost custody prior to DTC enrolment. The routinization of losing child custody in the court draws on classic notions that a woman who uses illicit substances (as opposed to prescription drugs or even alcohol) is a truly unfit mother (Boyd 1999; Campbell 2000). The logic here rests on the unfounded assumption that drug use is *de facto* child abuse, regardless of the woman's actual practices while she is using. At the same time, seizing children is thought to increase the chances a woman has of recovering because, unburdened by the day-to-day demands of childcare, a woman is free to devote herself to her own recovery. Severing the mother–child relationship is assumed to be the best way to liberate the woman so that she can pursue her recovery unencumbered.

Regaining access to children is a major issue for the women in the court and is often a basis for the negotiation of risks. In one instance, Carla was making plans to see her children who live in a nearby city. The plans worked around her court-imposed curfew and her daily treatment appointments. When the plan to see her children was presented to the court, the court team read it as placing both Carla and her children at risk. The judge explained to Carla, 'the reason we're all sitting here is that we don't want you to be placed in a situation where you relapse . . . we want to make sure that it's the best thing for you and your children'. A visit with her children was considered a risk factor for Carla. The judge anticipated that a visit with Carla's children would cause her stress and likely lead to relapse, jeopardizing her standing in the DTC.[9]

9 The women's children are also seen to be 'at risk' if they spend time with their mothers as demonstrated by the court's concern that visits are 'the best thing for you and your children'. Echoing Hannah-Moffat's observations in this collection, women's relationship and visits

Once a woman starts to do well in the court (remains drug free for a period, is attending court and treatment regularly, has started volunteering) the court will facilitate access to her children by easing her bail conditions. Women may, for example, have curfews lifted or geographic restrictions eased to facilitate travel and overnight visits. The celebration of a woman having her children returned to her is illustrative of the way in which the court views child custody. The following comes from research notes:

> Another example comes from a court graduation day.[10] Ming was called up and the Crown proceeded to read out Ming's accomplishments. She managed to remain free of crack for nine months, has a new job, a place to live, has reconnected with her family and her two children are living with her again. The judge made much of Ming's achievements, paying careful attention to her children, noted how pleased he was to see that Ming was able to get her children back and assured her that she is now in a position to 'be a good mother' to her kids.

The positioning of 'good motherhood' as so central to a woman's success in the DTC reveals a shadow story about the risks of DTC involvement for women with children. If regaining access to children is one of the rewards of successful navigation of the DTC programme, then having children removed must be part of the court's punitive edge. Women newly admitted to the programme or who are not doing well face the risk of being continually denied access to their children. At the same time, the significant emphasis placed on regaining access to children creates an environment in which a woman is no longer able to choose whether or not she wants to be a mother. To be a success in the DTC is to regain lost children. There is no space in the DTC for a woman who is no longer interested in or does not feel able to parent. We develop this point further in the next section.

The court's control over the parenting relationship becomes a second order risk the women in the court must manage. As mothers, women DTC participants face the risk of additional sanctioning, on the one hand, and state intervention with and control over their relationships with their children, on the other. Importantly, the court does not read its actions as harmful to the

---

with their children are considered central risk factors that could jeopardize a woman's chances of recovery. Exposing children to drug use is routinely read as harmful to children and also grounds for removing children from their mothers in the interest of child protection (Boyd 2004; Campbell 2000). The cultural relativity of such claims ought not to go unnoticed in such instances given that the consumption of alcohol and tobacco are not understood as necessarily dangerous.

10 Graduation ceremonies are major events in DTC. Each person who has successfully completed the programme is publicly celebrated through a series of speeches and applause as well as presented with a graduation certificate and given the promised non-custodial sentence.

women in the court. Rather, regulating motherhood is only understood as a benevolent prerogative of the court, designed to protect both mothers and children.

Even though Canadian civil law makes explicit the interdiction on incarcerating pregnant women to protect the foetus,[11] the practice of remanding pregnant women is well kept in the DTCs. Part of the exercise here involves reviving the foetus as a person worthy of protection and also as a person placed in harm's way by the woman, a relationship that, in many ways, reverts back to the kinds of governance described above, except that the foetus can not be seized for therapeutic purposes.[12] The courts routinely use incarceration as a means of seizing both mother and foetus. The justifications given here are solely therapeutic.

In one instance, a pregnant woman appeared in court in custody. She was arrested for breaching her bail conditions (she was found in her restricted area and also failed to report to treatment court). In reconnecting with her therapist the woman admitted to having relapsed into drug use while she was absent from the court programme. The judge decided to incarcerate her for the duration of her pregnancy, justifying the action as a means of protecting the woman's foetus. 'Jail will be a safer place for you,' the judge explained. 'This is for the good of your baby.' For this woman, being pregnant in the DTC constitutes a second order risk. The court reinvents the foetus as a baby in order to constitute the woman as a threat and justify her incarceration as a child-saving measure. At the same time, the woman's involvement in the court is risky for her as the court works to incarcerate her for stated therapeutic purposes. This is especially apparent given the court's dubious logic suggesting that jail is somehow a safe place. Far from therapeutic, prisons of any sort, and jails in particular, are notoriously dangerous spaces that have well documented ill effects on health (Carlen and Worrall 2004; Kilty 2006, Scraton and Moore 2005). This, compounded with the fact that prisons also have a wide range of substances readily available, calls into question the court's assertion that detention will somehow protect a woman from tempting exposure to illicit substances.

Women do not have to be mothers in order to experience harms associated with DTC involvement. Drug using communities are relatively small and homogenous, forming sub worlds with underground economies and relationships. Sex work is a major part of this economy for many women users. When members of these communities are placed in the community of criminal justice administered drug treatment, risks emerge for women, who are made

11 In the case of *Winnipeg Child and Family Services (Northwest Area) v G.*, (D.F.) 1997. 3 S.C.R. 925, the Supreme Court of Canada found that a pregnant woman could not be forced into treatment as a child-saving measure.

12 While the link here is never made explicitly, this practice draws on fears of the crack baby, a phenomena contested in academic literature (Humphries 1999; Roth 2000; Toscano 2005).

vulnerable to other people who are in the DTC programme. Women can be placed in the same health clinics, treatment centres, group counselling sessions, and courtroom as former or current pimps, johns, abusive partners, and/or men they fear (Benoit *et al* 2001). The potential for this scenario to unfold is particular to the Ottawa and Toronto courts where no gender-specific programming is offered to court participants. This may be one indication of why so many women in the Toronto DTC drop out of the court after their initial assessment which orients them to the Toronto DTC rules and programming.

Harkening back to our earlier housing example, placing women in non gender-specific groups puts them in double jeopardy. The woman who finds herself in treatment with a man who holds a problematic position in her life is left with two 'choices'. She can participate in a treatment setting where she is not comfortable or face court sanctions for non-compliance with court orders because she is not willing to participate in such a treatment milieu. Either way, she faces gendered harms that are particular to her DTC involvement. Of course, concerns about forced, mixed gender treatment settings need not be specific only to those women involved in the drug trade. Feminist therapy and women's own experiences suggest that mixed treatment settings can be difficult for women to negotiate at the best of times given the considerable numbers of women who have been victimized by men (DeChant 1996; Hodgins *et al* 1997; United Nations 2004).

To date, the Vancouver court is the only one to have made concerted efforts to respond to the problem of mixed gender treatment. In Vancouver the court is gender segregated (in theory) with one day of the week assigned to women and the other to men. Vancouver also offers women-only treatment groups. In Toronto, by contrast, women may find themselves in treatment with former pimps or johns.

Managing second order risk

In their study of agency and resistance in both men's and women's prisons, Bosworth and Carrabine (2001: 512) conclude:

> Irrespective of whether prisoners' actions are interpreted as acquiescence, resistance or violence, understanding prisoners as agents who, to some extent at least, make choices and actively negotiate power relations, challenges the tendency to view power in prisons as conditioned by an all-or-nothing set of binary relations. It facilitates, in other words, a more nuanced account of how small-scale, 'everyday' activities contribute to the maintenance or disruption of the status quo.

It is through this same lens that we attempt to understand women's attempts to manage their DTC involvement. Our point here is not so much to show

how women resist but rather, following Bosworth and Carrabine, how women's actions have an effect on the functioning of the courts.

One of the primary means by which women manage the risks they face by virtue of their involvement in the DTCs is simply to drop out of the court programme. Those who do stay exhibit certain self-management practices that we argue are designed to help them navigate the risks associated with DTC involvement. Often these strategies serve to maintain a woman's status in the court rather than to disrupt court processes.

Women who stay in the court programme manage second order risks by adopting and using the therapeutic language of the court. A woman who has relapsed into drug use, for example, explains to the judge about how she placed herself in a 'high risk' situation and offers an account of how she will manage her 'triggers' in the future. In describing the circumstances that led to her relapse, Monica said, 'I put myself at risk by smoking in front of the building where I live'. The judge and Crown commended her for her insight into her triggers and her identification of the high risk situation that led to her use.

When women speak to the court about what they are doing to avoid high risk situations which will trigger them they are rewarded for their insight. In one example, the judge asked Dana what she was doing to avoid using drugs. She said she was going to 12 step meetings and staying at a recovery house. When the judge asked if she liked it at the house Dana said 'yeah, [pause] it's not my home, but it keeps me safe'. The Crown responded: 'I'm sitting here listening to Dana and . . . the degree of insight and intelligence, boy, there must be a tremendous upside to this person.'

When women come before the court and do not display 'insight' into their triggers to use drugs and the high risk situations in which the rhetoric of addiction treatment suggests those triggers will be found (parties, drug using neighbourhoods, anywhere where drug trade is taking place) there is concern expressed by the DTC team. For example, when Sue was called up before the judge and questioned about her relapse the judge asked her why she used. Sue responded that she was having a hard time and she only had one hit off a crack pipe. The judge offers Sue a sharp reprimand, reminding her of the court's policy that 'a use is a use' and that her job is not to offer excuses for her relapse but rather understand why it happened and how she will prevent it from happening in the future. Sue was given community service hours as a sanction for failing to adequately process her relapse.

The development of insights by women has a performative quality which serves as a tool of risk management for the women. What is noteworthy about these displays, for our purposes, is not their authenticity but rather their technical utility as a means of managing court involvement. Second order risk management in the DTCs involves the appropriation of a particular argot. Dana's use of the therapeutic language of the court gains her praise from court officials, whereas Sue is taken to task and sanctioned for offering an account of her relapse in her own words. In speaking the court's language, women are able to convey to the court that they are taking care of themselves in a manner the court deems appropriate. Adopting the court's language is a way of managing court involvement and the risk of sanctioning.

Women also negotiate second order risks through performance of traditional womanhood. The deployment of the gendered persona of a fallen and remorseful woman is familiar to criminal justice where traditional and stereotypic notions of femininity routinely drive criminal justice practice (Hudson 2002; Smart 1995, 1989; Worrall 1990). In the DTCs, some women use traditional gender roles as a means of managing their second order risks. For example, facing potential bail revocation for a relapse, Laura flirted with a bailiff before court begins. As he walks away smiling, Laura said he is the one that will put her in handcuffs later so she needs to be nice to him. Laura is well aware that she is facing a sanction for her relapse and manages this risk by engaging with the bailiff through relying on traditional gender roles that define male/female relationships through coquettishness and sexual conquest. Women's statuses as women, particularly traditionally and heterosexually attractive women, are used to negotiate potential future harms and risks imposed on women by their participation in the DTC.

Some women in the DTCs also perform[13] the normative femininity of the 'good woman' (Naffine 1990; Smart 1995) to manage risks posed to them by their participation in the DTC. This performance often involves supporting, comforting and looking out for other participants in the DTC. For example, one woman ensures other DTC participants have food at their house and if not she brings them groceries. Another woman is very friendly and helpful to incoming DTC participants. She is a mentor, particularly for women who are new to the DTC. The 'good women' are also friendly with the DTC team members, showing them pictures of children and greeting them with smiles, pleasantries and compliments. One woman who performs the 'good woman' is told she is a positive presence in the courtroom and in the DTC programme in general. Another woman initiated applause and cheering for her fellow participants. When this 'good woman' missed a treatment session and a urine screen the Crown asked for a sanction of community service hours. He qualified this sanction with: 'we can't deny that she's a very enthusiastic and positive contribution to the courtroom and the drug treatment program . . . She supports others. She's cheering people on, clapping. We don't want to lose you.'

---

13 In describing these performances our intent is not to challenge the authenticity of women's actions in this context. We are interested in exploring the effects of women's actions, not their veracity.

Women also perform the good woman role by showing interest in regaining custody of their children and engaging in groups that support mothers who use drugs. An exchange in a DTC illustrates this:

Judge: I hear also that you're actively participating in programming . . . and that you had a visit with your children. How was it?
Paula: It was awesome, I needed to see them.
Judge: How old are they?
Paula: 2 and 6.
Judge: This calls for a coffee.
Paula is handed a coupon for a free coffee.

The positioning of women vis-à-vis their children is particularly troubling in the court as there is a clear assumption on the part of the court that a woman with children ought to want her children back. The fact that children are used as a carrot in the recovery/punishment process is testament to this. Without interviewing the women in the court it is difficult to provide concrete evidence about this phenomenon; however, interviews with treatment providers as well as members of community agencies working to support women in the court suggest that there is an undue pressure and expectation placed on women to want to regain custody of their children. The practitioners we spoke with shared their suspicions that the celebrated and favoured nature of mother-hood in the court leads some women to perform a desire to continue parenting that may not be reflective of their actual interests.

Women who perform the 'good woman' role seem to be given more lenience when it comes to breaches and sanctions. This is consistent with Naffine's (1990) analysis of how women perceived as 'good' are rewarded with more lenient sentences, while women diverging from this stereotypical construction (the 'bad woman') are punished more severely. Showing support and nurtur-ance for other court participants and/or children as well as a certain deference and sexuality to court personnel is clearly read by the court as an indication that a woman is committed to the programme and desires to change her substance use habits and thus her criminality. This may very well be an indi-cation of her commitment to the DTC treatment programme; however, this may also be a strategy that is used to resist punishment in the DTC. Since this work is based on court observations and not conversations, we are not making claims about the women's intentions. What we claim is that court personnel make decisions based on how women perform their femininity; women who perform the 'good woman' are rewarded in the DTCs.

Gendering the drug treatment court

In the face of the glaringly high attrition rates of the women in the DTCs the courts can no longer ignore the gendered problems they face in their attempts to cure criminal addicts. Most of the Canadian treatment courts are now implementing some form of gender-specific practices as a means of responding to the experiences of the women in the court. In Vancouver, for example, the court is, in theory, gender segregated, reserving Tuesdays as 'women's day' and Thursday for men. The Edmonton DTC started as a result of a sweep of sex trade workers in that city. Its first participants were all women.[14] The Toronto court, even though it has been in operation the longest, has only recently begun actively addressing the situation of the women in the court, through recruiting women participants by raising awareness through the criminal justice system, as well as only releasing women on Tuesdays so that they have enough time to 'stabilize' before the 'high risk' weekend sets in. In both Ottawa and Toronto the lack of gender-specific programming is attributed to the low numbers of women enrolled in the court. Perpetuating the 'too few to count' dilemma, court practitioners suggest that running a programme for three or four women is neither clinically nor financially viable.

While two of the courts we study (Toronto and Vancouver) have committed to some sort of gender sensitive practices on paper, the reality of these courts is much further removed from embracing this ideal. While Vancouver's court is meant to be gender segregated, in the six months of court observation, we never observed a women's day where a male participant was not present in the court (largely because men were either back in court on new charges or had to be released from custody). In addition, echoing concerns raised in response to the implementation of 'gender sensitivity' in the penal system (Hannah-Moffat 2004), gender segregation of the Vancouver court stops at court participants. In Vancouver the Crown, defence and treatment team liaison are all male.

The Toronto practice of releasing women on a specified day appears to have done nothing to alleviate the conditions for the women in that court. Women continue to drop out of the court programme at a considerable rate. While court officials in that court are making efforts to bring more women into the court programme through measures such as offering DTC information sessions at the local women's prison, comparatively little is being done to ameliorate the circumstances of women once they are enrolled in the court.

CONCLUSION

The DTCs offer a site through which to understand how attempts to cure those in conflict with the law, especially when linked up with the juridical power of the courts, can constitute particular harms that also need

---

14 Our future research will look more closely at the gendering effects of starting a court with only women clients.

management. The DTCs present a bifurcated governance regime in which the goal of curing the offender involves managing two different levels of risks: the risks the individual is said to pose to herself and society, and the risks criminal justice involvement poses to her. The existence of such risks is not necessarily gendered. However, within this broad category there are a number of risks faced exclusively by the women in the court. Pregnancy, motherhood and sex trade involvement are all factors that inform gendered risks. Because the court locates its own risk management/harm reduction practices in the context of a benevolent project of change, these second order risks are never acknowledged by the governing officials of the court. The women who are subject to such interventions work to deploy their own strategies of managing these risks.

The subject of risk is not a universal subject. The gendering of both first and second order risks in the DTCs reveals that governing through risk also means governing through contested identities of the targeted subject. The women in the DTC have risky pregnancies, are risky mothers and lead risky lives. So say the courts. The women in the courts do not necessarily contest these assessments. For these women, the point of contention is not whether or not they are at risk but rather what the origins of those risks are and how best to manage them. Understanding risk as something which occurs on more than one order or in different forms (Zedner 2006) helps us to see that risk is a strategy of governance that comes from both above and below. Notably, despite the fact risks are born out of these different orders, the responsibility for managing these risks does not shift. In the case of both first and second order risks, it is the woman in conflict with the law who is left to negotiate the risks she faces, regardless of whether they emerge out of her own choices or the juridical power of the justice system.

Seeing that women are responsibilized in such a way is important to forwarding our own understandings of how women manage in a gendered system that would place them in the way of amplified harms by virtue of their gender. Our work on the women in the DTC hopefully invites further exploration into such phenomena.

REFERENCES

Andrews, D.A., Bonta, J. and Stephen Wormith, J. (2006). 'The Recent Past and Near Future of Risk and/or Need Assessment'. *Crime and Delinquency*, 52(1): 7–27.

Benoit, Cecilia and Dena Carroll. With the assistance of Lisa Lawr and Munaza Chaudhry (1 March 1 2001). 'Marginalized Voices from the Downtown Eastside: Aboriginal Women Speak About Their Health Experiences'. Prepared for: The National Network on Environments and Women's Health A Centre of Excellence on Women's Health. York University.

Bosworth, Mary (2006) 'Self-Harm in Women's Prisons' *Criminology and Public Policy*, 5(1): 157.

Bosworth, Mary (1999) *Engendering resistance: Agency and power in women's prisons.* Aldershott: Ashgate Dartmouth.

Bosworth, Mary and Eamonn Carrabine (2001) 'Reassessing Resistance: Race, Gender and Sexuality in Prison' *Punishment and Society*, 3(4): 501–515.

Boyd, Susan C. (2004) *From Witches to Crack Moms: Women, drug law, and policy.* Durham, N.C: Carolina Academic Press.

Boyd, Susan C. (1999) *Mothers and illicit drugs: Transcending the myths.* Toronto: UTP.

Campbell, Nancy D. (2000) *Using Women: Gender, Drug Policy, and Social Justice.* New York: Routledge.

Canadian Human Rights Commission (2003) *Protecting Their Rights: A Systemic Review of Human Rights in Correctional Services for Federally Sentenced Women.* Ottawa: Canadian Human Rights Commission.

Carlen, Pat and Worrall, Anne (2004) *Analysing Women's Imprisonment.* Portland: Willan.

Chan, Wendy and Rigakos, George S. (2002) 'Risk, Crime and Gender' *British Journal of Criminology*, 42: 743–61.

Chunn and Lacombe (2000) 'Introduction' in Chunn and Lacombe (eds) *Law as a Gendering Practice.* Toronto: OUP.

Cruikshank, Barbara (1999) *The Will to Empower: Democratic Citizens and Other Subjects.* Ithaca: Cornell University Press.

DeChant, Betsy A. (1996) *Women and Group Psychotherapy: Theory and Practice.* Guilford Press.

Drug Treatment Court of Vancouver: Program Evaluation: Final Evaluation Report (30 November 2005) Orbis: Ottawa, ON.

Ericson, Richard V. and Haggerty, Kevin D. (1997) *Policing the Risk Society.* Toronto: University of Toronto Press.

Ericson, Richard V., Doyle, Aaron and Barry, Dean (2003) *Insurance as Governance.* Toronto: University of Toronto Press.

Feeley, Malcolm M. and Jonathan Simon (1992) 'The New Penology: Notes on the Emerging Strategy of Corrections and its Implication' *Criminology*, 30(4): 449.

Gliksman, Louis, Newton-Taylor, Brenda, Patra, Jayadeep, and Rehm, Jürgen (30 November 2004). 'Toronto Drug Treatment Court: Evaluation Project Final Report'. Centre for Addiction and Mental Health: Toronto, ON.

Hannah-Moffat, Kelly (2004) 'Losing Ground: Gendered Knowledges, Parole Risk, and Responsibility' *Social Politics*, 11(3): 363–385.

Hodgins, David C., El-Guebaly, Nady and Jean Addington (1997) 'Treatment of substance abusers: Single or mixed gender programs?' *Addiction* 92(7): 805–812.

Hudson, Barbara (2002) 'Gender issues in penal policy and penal theory' in Pat Carlen (ed.) *Women and Punishment: The Struggle for Justice.* Portland: Willan, pp. 21–46.

Humphries, D. (1999) *Crack Mothers.* Columbus: Ohio State University Press.

Kilty, Jennifer M. (2006) 'Under the Barred Umbrella: Is There Room for a Women-Centred Self-Injury Policy in Canadian Corrections?' *Criminology & Public Policy*, (5)1: 161–182.

Meyer, Jeff and Pat O'Malley. (2004) 'Missing the Punitive Turn? Canadian Criminal Justice, "Balance" and Penal Modernism' in Pratt *et al* (eds) *The New Punitiveness: Trends, Theories, Perspectives.* London: Willan.

Moore, Dawn (2007) 'Translating Justice and Therapy: The Drug Treatment Court Networks' in *British Journal of Criminology*, 43(1).

Moore, Dawn (2004) 'Drugalities: The generative capabilities of criminalized "drugs" ' *International Journal of Drug Policy*, 15(5): 419–426.

Moore, Dawn and Hannah-Moffat (2004) 'The liberal veil: Revisiting Canadian penality' in John Pratt *et al* (eds) *The New Punitiveness: Trends, Theories, Perspectives*. London: Willan.

Naffine, Ngaire (1990) *Law and the Sexes: Explorations in Feminist Jurisprudence*. Sydney: Allen & Unwin.

O'Malley, Pat (2004) *Risk, uncertainty and government*. London: Glass House.

Rose, Nikolas (1996) *Inventing Our Selves: Psychology, Power and Personhood*. Cambridge: Cambridge University Press.

Rose, Nikolas, Pat O'Malley and Mariana Valverde (2006) 'Governmentality' *Annual Review of Law and Society*, 2(1).

Roth, Rathel (2000) *Making Women Pay: The Hidden Costs of Fetal Rights*. New York: Cornell University Press.

Scraton, Phil and Moore, Linda (2005) 'Degradation, Harm and Survival in a Women's Prison' *Social Policy & Society* 5(1): 67–78.

Smart, Carol (1995) *Law, Crime and Sexuality: Essays in Feminism*. London: Sage.

Smart, Carol (1989) *Feminism and the Power of Law*. London: Routledge.

Toscano, Vicki (2005) 'Misguided Retribution: Criminalization of Pregnant Women who Take Drugs' *Social and Legal Studies*, 14(3): 359–386.

United Nations (2004) *Substance abuse treatment and care for women: Case studies and lessons learned*. New York: United Nations Office on Drugs and Crime.

Valverde, Mariana (1998) *Diseases of the Will: Alcohol and the dilemmas of freedom*. Cambridge: Cambridge University Press.

Wachholz, Sandra and Baukje Miedema (2000) 'Risk, fear, harm: Immigrant women's perceptions of the "policing solution" to woman abuse' *Crime, Law & Social Change*, 34: 301–317.

Worrall, Anne (1990) *Offending Women: Female Lawbreakers and the Criminal Justice System*. London: Routledge.

Zedner, Lucia (2006) 'Policing Before and After the Police: The Historical Antecedents of Contemporary Crime Control' *British Journal of Criminology*, 46(1): 78–96.

Chapter 10

'Getting mad wi' it'

Risk seeking by young women[1]

Susan A. Batchelor[2]

INTRODUCTION

Risk management and risk taking are an important part of young people's identity formation within late modernity (Mitchell *et al* 2001). 'Youth' is contemporaneously constructed as a period of dangerousness and deficiency (Muncie 2004). That said, whereas young men are more likely to be referred to as 'troublesome', young women are represented as 'troubled' (Green *et al* 2000). In other words, young women are more often portrayed as the passive victims of risk rather than as active risk seekers. This is clearly demonstrated in the literature on women and violence, which tends to focus on women's victimization, or explains their offending as a response to an abusive situation or past abusive experiences. The disadvantages of this approach are that it contributes to the falsehood that young women who actively seek risks are in some way abnormal or bizarre; it denies young women any agency or choice in their lives; and it leaves us with little understanding of the meaning of risk-seeking behaviour from the point of view of young women.

This chapter draws upon data from a recent Economic and Social Research Council (ESRC)-funded project exploring young women's violent behaviour.[3] Challenging conceptions of risk that focus solely on women's risk avoidance, the data point to the positive contribution risk-seeking behaviour can have in terms of young women's sense of self and self-efficacy. As Lyng's (1990) notion of 'edgework' acknowledges, voluntary risk taking can be used to achieve a semblance of control in a life that is experienced as out of control.

---

1 An early version of this chapter was presented at the ESRC Transdisciplinary Seminar on Law, Probability and Risk, hosted by the International Centre for Mathematical Sciences, Edinburgh, 2004.
2 Department of Sociology, Anthropology and Applied Social Sciences and Scottish Centre for Crime and Justice Research, University of Glasgow, Florentine House, 53 Hillhead Street, University of Glasgow, Glasgow G12 8QF, Scotland, UK. Tel: +44 (0)141 330 6167. E-mail: s.batchelor@lbss.gla.ac.uk.
3 ESRC studentship R42200034047.

However, an important criticism of early versions of this work is that it yielded conceptual models rooted in the experience of men (Miller 1991) and thereby failed to recognize the gendered nature of the edgework experience (Lois 2001). Through the use of direct quotations, the chapter will show that while young women are initially drawn to risk-seeking behaviour as a result of the shared adrenaline 'rush' or 'buzz' they experience, as their 'risk pathways' progress they increasingly come to rely on edgework as a means to *block out* powerful emotions. The data also show that, unlike men, who tend to retrospectively redefine their edgework experiences as an expression of exhilaration and omnipotence (Lyng 1990), young women are more likely to look upon their behaviour as irrational and therefore feel guilty about what they have done.

THE SOCIOLOGY OF RISK SEEKING

The most oft-cited analysis of risk-seeking behaviour is Stephen Lyng's (1990) article on 'edgework'. Lyng's analysis, which is grounded in his empirical research with male skydivers (Lyng and Snow 1986), departs from previous (predominantly psychological) approaches by conceptualizing risk taking from a sociological perspective and linking it to the alienated and over-socialized nature of the late modern period. According to Lyng, edgework activities involve 'a clearly observable threat to one's physical or mental well-being or one's sense of an ordered existence ... [and] the ability to maintain control over a situation that verges on complete chaos' (1990: 858–9).[4] In other words, he conceptualizes risk taking as a form of 'boundary negotiation' in which the point is 'to get as close as possible to the edge without going over it' (ibid: 862). Through the rational calibration of risk and skill, edgeworkers seek to push themselves to their mental and physical limits in order to encounter an intense sensory experience that gives them a feeling of agency and control. According to Lyng, individuals engaging in edgework 'experience themselves as instinctively acting entities ... with a purified and magnified sense of self' (ibid: 154). Despite being largely illusory, this heightened sense of control is psychologically *necessary*, Lyng argues, because of the shared absence of control individuals experience at this particular historical moment:

> The general tendency towards a 'deskilling' of work in economies dominated by mass production industries and authority structures means that workers at many different levels, ranging from service workers

---

4 The classic edgework experience is one where 'the individual's failure to meet the challenge at hand will result in death or at the very least debilitating injury' (ibid); for example, bungee jumping, hang gliding, skydiving, or motorbike racing.

to certain types of professionals, may be forced to work under alienating conditions.

(Lyng 1990: 876)

O'Malley and Mugford (1994) develop this idea further, arguing that edgeworkers seek excitement in response to the controlled emotionality of the modern industrial experience:

> The separation of reason from emotion, the identification of the former with the intellect and the latter with the body (carnality) was a crucial element of the Enlightenment project . . . one of the key assumptions that formed the modern world-view [was] the identification of emotions as being within the body, and therefore as base and subordinated to reason. Culturally constructed in this fashion, emotions become controllable or manageable. Indeed, the idea is that they *must* be controlled.
>
> (O'Malley and Mugford 1994: 197, emphasis added)

Thus, edgework can be seen as the 'flipside of modernity' (Lupton 1999: 156), a way of asserting control in the face of the alienating nature of work in the modern, rationalized age. Its seductiveness is linked both to the inherent thrill of the act and the feelings of 'self-realization' and 'self-determination' to which the thrill gives rise.

One of the key criticisms of the edgework model has been that it draws on examples that are 'engaged in by white men with attachment to the labor force' (Miller 1991: 1531). Yet understandings and experiences of risk are different for different groups. There can be little question that class, gender and ethnicity impact upon both the opportunities for edgework and its underlying imperatives. Socially excluded and socio-economically disadvantaged young people, for example, have little connection with the world of work, and typically lack access to pre-arranged excitements such as skydiving or base jumping. Rather, they spend much of their time 'bored', hanging about street corners with their peers. As Lyng (2005) has himself recently acknowledged, within this context '*criminal* edgework is a much more relevant and accessible means to re-enchantment than the pursuit of leisure edgework or postmodern consumption' (Lyng 2005: 29, emphasis added).

THE 'PATHWAYS THROUGH VIOLENCE' RESEARCH

In a society where concerns about crime are firmly embedded within a youth discourse, violent young women are increasingly presented as a new source of the 'youth problem' (Batchelor 2001/2002, 2005; Batchelor *et al* 2001). Increasing numbers of girls and young women are being drawn into both the criminal justice and the penal systems for violent behaviour (Batchelor and Burman

2004), leading to calls for more research on and surveillance of young women's risk taking, risk factors and risk profiles (Kemshall 2004). The relative infrequency and distinctive nature of female offending means that existing actuarial predictors, derived from studies of male offenders, are increasingly considered inaccurate and inappropriate (Hannah-Moffat and Shaw 2001; Hannah-Moffat and Maurutto 2001; Worrall 2001). Consequently there is a need for empirical evidence examining the ways in which young women who offend understand and respond towards risk-related discourses and strategies.

Funded by the ESRC, the 'Pathways through Violence' research sought to challenge existing portrayals of violence by young women through an examination of the feelings, beliefs and experiences of young women convicted of a violent crime. One of the key aims was to bring the voices of young women to the centre of theoretical and methodological debates about 'youth violence' and, in doing so, to acknowledge the often inconsistent and even contradictory ways in which subordination and agency are simultaneously realized in young women's lives. Methods employed by the study included in-depth oral-history interviews with young women detained in Her Majesty's Prison and Young Offenders Institute, Cornton Vale in Scotland, interviews with adults that work with such young women, and documentary analysis.[5] All of the young women in the interview sample were single and all were white; ages ranged from 16 to 24 years.[6]

RISK PATHWAYS

The research identified four pathways to violent offending among the women interviewed:[7]

---

5 Cornton Vale is Scotland's only all-female establishment, and the majority of Scotland's female prison population is housed there, including young offenders. Fieldwork was completed in August 2001, when there were 38 young women under the age of 25 serving a custodial sentence who had at least one previous conviction for violence. Each of these young women was sent a letter asking them if they would be interested in participating in the study and, of the 24 who agreed to be involved, 21 were eventually interviewed. These interviews ranged in length from one to two hours, all of which were tape-recorded, transcribed and analysed by the author.

6 In February 2005, minority ethnic groups made up 5 per cent of the female prison population in Scotland (Scottish Prison Service, personal correspondence, 24 Feb 2005). In the general population of Scotland, 98 per cent is white. The disproportionate number of ethnic minority women in prison in Scotland is therefore much lower than in England and Wales, where minority ethnic groups make up 26 per cent of the female average population (compared to 6 per cent of the population at large).

7 While it was developed independently, this classification has much in common with Daly's (1992) typology of women appearing at felony court. Daly identified five main groups: street women; harmed and harming women; battered women; drug-connected women; and economically motivated women.

1   The *abused adult*, who attacks her abuser whilst under the influence of alcohol. The abused adult has no previous convictions and considers her actions to be in self-defence. (Rare in current sample due to age range, but more common in the wider female prison population.)

2   The *teenage fighter*, who drinks heavily and experiments with recreational drugs and/or prescription medication, often as a means to avoid problems at home. Her violent offence typically relates to a street fight that is initiated whilst the offender is under the influence of alcohol and where things 'get out of hand', resulting in the victim receiving a severe injury. The (sub) cultural norms and values of this group promote pre-emptive violence and the defence of respect, and victims are generally (but not solely) other young women.

3   The *drug offender*, who engages in property crime and/or prostitution as a means to support her drug habit. Her violent offence typically relates to an assault on a police officer/security guard/householder who has attempted to apprehend her. Often abused as a child, the drug offender relies on substance abuse to dull emotional pain. She is generally intoxicated at the time of the offence and considers her violent actions to be in self-defence.

4   The *hurt and hurting child*, who assaults and robs unknown victims, often threatening them with a weapon. This group of offenders represent perhaps the most 'damaged' young women: they have extensive histories in care, poor family relationships and significant experience of physical and sexual abuse within the family. This small group of young women experience overwhelming feelings of anger and rage and express these feelings by hurting other people.

As these pathways suggest, one of the central findings of the research was that young women's violent behaviour was motivated by a complex interaction involving active risk seeking and risk management. Further, young women made a distinction between their motivations for starting and maintaining risk-seeking behaviour. As the sections that follow demonstrate, most of the young women initially became involved in violence and other forms of offending for non-pecuniary reasons: to have fun, to impress their mates, to stand up for themselves (pathway 2). For the three-fifths whose substance use progressed to dependence, however, the importance of excitement sharply declined as drug addiction replaced peers as a central organizing feature (pathways 3 and 4). For this latter group of women, risk-taking behaviour principally became a means of managing emotional pain.

'Jist wan o' the troops'

The significance of the peer group as a source of identity and status is well documented. Young women in particular commonly describe their friendships as 'the most important thing' (Burman *et al* 2003; Griffiths 1995; Hey 1997). Spending time with friends is a prime social activity for most young people and – according to the literature – young people often congregate in groups for a sense of belonging, as well as sociability. As Quicker (1983: 80) summarizes: 'To be in a gang is to be part of something. It means having a place to go, friends to talk with and parties to attend. It means recognition and respected status.' Research also points to the protective functions of 'gangs' (Seaman *et al* 2006), especially for young women (Joe and Chesney-Lind 1995; Miller 2001). Most of the young women in the current study came from families characterized by problems such as domestic violence and/or parental drug or alcohol abuse (Batchelor 2005). Two-fifths had been the victims of physical abuse and two-fifths had been sexually abused, usually by a family member. As a result, the young women turned to their peers as a source of emotional and social support, spending much of their time away from the family home.

Most of the young women had been persistent truants who spent their teenage years 'hanging round' drinking and taking drugs with friends. Four-fifths reported 'heavy' alcohol consumption during this period (drinking daily or partaking in regular binge drinking, for example) and a similar proportion reported experience of illicit drug use (initially 'recreational' drugs, such as cannabis, speed, acid, or ecstasy, along with tranquillisers and/or sleeping tablets). Joanne's experience was fairly typical:

> Ah was a pure terror at school. Ah was ayeways getting into fights a' the time. Just being a pure little brat! Just ayeways arguing wi' ma teachers and stuff and never listening to anybody . . . They started expelling me, throwing me oot. By the time Ah got tae fourth year, Ah ended up havin' to go to tae stay in a [children's] home.
>
> 'Cause Ah didnae get any guid grades fae school and because Ah wasnae settled anywhere, livin' rough, Ah just ended up hangin' aboot wi' the wrong people. Ken, people who obviously werenae workin' or goin' tae college or any'hin'? It was all people sittin' aboot, gettin' drunk, daein' 'hings like that. Ah just thought it was cool tae be hangin' aboot wi' all the big boys.
>
> Ah started drinkin' when Ah was 13. Like at nights after school, hanging round. That was just like bottles o' cider, 'hings like that, ken, a bottle o' Buckfast. Then it was like Ah was runnin' aboot wi' ma pals all during the day and drinkin' wi' these aulder folk. And they're drinkin' bottles o' vodka and Ah would drink it as well. And that's when Ah started offending real bad. Ah was drinkin', like 24 hours a day. Drinkin' fae when Ah opened ma eyes until Ah closed them, a' the time. Takin' vallies and jellies and stuff like that.
>
> (Joanne)

While most young women refuted the influence of 'peer pressure' (this was something that was seen to affect other people), they spoke about not wanting to be 'left out' and said that they started drinking/taking drugs/offending because 'everyone else was doing it'.

Almost three-quarters of the young women in the study reported previous social work involvement and over half had experienced being looked after by the local authority (e.g. in a children's unit). Powerful peer group cultures are a common feature of residential care (Reynold and Barter 2003; Wade *et al* 1998), and young people who spend time in care are often subject to multiple changes of placement (Triseliotis *et al* 1995). Interviewees frequently remarked that they 'went along with' risky behaviours in order to 'fit in' with a new peer group and said that taking drugs, 'being pure cheeky tae the staff', and/or offending, provided a way to instantly 'bond' with existing residents. Alternatively they would initiate violence, drug use or offending in an attempt to establish respect or status. Stephanie, who was placed in local authority care for a second time at age 13, gave the following account:

> See since I got put in a home, that's when I started getting wilder and wilder and wilder. See the home I was in, I was wi' aulder people. So we were getting brought up wi' older people and I was watching them daein' things and I was following along, ken just watching them taking drugs and going aboot mad wi' it, battering people, and I was going along wi' them, eh? You see them daein' 'hings and you're like that, 'Aww, I want tae dae what they're daein' and you just keep on going wi' them.
>
> (Stephanie)

Again Stephanie didn't feel *pressured* into offending; she 'followed along' because she looked up to, and wanted to emulate, her residential peers. Like a number of the young women, she suggested that while she 'learned' to offend through the tutelage of older residents the *decision* to offend was ultimately her own: 'at the end of the day I know what I am daein'. I know I'm getting the jail, but I still dae it.'

This emphasis on personal responsibility was reflected in Pauline's account of her entry into prostitution. Pauline was an only child, born and brought up in a 'good working-class' area of a large Scottish city. After her parents' separation (when Pauline was five), she spent much of her childhood in and out of residential school. At age 17, she left care and moved into supported accommodation:

> Ah was in flats run by the social work department ... Ah wis gettin' aulder, so that jist made me mature a bit, 'cause Ah started to fend for masel', basically ... That's when Ah went into prostitution. Money. Curiosity. Ah was younger – Ah was aboot 17 – and two lassies that Ah was pally wi', Ah wondered where they were gettin' their money fae.

Jealousy, basically. Ah was wonderin' 'How the hell are they comin' in here wi' loads o' money and clothes?' Ah didnae know anything like that. And Ah spoke to the guy they were workin' wi' and that was it. Ah did it a couple o' times, liked the money, it was easy money and that was it.

(Pauline)

Unlike Stephanie, Pauline's involvement in offending wasn't motivated by a desire to be the same but rather to *have* the same. Acknowledging her lack of educational qualifications and non-existent family support, she made what she saw as a rational choice to become involved in prostitution.

Karen's account demonstrated a similar weighing of options. Karen initially became involved in shoplifting after moving to a new primary school. Like Pauline, she said her offences were driven by a desire to 'keep up with the Joneses' and show she was 'as good as' her new peers. As she grew older, however, her motives changed and she began using the skills gained to impress new peers:

I haven't lived in any one place for a long time . . . My mum and that stayed in Linncraig until I was five and then I lived in England. I spent nine years travelling England and then back up here to jump fae place to place for the past few years.

I had been like shoplifting since I was seven or something, ken, *really* young. See ma pals at school, we used to all walk to school thegither because it was a dead safe little town doon in England. It was dead posh . . . And they all used to get money for sweeties, but me and my sister didn't used to get any . . . So I used to steal things. Like I used tae steal things for my wee sister, because she was only at nursery and I couldnae send her to school without sweeties because *everybody* had sweeties.

Up until I went to the high school I was top of the class. I was not a bad kid. I was a good kid. I was quite a loner, but I wasn't . . . a bad kid. When I went to high school, for the first time in ma whole life it wasn't just me that was the new kid. *Everybody* was the new kid. I seemed to– I don't know, my personality just– and everybody respected me.

That's when I started shoplifting all the time . . . I used to steal all these tapes and toiletries and make-up and stuff and then clothes, just anything ma pals wanted. If any of ma pals needed stuff I would steal them for them.

(Karen)

One explanation for young women's risk taking, then, is the desire to establish new and maintain existing peer relationships. Theories of women's psychological development propose that women cultivate a sense of self and self worth via their connection with others (Chodorow 1978; Miller 1976; Gilligan 1982). For young women whose home experiences are characterized by disconnection and violation, peers offer an important source of social and self-identity.

'Daein it fer the buzz'

The thrill of transgression was another central theme. In line with the findings of Matza and Sykes (1961), along with work carried out under the rubric of 'cultural criminology' (for an overview, see Ferrell 1999), young women often cited the adrenaline 'rushes' involved in offending behaviour, stating that offending was 'fun, something to do'. As Annie put it, 'Ah wasnae wanting to hurt anybody, it was just *boredom*'. Likewise, Kelly said, 'Offending was jist some'hin tae break up ma day, it gied us something to pass the time'. She gave the following example:

> When we was drinkin' we used to jist . . . cause a fight wi' somebody. Lassies that never even done nothing to us, for the sake ay it. Eh, one night it was me and ma pals, and there was this lassie sittin' in the grass, an' they were all like pushin' me an' sayin' like, 'Go on, Go on!' . . . makin' oot she'd took the cunt oot me an' all that when she hudnae. So jist for the sake ay it Ah went an' done it. Even though Ah knew it was wrong. Ah jist went up an' battered her for nae reason. Jist fer some'hin tae dae.
>
> (Kelly)

The excitement associated with violence was emphasized more forcefully by Zoë:

> I get very excited. I get sick. I get– I take the bile I get that excited aboot it. See aifter I dae something in all, I always need a pee wi' excitement. That's terrible, innit? I get a buzz aff it. I get a buzz aff of being violent, *when I am violent*.
>   I'd love tae [bite someone's ear off]. I've thought aboot ripping it off. But I've naw. I don't know. With ma teeth. [Laughing, embarrassed] Just imagining all the blood popping oot. That's terrible innit? Aw naw!
>
> (Zoë, emphasis added)

Both Kelly and Zoë took pleasure in remembering and describing their violent escapades, and became visibly agitated when recounting stories of fights between groups of young people. This is significant because, while accounts of male offenders have emphasized their thrill-seeking and controlling nature (c.f. Katz 1998), dominant discourses depict young women as risk averse, and women's violence tends to be explained as loss of control, about which women feel guilty and ashamed (c.f. Campbell 1993). Yet for young women in the current study such violence was considered deeply meaningful; it served to maintain group solidarity, reinforce friendships, affirm allegiances, and enhance personal status within the group.

Violence wasn't the only criminal activity that the young women referred to as exciting. Angela referred to 'the buzz' associated with stealing cars, for example, while Lesley discussed feelings of elation after a successful housebreaking:

> I used tae dae it fer the buzz! Because you were daein' something you werenae supposed tae be daein' and you thought, 'Oh, if I get caught here I'll get a chase!' Everything starts running through your mind. You don't actually sit and think, 'Well, if I take this car, this person's gonna be "Ma car, ma insurance!"' You don't think o' how the person's gonna feel; you just think aboot how you're gonna feel inside yourself.
>
> (Angela)

> Your adrenaline is going and stuff like that. . . . Because you know that you could get caught or they could wake up and you're fucked. But it's a buzz. It's a good feeling. See when you come oot that hoose and you open up a purse or a bag and you see all this money, you're like that: 'Oh my God! It takes some people a week to earn that amount of money and I've just earned it in five minutes.' So you don't think of the consequences or the hurt you're causing or anything like that.
>
> (Lesley)

For Karen, the value of the goods stolen was of less importance than the sense of euphoria and exhilaration associated with 'pulling a fast one' or 'putting one over' on someone:

> I lost my bottle for shoplifting . . . One day I put on a black hat and a black jacket and broke into a house. I found it dead easy. And the adrenaline rush I got off it was *amazing*. It was much better than shoplifting. I used to *love* shoplifting. I still do . . . When you're waiting fer somebody to grab you and they don't, it's like, 'Cool!' When you're breaking into a hoose it's even better 'cause it is *dark* and just the sneakiness o' it. I liked breaking into the houses better than I liked the money and the drugs. I actually enjoyed the thieving better than I enjoyed the takings.
>
> (Karen)

Thus offending presented some young women with a measure of self-esteem and self-efficacy; a sense that they had crossed the boundaries into someone else's world and 'gotten away with it'.

The status and sense of superiority young women said they felt was sometimes linked to the 'masculine' nature of the offences they committed. Karen, for example, took pride in her status as 'the only female housebreaker in

Midvale', while Zoë claimed to be one of the few prisoners 'that's been done fer car theft'. Committing traditionally 'male' offences made both women feel special or unique. It also afforded them respect amongst their male peers:

> I used to be at the high school with five of my male pals, ken, there was six of us, and we used to wrestle . . . Like we would take it in turns and whoever wasn't wrestling was drinking. It started off quite mild, but by the end of the night we would have black eyes and we would basically be battered to death. And not one of them made an allowance for me being a female, not one of them. There was only two of them that could actually beat me . . . I just preferred the company and liked the things that guys done better than the things that lassies done.
>
> (Karen)

Hence some young women initially engaged in offending, particularly violent offending, because it carried with it an excess of masculine meanings (e.g. independence, strength, emotional stoicism, toughness), and confronting expectations that women should not steal cars, break into houses, engage in violence and so on provided an additional source of excitement, pleasure, self-respect and status. That is not to say, however, that the young women embraced a masculine *identity*. Rather, they appropriated an ideology of femininity according to which the use of violence was socially sanctioned. As reported below, one of the primary motivations young women in the current study gave for engaging in violent behaviour was to protect and/or prove their allegiance to their family, their friends and/or their local area. In other words, they justified their behaviour by reference to norms of emphasized femininity (e.g. selflessness, loyalty and caring for others).

'Better a sair face than a red face'

Like the North American street youth studied by Anderson (1999) and Bourgois (2002), young women placed a high premium on being treated with 'respect', believing that if you allowed other people to disrespect you, you would be left with nothing:

> I've realized now that I've got to defend for masel' [sic]. And if that means doing anything, that means doing anything, no matter what it takes.
>
> If you let folk think that they can just come up and they can just smack you, you're gonnae get that all the time, you're gonna get treated like a pure bam. And you are gonnae get targeted and targeted and targeted. You cannae just stand there and let somebody punch you, or stick the head in ye, know what Ah mean? You're obviously gonnae hit them back.
>
> (Carol)

Much of the young women's violence, then, was motivated by a desire to gain respect, but this search for respect was in itself a form of risk management, an attempt to pre-empt bullying or victimization through the display of an aggressive or violent disposition. Almost without exception, the young women expressed the importance of being *seen* to 'stand up for yourself', repeating the mantra: 'I'd rather take a sore face than a red face.' Adopting a tough, aggressive approach was regarded as an *unavoidable* aspect of life growing up in a 'rough' area and was something that many of the young women said that they were explicitly taught by their parents from a very early age.

Against this backdrop, some of the seemingly trivial sources of young women's anger and annoyance are rendered intelligible. Within the prison setting, for example, Zoë attacked a fellow inmate for lifting a slice of bread that she put in the toaster: 'I'd toasted it and she's just buttered it and taken it away. That's treating ye like a daftie'; while Stephanie got involved in a fight over a cigarette:

> I got put in with this girl and her fag went oot and I says, 'Cool doon! You'll get a light. We've only got 10 minutes to go!' and she went, 'You shut up!' I went, 'Who are you telling to shut up, you bam?!' She went, 'You're the bam!' I says, 'Prove me the bam!' and she went, 'Naw, *you* prove me the bam!' I says, 'Naw, *you* prove *me* the bam!' . . . and she jumped up and grabbed us. I was like that, 'I'll have tae fight fer maself here' and I just started punching fuck oot 'er.
>
> (Stephanie)

Both women felt that they *had* to react in such circumstances or they would be seen as 'a daftie' or 'a bam' (i.e. easy prey). Far from being irrational, then, viewed within the hostile world of the prison setting their behaviour could be regarded as a 'necessary survival strategy' (Maher 1997). The young women confronted real danger on a daily basis. At any given moment, their victim, their offending peers, or various agents of the state, could attempt to take advantage or 'put one over' on them (Katz 1988). By communicating that they were prepared to stand up for themselves, physically if necessary, the young women maintained a level self-respect and status, and in doing so protected their emotional and physical selves.

'Just tae black oot'

Young women also engaged in risk-seeking behaviour as a means of managing negative feelings. As previously stated, disruptive family backgrounds, histories of physical and sexual violence, and childhood experiences of institutional care were common among the young women interviewed. As a result of these experiences, many of the young women expressed feelings of unresolved grief and rage, and said that these emotions contributed indirectly to their offending. Clear correlations exist between the victimization of young women and high-risk behaviours such as substance misuse, suicide and self-harm (Acoca and Dedel 1998; Howard League 1997). One third of the sample were drinking daily and half described a pattern of regular binge drinking prior to their 'current' offence. Three-fifths of the young women were addicted to heroin. Most said that while they initially started drinking, or taking drugs, because it made them feel good, they soon came to rely on it as a way to avoid unpleasant memories. As Joanne explained:

> When Ah started off taking everything it was just tae be the same as every-body else and just fer the buzz. But then through time, as each year went on, Ah was taking mair and mair different 'hings and that was just to black oot, forget a' the stupid 'hings Ah'd obviously already done, eh? 'hings like that.
>
> (Joanne)

Similar themes pervaded Cathy's account. Cathy had been sexually abused by her paternal grandfather between the ages of seven and 11. Following a fight with her father, she was received into local authority care aged 11, at which point she started experimenting with drugs (temazepam, ecstasy and cannabis). As her drug use escalated, Cathy became involved in offending to get money for drugs. She was eventually sent to residential school after being caught stealing charity boxes:

> Wi' ma friends I would take, like, jellies and eccie and then when I was sitting on ma own I would smoke hash. I done it to blank everything oot. But then when I woke up in the morning it was still there, so I just took drugs again. And that's how I started getting intae committing crime. And the crimes that I were committing were shoplifting, thefts, just so I could get money, just tae get me them drugs, just tae forget fer a wee while.
>
> See at the start, it was a really positive thing. It was making me happy and it was making me forget and it was gieing me a laugh wi' ma pals and then it started to get beyond a joke. I got caught stealing . . . and put in residential school.
>
> (Cathy)

As their drug use progressed, then, the young women's offending pattern altered. Offences that were initially engaged in alongside peers for the buzz or a shared sense of experience became financially motivated – driven by the need to fund escalating drug problems. When the young women attempted to reduce their consumption, in an effort to regain some degree of control, negative feelings resurfaced and were often compounded by guilt and shame arising from their own behaviours (hurting others, for example, or allowing their children to be put up for adoption). This became a self-perpetuating cycle, as Angela, who was sexually abused by her uncle over a 12-year period, explained:

> When I took drugs I didnae have the thoughts, I didnae have the night-mares, or the flashbacks. So I was free. And then for a while I wasnae able to get drugs, em, I was working. I'd got masel a job and I wasnae able to get the drugs. And that's when it started coming back and I couldnae handle it.
>
> If I took the drugs the abuse was gone, and if I didnae have the drugs the abuse was there. And I thought, 'If I take these drugs, and I keep taking them, I'll no need to think about it and it will no be in ma mind'.
>
> (Angela)

A major draw of drugs, then, was that they prevented conscious thought and provided temporary relief from intense feelings. In contrast to the reflexive actors depicted by Giddens (1990, 1991) and Beck (1992, 1994), the majority of young women in the current study gave little thought to the past, or indeed the future, preferring instead to take themselves out of themselves, living their lives in the moment, focusing on the next hit.[8]

'A way to make you feel'

Some of the young women said that they felt emotionally 'numb' much of the time and no longer experienced 'natural' or 'normal' feelings. Joanne's account was typical of this group:

> Through drugs Ah've become totally immune. Ah don't feel the way normal folk feel. Ah've just lost every bit o' confidence and every'hin' . . . Ah'm all withdrawn fae everybody. Ah'll no sit wi' anybody, Ah'll just sit masel'. Ah 'hink that's just like wi' havin' heroin, because Ah've been that used tae it.
>
> (Joanne)

Carol, too, said she felt 'detached'. She spoke about 'closing down' emotion-ally so that no one could hurt her, and of no longer knowing how to react appropriately to someone else's distress:

> It just doesn't hurt anymore . . . Ah used tae be dead, dead quiet and just used to never bother and then Ah just got sick o' it. You just think to

---

8 In this sense, they can be characterized as 'reflexivity losers' (Lash 1994).

yersel', 'Awff, what else can anybody else do tae ye?' So you just start getting immune tae things. I'll be honest, see when Ah see people crying in here, Ah laugh. But it's not because Ah'm thinking they're pure pathetic, it's just Ah dae ken [don't know] what tae dae.

(Carol)

Risk seeking, in this context, was understood as 'a way to make you feel' and reminded young women that they were 'alive'.

Self-harm was a relatively popular method of *expressing* negative emotions. In much the same way that Karen and Lesley talked about housebreaking in order to experience the 'buzz' or 'rush' that comes with a successful theft, young women who self-harmed said it gave them a 'release', a sense of omnipotence and self-control. Others engaged in violence for the same reasons:

To be honest wi' you Ah like rollin' about wi folk! [Laughs] It's like seeing how much Ah can tolerate. Like say in here, there's been fuckin' times when they've like jumped on me, prison officers, they jumped me right and it is bloody sore. And your mind just goes intae somewhere else so that you're tolerating it. And it makes them worse because you are tolerating it. They're like that, 'Why the fuck is she no squealing?' Ah just sit there and smile, but it fucking hurts, you're like that, 'Mmm'. But it's like seeing how much Ah can tolerate.

(Carol)

For certain young women, then, violence (whether directed at the self or at others) was motivated by a desire to feel physical pain, and the ability to endure physical pain was in turn understood as an assertion of power and control.

Another means of expressing negative emotions was hurting others. All three of the young women convicted of robbery, for example, cited vengeance as a basis of their actions. Debbie said she liked 'robbin' boys' as a way of exacting retribution on her abuser:

Ah robbed somebody. And it *wisnae* for money 'cause Ah *had* money . . . Ah *liked* robbin' people. . . . Ah *liked* the feelin'. Ah felt kinda relieved . . . Ah wanted people tae hurt. 'Cause Ah wis hurtin. Selfish. [Short pause] Ah think it wis tae get some o' ma anger oot. Like [when] some people cut thairsels, sort o' hing.

(Debbie)

This account supports Katz's (1988) theory of robbery as learned. Katz argues that those who persistently engage in robbery are making a choice to continue involvement in a form of behaviour they have previously discovered to be instrumentally and expressively useful. Against structural explanations and cost-benefit analyses, both of which regard monetary gain as the robber's prime motivation, Katz argues that most robberies result in relatively low levels of financial recompense and, further, have a comparatively high rate of detection. Put another way, if the offender's aim is the rational pursuit of cash, then there are easier, safer and more lucrative ways to make a living, both legal (working in McDonalds, for example – see Goode 1990: 8) and illegal (e.g. burglary). Both Debbie's and Carol's offences were largely prompted by anger. Their primary aim was to attack 'somebody . . . anybody' and the level of violence utilized often exceeded that which was required.

THE ILLUSION OF CONTROL: DIFFERENT FOR YOUNG WOMEN?

As the preceding data have hopefully made clear, young women in the current study employed risk-seeking behaviour in a deliberate attempt to exert control over lives that were experienced as out of control. However, unlike Lyng's (1990) edgeworkers, who engaged in voluntary risk taking in response to the dehumanizing, alienating nature of work in the post-industrial era, they cited *families* as the source of estrangement and disaffection. This is unsurprising considering that 'emphasised femininity' is associated with the intimate emotionality of family rather than the competitive rationality of work (Connell 1987). Disruptive family backgrounds, histories of physical and sexual abuse, and childhood experiences of institutional care were common among the young women interviewed, and many claimed that they did not feel 'wanted' at home or that their parents were emotionally distant or didn't pay them enough attention. Consequently they turned to their peers for an enhanced sense of sociability and belonging. Risk seeking, in this context, permitted the young women to construct an enhanced sense of self and self-efficacy, 'a realisation of immediacy and a reassertion of identity and ontology' (Hayward and Young 2004: 267). As their risk pathways progressed, however, risk seeking became a coping mechanism to manage overwhelming emotions.

This raises an important question of how we should understand the term 'voluntary' in relation to young women's risk-seeking behaviour. According to Lyng's (1990) definition, edgework involves the *active* pursuit of risky situations, rather than these situations being forced on the individual. As Miller (1991) acknowledges, women's ability to make choices is bounded by structural constraints and so it could be argued that they are not entirely free to engage in risk taking voluntarily. This means that 'We have to be very careful . . . about what we mean when we say risk so that we do not confound this concept a priori with simply being male' (Chan and Rigakos 2002: 750). Chan and Rigakos (2002) argue that women are required to engage in *instrumental* risk in the course of their daily activities, where they are exposed to risks such as harassment, intimidation and/or assault on a routine basis. Voluntary (i.e. non-instrumental) risks, Chan and Rigakos claim, are almost exclusively 'the purview of the privileged' (i.e. white middle-class males). That said, there was undoubtedly evidence of some young women pursuing especially risky situations, above and beyond the level necessitated by their social position: deliberately offending in front of security cameras, for example, or electing to engage in robbery as opposed to burglary. Young women like Zoë, Stephanie, Karen, Carol and Debbie clearly took pride in their ability to 'push the edge' and make it home unscathed, but they did so in ways that were stereotypically feminine – just as Lyng's skydivers behaved in ways that were stereotypically masculine.

In her influential work on aggression, Anne Campbell (1993) demonstrates that whereas for men aggression is often regarded as 'a means of exerting control over other people when they feel the need to reclaim power or self-esteem', women typically describe aggression as 'a temporary loss of control caused by overwhelming pressure and resulting in guilt' (Campbell 1993: viii). On the basis of these findings, Campbell claims that men's aggression is 'instrumental' and that women's is 'expressive', emerging as a release only after they can no longer control their pent-up frustration and anger. Not only does this construction – of the relationship between gender and aggression as a duality – reinforce a stereotypical conception of women's true nature as irrational, emotional, out of control and so on, it oversimplifies what is in fact a complex issue. Whilst my own data would seem to support Campbell's assertions about the sense of guilt and humiliation some women feel after perpetrating a violent act, the young women's remarks about the relationship between control and aggression were more contradictory. For example, 13 of the 21 young women said that feeling or doing something aggressive made them feel guilty, while 12 said that it made them feel better. Twelve reported feeling 'out of control', nine reported feeling 'in control', and seven said that feeling or doing something aggressive made them feel both 'in' and 'out of control', depending on the time frame. This last group of young women usually clarified their responses by explaining that they felt in control during the violent act, but out of control when they looked back at what they had done. Some of the young women were also able to distinguish between different forms of violence, i.e. violence that was controlled (usually pre-meditated, for example against someone perceived to be a deserving victim), and violence that was out of control (or committed 'in the heat of the moment'). Negative feelings (guilt, remorse etc.) were usually attributed to events in the latter category, because the young women felt that they had 'gone too far' and couldn't explain or sometimes even remember what had actually happened. Conversely, 'controlled' violence, which was generally violence that was regarded by the interviewees as justified, was more likely to be described as enjoyable.

The significance of 'retrospective interpretation' to the experience of

edgework is explored by Jennifer Lois (2003) in her work on search and rescue volunteers. Lois demonstrates that, while edgeworkers are often drawn to risk-seeking behaviour as a result of the adrenaline 'rush' or 'buzz' it affords, the prominent 'emotional culture' of edgework is emotional suppression, what Lois terms 'emotional cool':

> Edgework challenges individuals' ability to retain self-control by invoking intense, life threatening emotions that *must* be suppressed. Failing this, the consequences are dire. Thus, it appears that edgework is the ultimate test of emotional cool . . .
>
> (Lois 2003: 181, original emphasis)

Lois's analysis offers a four-stage model through which rescuers prepare for and experience their work. During preparations for and performance of their mission, volunteers share the belief that all emotions (but especially negative emotions) should be suppressed. Pent-up stress is released in the third stage by laughing, joking, drinking, or crying. On the one hand, rescuers feel energized, and this is generally associated with positive feelings of control and competence. On the other hand, they may experience negative emotions such as fear or alarm, or have to deal with emotionally disturbing memories of dead or maimed bodies. In order to safeguard their future edgework ability, these negative feelings have to be redefined, thus in the fourth and final stage of edgework, rescuers engage in what Hochschild (1983) calls 'deep acting', deliberately visualizing a substantial portion of reality in a different way.

One of Lois's key findings was that men and women interpreted and managed the emotions associated with edgework differently. For example, she found that while male rescuers thrived on the 'excitement' of missions, interpreting adrenaline rushes as urgency, female rescuers were more likely to express trepidation, interpreting heightened arousal as fear or anxiety (gender appropriate, but socially devalued emotions). Cultural norms in Western societies make strong distinctions between the ways in which men and women are permitted to express emotions. Masculinity norms dictate that men are 'emotionless' and may only display 'powerful' emotions such as anger, excitement or thrill – hence their proclivity for edgework, which allows them to act out their emotions in a socially acceptable context. Feminine gender norms, on the other hand, encourage women to be 'emotional' and to express such emotions as grief, anxiety or fear, but not anger or aggression. Women internalize these standards, which in turn impact upon their tastes for risk, likelihood of shame, level of self-control, and assessment of the costs and benefits associated with 'risking it'. As Lois's work demonstrates, although female rescuers *actually* perform edgework competently (i.e. they manage their anxiety in a relatively effective way during their missions), they still come to *believe* that they are 'emotional deviants', viewing their lack of confidence as problematic and declining tasks they think might overwhelm them.

Lois's work sheds light on the current findings in two important ways. Firstly, she shows that while edgeworkers initially seek situations of risk for a sense of danger and excitement, during the experience itself 'they narrow their focus so dramatically that they lose awareness of everything extraneous to the risk activity itself' (2001: 393). It is precisely this sense of dissociation that the young women in the current study come to learn as expressively useful. While their initial drug use is described as 'exciting' and 'fun', for example, the progression to more regular use is motivated by a desire to 'lose it' or 'to forget'. These young women do more than 'crowd the edge', they go over it – in much the same way as Katz's (1988) 'badass' loses control in order to take control. By deliberately pursuing a path of drug use, offending and/or self-harm, young women were able to master an internal sense of helplessness and anger. While their actions may ultimately be misguided, reinforcing alienation and exclusion, the young women took comfort from the fact that they were creating a situation of their own making. As Annie explained, 'It's like you cannae control what's happening around you, so you control what you dae to yoursel'. Hence risk seeking was not regarded as something that is imposed on the offender, but rather a lifestyle that has been *chosen*.

By showing that the emotional rewards of edgework only take place after the experience itself is actually over, Lois's work also demonstrates the way in which feelings are constructed according to gendered cultural norms. As young people, young women are controlled by a set of ideological forces that encourage them to 'live for today', 'let go', 'give in' and take risks, but as females a contrary force cautions them to avoid risk and exercise self-control. Where young women, looking back on their past behaviour, feel unable to explain their actions by recourse to (sub)cultural norms and values, 'scripts' regarding deserving victims for example or the need to stick up for friends, they are more likely to rely on discourses of normative femininity, which interpret their behaviour as pathological and/or irrational, and therefore feel guilty about what they have done. This perhaps explains why younger women (mainly those in the 'teenage fighter' category) were more likely to experience risk seeking as exciting, viewing violence in particular as an expression of control, while older offenders' accounts were more likely to characterized by ambivalence, shame and embarrassment. Risk seeking was very much considered 'a younger lassie's game', something that 'normal' women should 'grow out of'.

CONCLUSION

There is a paucity of literature exploring the risk-seeking behaviour of girls and young women. The current study suggests that young women can be involved in the same range of risky behaviours as young men, often for what seem like very similar reasons (i.e. fun, excitement, self-respect and status).

However, the young women in the current study were acting in a different social, familial and personal context than the male skydivers described by Lyng (1990), and families and peers appeared to have a greater impact on their pursuit of risky situations, in part reflecting the greater awareness women have about the importance of relationships compared with men. In line with research into the backgrounds and characteristics of young women convicted of violent offences in North America (e.g. Baskin and Sommers 1998; Miller 2001; Ryder 2003), the current study suggests a pattern of female risk seeking that begins with family problems and experiences of abuse. Hence, while young women are initially drawn to risk-seeking behaviour as a result of the shared adrenaline 'rush' or 'buzz' they experience, as their 'risk pathways' progress they increasingly come to rely on edgework as a means to *block out* powerful emotions. The data also show that, unlike men, who tend to retrospectively redefine their edgework experiences as an expression of exhilaration and omnipotence (Lyng 1990), young women are more likely to feel ambivalent, for example looking upon their behaviour as irrational and therefore feeling guilty about what they have done. However, this is not the same as saying that their behaviour is in actual fact 'a loss of control'. Quite the contrary: for many it can be the most integrative and self-preserving *choice*, albeit from a very limited field of options. Young women are perhaps more tightly regulated than any other social group. As young people, adults control nearly every aspect of their lives and they rarely, if ever, have the chance for 'genuinely free, creative, exciting, self-directed behaviour' (Miller 2005). As women, they are also subject to powerful disciplinary discourses of domesticity, sexuality and pathological 'otherness' (Carlen and Worrall 1987). In particular, they are acculturated from an early age not to express anger, to avoid risk and thereby to prevent their own violent victimization. By challenging dominant discourses of femininity, female risk seeking is thus an important source of 'gender trouble' (Butler 1990). For the young women in the current study, it was a vital survival strategy.

REFERENCES

Acoca, L. and Dedel, K. (1998) *No Place to Hide*, San Francisco: National Council on Crime and Delinquency.
Anderson, E. (1999) *Code of the Street: Decency, violence, and the moral life of the inner city*, New York: WW Norton and Company.
Baskin, D. and Sommers, I. (1998) *Casualties of Community Disorder: Women's careers in violent crime*, Oxford: Westview.
Batchelor, S. (2001) 'The myth of girl gangs' *Criminal Justice Matters* 43: 26–27 (Reprinted in Y. Jewkes and G. Letherby (eds) (2002) *Criminology: A reader*, London: Sage).
Batchelor, S. (2005) ' "Prove me the bam!" Victimisation and agency in the

lives of young women who commit violent offences' *Probation Journal* 52(4): 358–375.

Batchelor, S. and Burman, M. (2004) 'Working with girls and young women' in G. McIvor (ed.) *Research Highlights in Social Work: Women who offend*, London: Jessica Kingsley.

Batchelor, S., Burman, M. and Brown, J. (2001) 'Discussing Violence: Let's hear it for the Girls' *Probation Journal* 48(2): 125–134.

Beck, U. (1992) *Risk Society: Towards a new modernity*, London: Sage.

Beck, U. (1994) 'The reinvention of politics: towards a theory of reflexive modernization' in U. Beck, A. Giddens and S. Lash (eds) *Reflexive Modernization: Politics, tradition and aesthetics in the modern social order*, Cambridge: Polity Press.

Bourgois, P. (2002) *In Search of Respect*, 2nd edn, Cambridge: Cambridge University Press.

Butler, J. (1990) *Gender Trouble: Feminism and the subversion of identity*, London: Routledge.

Burman, M., Brown, J. and Batchelor, S. (2003) ' "Taking it to heart": Girls and the meanings of violence' in E. Stanko (ed.) *The Meanings of Violence*, London: Routledge.

Campbell, A. (1993) *Men, Women and Aggression*, New York: Basic Books.

Carlen, P. and Worrall, A. (eds) (1987) *Gender, crime and justice*, Milton Keynes: Open University Press.

Chan, W. and Rigakos, G. (2002) 'Risk, crime and gender' *British Journal of Criminology* 42: 743–761.

Chodorow, N. (1978) *The Reproduction of Mothering: Psychoanalysis and the sociology of gender*, Berkeley: University of California Press.

Connell, R. W. (1987) *Gender and Power: Society, the person and sexual politics*, Stanford, CA: Stanford University Press.

Daly, K. (1992) 'A women's pathway to felony court' *Review of Law and Women's Studies* 2: 11–52.

Ferrell, J. (1999) 'Cultural criminology' *Annual Review of Sociology* 25: 395–418.

Giddens, A. (1990) *The Consequences of Modernity*, Cambridge: Polity Press.

Giddens, A. (1991) *Modernity and Self-identity: Self and society in the late modern age*, Cambridge: Polity.

Gilligan, C. (1982) *In A Different Voice: Psychological theory and women's development*, Cambridge, MA: Harvard University Press.

Green, E., Mitchell, W. and Bunton, R. (2000) 'Contextualising risk and danger: An analysis of young people's perceptions of risk' *Journal of Youth Studies* 3(2): 109–126.

Griffiths, V. (1995) *Adolescent Girls and their Friends: A feminist ethnography*, Aldershot: Avebury.

Goode, E. (1990) 'Crime can be fun: The deviant experience' *Contemporary Sociology* 15: 5–12.

Hannah-Moffat, K. and Maurutto, P. (2001) *Youth Risk/Need Assessment: An Overview of the Issues and Practices*. Report submitted to the Department of Justice, Canada.

Hannah-Moffat, K. and Shaw, M. (2001) *Taking Risks: Incorporating gender and culture into classification and assessment of federally sentenced women*, Ottawa, Canada: Status of Women Canada.

Hayward, K. and Young, J. (2004) 'Cultural criminology: some notes on the script' *Theoretical Criminology* 8(3): 259–273.

Hey, V. (1997) *The Company She Keeps: An ethnography of girls' friendships*, Buckingham: Open University Press.

Hochschild, A. (1983) *The Managed Heart: Commercialization of human feeling*, Berkeley: University of California Press.

Howard League (1997) *Lost Inside*, London: Howard League.

Katz, J. (1988) *Seductions of Crime: Moral and sensual attractions in doing evil*, New York: Basic Books.

Kemshall, H. (2004) 'Risk, dangerousness and female offenders' in G. McIvor (ed.) *Research Highlights in Social Work: Women who offend*, London: Jessica Kingsley.

Joe, K. and Chesney-Lind, M. (1995) ' "Just every mother's angel": An analysis of gender and ethnic variations in youth gang membership' *Gender and Society* 9(4): 408–430.

Lash, S. (1994) 'Reflexivity and its doubles: Structure, aesthetics, community' in U. Beck, A. Giddens and S. Lash, *Reflexive Modernization: Politics, tradition and aesthetics in the modern social order*, Cambridge: Polity.

Lois, J. (2001) 'Peaks and valleys: The gendered emotional culture of edgework' *Gender and Society* 15(3): 381–406.

Lois, J. (2003) *Heroic Efforts: The emotional culture of search and rescue volunteers*, New York: New York University Press.

Lupton, D. (1999). *Risk*, London: Routledge.

Lyng, S. (1990) 'Edgework: A social psychological analysis of voluntary risk-taking' *American Journal of Sociology* 95(4): 876–921.

Lyng, S. (2005) 'Sociology at the edge: Social theory and voluntary risk-taking' in S. Lyng (ed.) *Edgework: The sociology of risk-taking*, London: Routledge.

Lyng, S. and Snow, D. (1986) 'Vocabularies of motive and high-risk behavior: The case of skydiving' *Advances in Group Process* 3: 157–179.

Maher, L. (1997) *Sexed Work*, Oxford: Oxford University Press.

Matza, D. and Sykes, G. (1961) 'Juvenile delinquency and subterranean values' *American Sociological Review* 26(5): 712–719.

Miller, E. M. (1991) 'Assessing the inattention to class race/ethnicity and gender: Comment on Lyng' *American Journal of Sociology* 96: 1530–4.

Miller, J. (2001) *One of the Guys*, New York: Oxford University Press.

Miller, J. B. (1976) *Toward a New Psychology of Women*, Boston: Beacon Press.

Miller, W. J. (2005) 'Adolescents on the edge: The sensual side of delinquency' in S. Lyng (ed.) *Edgework: The Sociology of Risk-taking*, London: Routledge.

Mitchell, W., Crawshaw, P., Bunton, R. and Green, E. (2001) 'Situating young people's experiences of risk and identity' *Health, Risk and Society* 3(2): 217–233.

Muncie, J. (2004) *Youth and Crime*, 2nd edn, London: Sage.

O'Malley, P. and Mugford, S. (1994) 'Crime, excitement and modernity' in G. Barak (ed.) *Varieties of Criminology*, Westport: Praeger.

Quicker, J. C. (1983) *Homegirls: Characterizing Chicana Gangs*, San Pedro: International Universities Press.

Reynold, E. and Barter, S. (2003) ' "Hi, I'm Ramon and I run this place": Challenging the normalisation of peer violence in children's homes' in E. Stanko (ed.) *The Meanings of Violence*, London: Routledge.

Ryder, J. (2003) 'Antecedents of Violent Behaviour' Unpublished doctoral thesis, City University of New York.

Seaman, P., Turner, K., Hill, M., Stafford, A. and Walker, M. (2006) *Parenting and Children's Resilience in Disadvantaged Communities*, London: National Children's Bureau.

Triseliotis, J., Borland, M., Hill, M. and Lambert, L. (1995) *Teenagers and the Social Work Services*, London: HMSO.

Wade, J. and Biehal, N. with Clayden, J. and Stein, M. (1998) *Going Missing: Young people absent from care*, Wiley: Chichester.

Worrall, A. (2001) 'Girls at risk?' *Probation Journal* 48(2): 86–92.

Chapter 11

Gendering dynamic risk

Assessing and managing the maternal identities of women prisoners

Kelly Hannah-Moffat

Risk/need principles are internationally accepted as central to the classification and treatment of offenders, and the increasing emphasis on risk/need/responsivity (RNR) over the past 15 years has reshaped dominant strategies of offender management. In fact, risk/need assessment is considered by many to be 'the spinal column of the correctional system' (Williamson 2000: 2) and 'the cornerstone of good correctional/forensic practice. It is the engine of case planning, decision-making and rehabilitative measurement' (Simourd 2002: 351). Practically, risk assessments are used to determine levels of custody, recidivism, risk of suicide or escape, and to classify prisoners for case management and treatment purposes.

Empirical research supporting these principles is almost exclusively based on white male correctional populations, and yet these empirical findings are routinely used to assess women and non-white populations and to legitimate correctional programmes without recognition of the fact that strategies of risk management differently impact gendered, stratified and racialized groups. Moreover, in the field of punishment, risk theorizations have largely missed the specific gendered and racialized character of risk governance and how institutional understandings of risk and their effects influence more global theorizations of risk. As this chapter will show, there is a need to recognize the situated nature of risk and its interpretations. Without such critical consideration, a disjuncture between theory and how risk is practised in local institutional contexts seems inevitable.

At the root of the problem is that few analyses of punishment and/or risk consider the co-existence and interrelatedness of governing ideologies that act to alter the practice of punishment and/or risk and their accompanying discourses. As David Garland's (1990) analysis of modern punishment astutely observes, penal governance is a rich and flexible tradition that has always contained within itself a number of competing themes and elements, principles and counter principles. Because these themes play a critical role in establishing and legitimating technical apparatuses designed to punish and control 'deviants,' while simultaneously furthering the social engineering of a 'good' society, Garland (1990: 6) suggests that:

[a]dministrators and employees of a penal system understand and justify their actions within the established ideological framework – a working ideology. This official ideology is a set of categories, signs and symbols through which punishment represents itself to others. Usually this ideology provides a highly developed rhetoric which can be used to give names, justifications, and a measure of coherence to a vast jumble of things that are done in the name of penal policy.

The current chapter analyses how two such ideologies – dynamic risk and gender responsivity[1] – are often combined to justify interventions that gender female criminals vis-à-vis their maternal relations. While the centrality of motherhood to the lives of incarcerated women is often cited in aggregate descriptive data,[2] my concern here is not with the adequacy or inadequacy of institutional provisions for incarcerated mothers in terms of visitation, contact and reunification with their children. Rather, my focus is on how maternal relations are constituted as risky and how maternal relations are mobilized by correctional organizations to govern risk and enable a gendered governance of risk through women's relationships.

Rather than simply examining how risk technologies are currently being applied to previously gendered subjects (cf. Smart 1998), I expand the critical focus to illustrate how institutional risk practices actively produce gendered penal subjects. I argue that institutional risk practices operate as gendering strategies that produce gendered subjectivities that, in turn, make women responsible for their children's future risk of criminalization.

I show how normative understandings of motherhood, implicit in which is the notion that good mothers are expected to control and discipline their children and be self-disciplined, are (re)produced in risk assessment and used to govern risk.[3] In so doing, I focus on the risk assessment practices used in

---

1 The term gender responsive refers to 'progressive' penal strategies that try to create 'an environment . . . that reflects an understanding of the realities of women's lives and addresses the issues of the women' (Bloom, Owen and Covington 2003: v). Advocates of this model maintain that '[a]s the criminal justice system becomes more responsive to the issues of managing women offenders, it will become more effective in targeting the pathways to offending that both propel women into the criminal justice system and return them to it' (Bloom *et al* 2003: v). While many feminist scholars and advocates support this model, few have assessed the representations of gender that sustain this model and its related penal policies.

2 Most studies indicate that 80 per cent of incarcerated women have children and that most are single mothers and the primary caregivers of their children before and after their incarceration. An equal number of women have histories of violent victimization and trauma.

3 Admittedly, an emphasis on the family and women's maternal responsibilities is not new within the field of punishment: this theme has a long tradition in social and penal programming (Hannah-Moffat 2001) and law (Zedner 1991; Carlen 2002; Smart 1998; Fineman and Karpin 1995). Numerous historical accounts of the governance of criminalized women document how, in their roles as mothers, criminal women have been seen as perpetuating corruption and 'identified as biological sources of crime and degradation' (Worrall 1990;

prison classification and treatment. This type of risk assessment stresses *dynamic risk factors* (also known as criminogenic need factors), which are a subset of offender 'needs' that are statistically co-related with recidivism *and* amenable to intervention. Risk/need assessments that include evaluations of women's parental capacities enable moral evaluations of women as 'bad or neglectful' mothers and loosely link these moral determinations to risk/need areas requiring intervention with parenting programmes used as regulatory tools through which maternal and feminine ideals are promoted.

I show how discipline and responsibility are fostered on two levels. First, women prisoners are expected to adhere to the middle-class, white normative ideals of motherhood by properly training and regulating their children to ensure they are nurtured and 'behave' appropriately. Second, by teaching women how to govern their children, parenting programmes govern the women themselves. Women are expected to take responsibility for putting things right in the future.

DYNAMIC RISK/CRIMINOGENIC NEED

In 1994, the Correctional Service of Canada (CSC) formalized the use of structured risk/needs assessment with the introduction of the Offender Intake Assessment (OIA). The OIA was adopted to provide a standardized, efficient and comprehensive method of evaluating all newly admitted federal prisoners. The OIA has two central components: criminal risk assessment and needs (dynamic risk) identification (Case Needs Identification and Analysis). Criminal risk assessment refers to a series of static factors, including previous youth/adult charges, sex offending history, sentence types, number and severity of convictions, victim characteristics, detention criteria, and the Statistical Inventory on Recidivism (SIR scale).[4] The analysis of needs entails a detailed evaluation of the offender's background, personal characteristics, interpersonal relationships, situational determinants, and environmental conditions. Typically, the needs assessment targets seven 'domain' areas:

1   marital and family;
2   employment;
3   associates and social interaction;
4   substance abuse;
5   community functioning;

Zedner 1991: 308; Hannah-Moffat 2001). Where the current analysis breaks new ground is in its connection of women's moral, domestic and maternal responsibility to risk, and in its addition of a newly configured 'feminist' emphasis on relationships.

4   This tool is not valid or used for women and aboriginal offenders.

6 attitude; and
7 personal and emotional concerns.

Since the concept of dynamic risk constitutes a set of offender needs as risks that are amenable to intervention, by default, this logic categorizes some needs as illegitimate targets or 'lacking in criminogenic potential'. Thus, within this assessment, a clear distinction is made between criminogenic and non-criminogenic need. Non-criminogenic needs are dynamic and change-able variables that are significant, but not necessarily related to recidivism (i.e., poverty, health) and are thus considered a low priority in terms of inter-vention, except for 'humane' consideration. Criminogenic needs, however, are the dynamic attributes of an offender that, when changed, are associated with shifts in the probability of recidivism.

Needs are constructed within narrowly defined parameters and are not necessarily linked to a prisoner's perception of what he or she requires, but are thought of in terms of risk reduction and 'intervenability'. As Hannah-Moffat (2004a) notes, an intervenable need is not an individual's self-perceived need, but a characteristic someone shares with a population that is statistically correlated with recidivism. An intervenable need, then, is defined not only through the availability of resources and structural arrangements that allow for intervention and possible amelioration, but also through stat-istical knowledge of it as a variable that is predictive of an undesirable and preventable outcome: recidivism. It is this narrow understanding of risk/need that is applied to the assessment of marital/family relations in institutional risk assessment practices. Importantly, the focus on needs is about reducing further crime or incidence of disruptive behaviours in prisons, *not necessarily* a general enhancement of a prisoner's well-being.

Assembling criminogenic relationships: assessing the marital/family domain

The identification of marital/family relationships as criminogenic and thus risky is contingent upon practitioners' reconstruction and interpretation of offenders' relationships. Operational manuals for risk tools outline a series of normative questions designed to determine if the risk/need area of marital/family is a problem (i.e., criminogenic). The specific nature and type of ques-tions varies across tools; however, thematically, the questions are designed to gather information about relevant relationships for practitioners to assess risk of recidivism and treatment needs. The questions contained in the 'marital/family' domain structure interpretations of these relationships. For women in particular, an emphasis is placed on parenting. The OIA questions the nature and type of parental responsibilities, asking whether the offender:

1   can handle the parental responsibilities;

2   controls the child's behaviour appropriately;
3   supervises the child properly;
4   participates in programmes/activities with the children;
5   understands child development;
6   has been arrested for child abuse/incest; and
7   perceives self as able to control the child's behaviour.

The supplementary intake assessment guidelines for women instruct assessors to 'record any problem related to the offender's children'.

For women prisoners, issues concerning their families and relationships are captured in other dynamic risk domains as well. For example, supplementary gender responsive assessment scripts used in some jurisdictions for the domain 'community functioning' ask the following about parenting capacity and maternal fitness:

1   How did she learn to be a mother?
2   What would her family and friends say about her as a mother?
3   What would her children say about her as a mother? and
4   Who is caring for the children?

Answers to such questions establish if the dynamic risk categories 'marital/ family' or associates are problematic and rank these risk factors along with other identified factors to produce a risk score. A range of similar marital/ family relationship questions are included in commonly used risk instruments such as the Level of Service Inventory (LSI). Practitioners use this informa- tion and their individualized gendered knowledge of dynamic risk to deter- mine if this area requires intervention. Practitioners' interpretations of dynamic risk also intentionally consider available knowledge about differ- ences in men's and women's criminality and life circumstances (Hannah- Moffat 2004b, 2006). Collectively, this evidence is used to produce categorical understandings of relationships as 'negative' or 'dysfunctional' versus 'pro- social', and to designate the type and amount of intervention needed to 'teach' women how to develop positive, respectful, supportive relationships that do not repeat their own histories of loss, neglect, disconnection and violence. 'Recovery' and learning about 'healthy relationships' thus becomes an important part of the risk management process.

Case managers interpreting the data generated from the risk/need assess- ment develop a correctional plan that recommends an offender take pro- grammes designed to target need areas. Not surprisingly, a large number of women are identified as having high risk/need levels in the marital/family domain.

Feminist and mainstream correctional research on the relevance of complex marital/family relationships is restricted by this narrow statistical interpreta- tion of criminogenic need (dynamic risk). For instance, parental capacities are speciously linked to recidivism as a consequence of being constituted as a criminogenic need. Increasingly, the evaluation of parenting is equated with risk management and normative assessments of parental capacities are being included in a range of risk assessment instruments. Intimate and familial relationships are constituted as criminogenic through gendered risk principles and are positioned as relevant to the governance of women who are increasingly characterized as 'relational'. The emphasis on marital and family relationships and the alignment of dynamic risk with certain relationships defines these intimate areas as sites of intervention and targets of correction. In this context, the statistical relevance of dynamic risk factors is overlooked in favour of a moral intuitive understanding of the connection between the family and risk. To stratify penal interventions and label particular offenders as 'risky' or not, these interpretive risk practices make use of a range of different femininities and masculinities to constitute the ideal of responsible parenting and stable motherhood. Normative gender ideals inform and structure risk practices. The gendered emphasis on maternal identity and responsibility reinforces a normative femininity and idealized motherhood that is inconsistent with the lived experiences of criminalized women, yet used to identify and govern women's risk.

Relationships are intuitively important to the assessment and treatment of criminal women. To garner such acceptance as 'criminogenic/dynamic risk areas', marital/family factors should, by definition, be statistically co-related to recidivism and thus legitimate intervention targets. Interestingly, the correctional literature has not clearly established this link. Within the correctional and academic literature, there continues to be a debate about the importance of various marital/family factors to offender treatment, reintegration and recidivism (Blanchette 2000; Blanchette and Brown 2006). Correctional researchers note that 'various family factors (e.g. family psychopathy, quality of parent-child relationships, experiences of childhood victimization, marital status and the quality of the relationship) have been implicated as *potential predictors* of criminal recidivism among adults . . . [but] much remains to be learned about whether family life can alter a delinquent career and can buffer against criminogenic influences in adulthood' (Oddone-Paolucci, Violato and Schofield 2000: 33). Others claim family ties are documented 'stability factors' that are purported to have a positive impact on offender reintegration and desistance (Maruna and Immarigeon 2004; Farrington 2003; Oddone-Paolucci, Violato and Schofield 1998). Some US scholars[5] suggest parenting

---

5 Using data from the *Adult Adolescent Parenting Inventory* (Bavolek and Keene 1999) and interviews with women, Green *et al* (2005: 145) claim that two-thirds of women prisoners scored in the 'impaired range' on a measure of parenting capabilities and that their scores were particularly low in terms of the expectations of obedience and submission. Further, it is suggested that women have 'quite unrealistic views about what are reasonable expectations for children and what it means to be a parent' (Green *et al* 2005: 147).

roles can be actively mobilized to reduce recidivism and transmit pro-social attitudes to a future generation. While these relationships are obviously important, the empirical evidence of their significance is ambiguous.[6]

The rise of risk-based penality, which espouses the criminogenic significance of needs as they manifest in particular relationships, occurs in tandem with gender responsive penality, and consequently elevates the status of relationships. Advocates of gender responsive penality begin from the premise that women are relational. They argue that relationships are essential to women's lives and 'when the concept of relationship is incorporated into policies, practices and programs the effectiveness of the system or agency is enhanced' (Bloom *et al* 2003: 53). Relational theory focuses on the psychological development of women and suggests women 'develop a sense of self and self worth when their actions arise out of and lead back into, connections with others' (ibid: 53). Relational theorists argue that 'such connections are so crucial that many of the psychological problems of women can be traced back to disconnections or violations with in relationships, whether in families, with personal acquaintances, or in a society at large' (ibid: 55). This logic is extended to claim that criminalized women, who have experienced considerable marginalization, disconnection and violation in their primary and social relationships, are more likely than men to be motivated by relational concerns and situational pressures, such as the threatened loss of valued relationships (ibid: 55; Covington and Surrey 1997; Steffensmeier and Allan 1998; Coll and Duff 1995). Consequently, it is argued that 'effective' gender responsive correctional interventions must acknowledge and focus on women's relationships and that 'a relational context is critical to successfully address the reasons why women commit crime, the motivations behind their behaviours, how they can change their behaviour, and their integration into the community' (Bloom *et al* 2003: 5).

In an effort to be more gender responsive, Canadian penal policy narratives such as CSC's 2004 *Program Strategy for Women Offenders* – as well as training materials and publications for the (American) National Institute for Corrections (Bloom *et al* 2003) – underscore the feminist literature on relational theory. Women's relationships are elevated in gender responsive risk/need discourses. For example, the new 2004 *Program Strategy* states:

> Gender-specific programming must reflect an understanding of the psychological development of women. Current thinking in this area suggests that women place great value in the development and maintenance of relationships. Consequently, 'situational pressures such as the loss of valued relationships play a greater role in female offending' . . . [S]ome

---

6 It is instructive to note that the data collected for risk assessment is as much about research as it is 'diagnosis'.

academics believe that relational theory is an approach that adds effectiveness to programming for women. Relational theory focuses on building and maintaining positive connections and relationships. The main goal is to increase women's capacity to engage in mutually empathic and mutually empowering relationships. To enable change, women need to develop relationships that are not reflective of previous loss or abuse.

(Fortin 2004: 5)

References to the significance of women's relationships are evident throughout this document, underscoring the belief that understanding the role of relationships is fundamental to managing the female offender.

The emphasis on relationships reproduces normative gender scripts. While it is obviously important to recognize the significance of maternal and intimate relationships, on a practical level it is also important to think about how an emphasis on such relationships is conflated with broader concerns about risk, need and interventions. Canada's revised 2004 programme strategy for federally sentenced women places equivalent emphasis on the correctional trinity: risk, need and responsivity. It is not surprising given the primary role these principles play in correctional assessment and programming. The 2004 programme strategy makes a strong link between the importance of relationships and intervention. It clearly frames parenting programmes as a 'social' rather than 'correctional' or 'mental health' programme. As a social programme, 'parenting skills' is supposed to 'help offenders to identify pro-social lifestyles, [and] to choose activities that will integrate them as productive members of society and law-abiding citizens' (Fortin 2004: 17). Federal correctional agencies are required to offer programmes 'that are deemed essential to CSC's efforts to safely and successfully reintegrate offenders' (Fortin 2004: 17). Parenting programmes[7] are so designated.

This trend toward governing women through their maternal and intimate relationships occurs in many international social, welfare and penal settings. For instance, of comparable interest are recent statements by the US National Institute of Corrections, such as:

There is significant evidence that the mother-child relationship may hold significant potential for community reintegration. Incarcerated women tend to experience a sense of isolation and abandonment while in prison because of their inability to keep their families together. . . . *Recognizing the centrality of women's roles as mothers* provides an opportunity for

---

7 According to Fortin (2004: 17), 'Parenting Skills Programs are designed based on the 1995 Guidelines for Parenting Skills Programs for Federally Sentenced Women. The Guidelines were designed to help CSC plan, develop, implement, and evaluate parenting skills programming for women. The Guidelines were also meant to help program developers design and deliver material that would best match the needs of this specific population'.

the criminal justice, medical, mental health, legal and social service agencies to develop this role as an integral part of the program and treatment interventions for the female offender population.

(Bloom *et al* 2003:57; emphasis added)

Increasingly, parental status is used to regulate women and to promote prosocial values. For example, the NIC report notes, '. . . because most female offenders are mothers, visits with children can motivate them to change their behaviour' (Bloom *et al* 2003: 29). This quote illustrates how children are centrally positioned in the regulation of women.

MENDING FAMILIES AND RESPONSIBILIZING MOTHERS

The actual provision of parenting programmes is gendered vis-à-vis difference (from men) and through the use of normative understandings of white middle-class femininity, behaviours and roles in the family. Fatherhood is rarely examined in studies of criminalized men. Male institutions rarely offer parenting programmes and when they do the parental roles and responsibilities are differentially constructed. If parenting is problematized for men, typically it is in the context of sexual or physical violence. The male offender is not primarily positioned as a mentor, provider or caregiver; rather, he is seen as a predator in cases of incest or intimate partner violence. Programmes may teach men coping strategies to help them deal with the loss of family relationships and with family reunification in the event that it occurs. Some initiatives[8] are underway to help men in prisons become more involved and supportive, responsible fathers;[9] however, they are not as widely accepted as those in women's prisons. The sparse material that is available on fatherhood

---

8 See, for instance, Waldman and Hercik (2002). This report claims the promotion of 'responsible fatherhood has become a top priority for States. All fifty States have responsible fatherhood programs and many States are designing programs to enhance the parenting skills of incarcerated parents. . . . States can use [government Temporary Assistance for Needy Families (TANF)] funds for programs that assist incarcerated parents as long as the services provided meet the purposes of TANF. Two of these purposes include: ending the dependence on government benefits by promoting job preparation, work, and marriage; and encouraging the formation and maintenance of two-parent families'. The emphasis on parenting in the US is in many instances linked to the re-emergence of multifaith-based programmes that promote personal responsibility, family responsibility and employability.

9 Information about the Long-Distance Dads (LDD) Program at the State Correctional Institution in Albion, Pa. can be found at: http://www.outreach.psu.edu/news/magazine/Vol_4.2/prison.html, and parenting programmes (including those for fathers) offered by the Texas Department of Criminal Justice. For a discussion of two parenting programmes for men, Family Man and Fathers Inside, see: Halsey, Ashworth and Harland (2002).

programmes emphasizes the impact of men's incarceration on the family unit, not his parental responsibilities. Men are not positioned as equal partners in parenting. Such an emphasis on parental responsibilities draws on romanticized forms of nurturing masculinity not typically associated with male prisoners. The limited characterizations of fatherhood in risk-based penal policy evoke dichotomous constructions of masculinity: the predator versus nurturer and deadbeat father versus provider. For men, the ability to return to a family is seen as a stability factor that functions to reduce potential recidivism by discouraging risk taking and fostering normative intimate and provider roles that encourage sobriety, heterosexual relationships, employment stability and social integration.

Whilst increasing in importance, fatherhood does not play the same disciplinary role as motherhood plays in penality. Few institutions have parenting programmes that target men's familial role and parental responsibilities. Programmes that exist are often sponsored by religious organizations. This gap is partly due to the gendered belief that men and women 'do time' differently and have different bonds with their families. Consistent with stereotypical masculinities and femininities, it is argued that 'men concentrate on 'doing their own time', relying on feelings of inner strength and their ability to withstand outside pressures to get themselves through their time in prison. Women, on the other hand, remain interwoven in the lives of significant others, primarily their children and their own mothers, who usually take on care of the children (Bloom *et al* 2005: 57). These gender differences legitimate different types of intervention.

Parenting programmes have multiple functions. Most basically they are meant to teach women 'how to parent', but they are also designed to target risk. Parenting programmes place women's primary relationships under a microscope and compare them to normative feminine ideals of motherhood, domesticity and intimacy. These ideals are the vehicles through which women's criminality and risk are interpreted. Programmes that target relationships and parenting skills, as well as those designed to address past abuse and trauma, seek to normalize women and teach them how to relate better and to identify and avoid 'negative' relationships with men.

On the surface, parenting programmes are appealing in that they claim to accommodate women prisoners' self-reported need for recognition of their maternal identities, of victimization in their formative relationships, and of women's desire to provide for their children. The emphasis on family reunification as a correctional goal and parenting in particular clearly recognizes this gendered pain of imprisonment. However, it is also a gendered strategy of risk governance wherein domesticity and motherhood are centrally positioned in the detection, prevention and management of risk. Embedded in narratives and assessment of parenting is a complex network of meanings and behaviours used to constitute proper mothering.

Cycles of poverty, violence, substance abuse and criminalization frame the histories of imprisoned women (Comack 2006) and their relationships. The reality of many incarcerated women's lives significantly departs from normative scripts of domesticity and 'civility', and the matrix of behaviours deemed to constitute good mothering. The ideal mother is 'always available to her children, she spends time with them, guides, supports, encourages and corrects as well as loving and caring for them physically' (Smart 1992: 38, in Kline 1995: 119). Many criminalized women have worked in the sex trade and developed additions to drugs and/or alcohol. Addicted mothers are culturally denounced, criminalized and ostracized. They are characterized as irresponsible, hedonistic and selfish – the antithesis of dominate cultural images of the 'good' working mother or the stay-at-home mother.

Pregnant addicts are particularly vulnerable and often demonized for exposing the children to the horrors of addiction and risk of physical and/or mental disabilities. Narratives of maternal addiction are also deeply racialized. Recently, correctional research has emphasized the important role of addictions and more specifically the prevalence of Foetal Alcohol Spectrum Disorder (FASD) and associated risks (Bell *et al* 2004). Women with children who have FASD are seen as requiring specialized instruction and support to parent their children. Having FASD children is often characterized as an 'aboriginal problem'. As mothers, all criminalized women are expected to provide for their children, and in doing so, there are normative expectations of prudence and self-sacrifice. Maternal ideals position hedonistic pleasure as secondary to children's health and happiness. Criminalized women who spend scarce resources on drugs, alcohol and partying, and engage in multiple, casual sexual relationships, do not fit hetero-normative tropes of middle-class motherhood, domesticity or decency. Criminalized women are characterized as 'unfit'; consequently, when they 'have and raise children, it is difficult, if not impossible for them to meet [the] societal image of the good mother' (Kline 1995: 120).

Motherhood is tacitly accepted as the natural desired and eventual ambition of all *normal* women. The desire to improve and be a good mother is naturalized and normative. The pressure to resume mothering, and the expectation that this role will result in compliance, conformity and risk reduction, fails to acknowledge the less than ideal circumstances in which many of these women are compelled to parent. As Gieger and Fischer's study (2003: 511) shows, motherhood does not insulate women from criminal opportunities, as evidenced by their own mothers. Many incarcerated women had abusive formative relationships and mothers who sent them into prostitution or were involved in crime and drugs. This study's observations of imprisoned mothers and identity also suggests that 'female offender's attachment and commitment to the cardinal value of motherhood led to self-condemnation . . . for failing to fulfill the "sacred duties" of motherhood. They had neglected their children. They had failed to keep their promises to their children and to be there when their children needed them. They had numerous times disappointed and betrayed their children' (Gieger and Fischer 2003: 511). Instead of accommodating and legitimating these experiences, it is expected that imprisoned women feel regret and loss with respect to their children. In policy narratives, women are typically characterized as experiencing grief and guilt about the separation from their children while imprisoned. Their desire to be mothers and resume the role of mothering is naturalized in most penal policy. A woman's desire to sever her maternal bonds is often misread as escalating risk.

Women's feelings or the context of maternal relationships with children are rarely explored. Often, the offender's life in drugs, crime and prostitution and resultant convictions lead to women's separation from children and their loss of custody. On some occasions, women *actively choose* to sever relationships with their children. The narratives of some imprisoned women reveal that 'after years of drug abuse, incarceration, and separation from their children, female offenders end up feeling nothing for the very children who would have given meaning to their existence' (Geiger and Fischer 2003: 511). This 'reality' is typically silenced and often pathologized through an essentialized femininity. Motherhood is idealized and embraced. Women who distance themselves from their children are seen as 'bad or neglectful mothers'. They are 'risky' women who resist particular normative femininities. Their resistance and gender deviance is not easily accommodated in penal logics that emphasize positive stable relationships. Nevertheless, women (mothers) are expected to learn how to conform to these normative scripts of essentialized femininity and to assume naturalized maternal identities. As feminist scholarship has repeatedly shown, although domesticity is central to 'keeping women in their place', the family is often not a place of safety or stability for women.

An objective of relational-based programming is to teach women how to overcome their relationship failings through the creation of stable, secure family structures and positive mutually reinforcing relationships. The norm for many incarcerated women is that of dysfunctional and abusive families of origin, and many failed intimate relationships characterize their lives. Middle-class nuclear families are not the norm, but rather are the standard with which women are compared and disciplined. Implicitly, 'stable families' include both mothers and fathers, but ideal families are not single parent families. The norm for many incarcerated women prior to conviction and upon release is unsupported single parenting.[10] Safe and healthy families are economically independent. Mothers are expected to create conditions of safety and to provide for basic necessities. The ability to do so reflects back onto perceptions of risk. If a woman is seen as unstable, immature or deficient in the skills needed for economic self-sufficiency, she remains a risk to herself,

10 See Comack (2006) for a statistical breakdown of single parenting, the feminization of poverty and the socio-economic context of aboriginal families.

her family and her community. Even more troubling is that risk practices typically characterize these problems as evidence of individual failings.

In sum, dominant penal ideologies link maternal capacity to rehabilitative success which is then equated with risk minimization. Female offenders are socialized to the norms and roles ascribed to mothers, but they are often not afforded the opportunity to fulfil the obligations attached to these roles. For many criminalized women, the ability to function as an emotional centre for their children, achieve economic independence, and live drug free in stable relationships are unrealistic expectations, given the feminization of poverty, the absence of safe, affordable housing, childcare and employment. Admittedly, many advocates of gender responsive approaches recognize these barriers. For example, as Bloom *et al* (2005: 57) note, 'without attention to the capacity of women to improve themselves responsible connections between mothers and their children can not be maintained'. To reconcile this concern most gender responsive initiatives are holistic. By definition, holistic approaches address the whole woman within the social context of her life, her relationships, the systems she encounters, and the society in which she lives. This 'holistic' attentiveness to women's capacities for improvement often amount to increased surveillance and layers of extra-legal regulation by medical, mental health, welfare and social services, as evidenced by the emphasis on aboriginal families.

Risk and aboriginal mothers

The emphasis on aboriginality and culturally sensitive programming suggests that the mobilization of motherhood is racialized (Kline 1995; Roberts 1995; Monture-Angus 1999). Hegemonic ideologies of motherhood, womanhood and family operate to impose dominant white, Western cultural values on aboriginal (Kline 1995) and non-white women. Aboriginal men and women are over-represented in Canadian prisons. Alongside efforts to gender women's penality, steps are being taken to ensure punishment is culturally sensitive. CSC policy narratives on families include a separate definition of the 'family' for aboriginals. Correctional narratives routinely document the generational impact of colonization, drug and alcohol abuse, foster care and residential schools on aboriginal communities. In terms of parenting, this history contributes to the view that aboriginal women typically come from 'dysfunctional families' and thus have more acute parenting skill deficits (Bell *et al* 2004: 23–24, 40). Socio-cultural histories, while tacitly acknowledged, rarely translate into correctional programming which by design blame and accentuate women's deficiencies. More often than not, aboriginal women are 'characterised as beset by a chaotic lifestyle resulting from an abusive relationship and alcoholism' (Kline 1995: 125).

Risk assessments draw on white ideologies of family and motherhood and, as expected, confirm that aboriginal women have a high degree of need in the marital/family domain. Perhaps more interesting than these predictable results is how risk is framed with in this domain. In addition to examining the 'needs' (dynamic risk) of individual aboriginal women, correctional research advocates an attentiveness to the *needs of the family*. The aboriginal family is targeted because it represents a major source of support and linkage to the community and because these families are typically portrayed in correctional narratives as inherently dysfunctional. Aboriginal families are differentiated from the families of non-aboriginal prisoners and seen as requiring family counselling, financial support, assistance with childcare and help maintaining contact with incarcerated family members (Bell *et al* 2005: 40; Dowden and Serin 2000). The governance of risk in this context is holistic and racialized. While many 'white' families have similar needs they are not similarly positioned as requiring such intervention.

Gender is a form of inequality that intersects with other forms of social inequality: namely, race, ethnicity, class and sexuality. The complex, intersectional nature of these inequalities is crucial to our understanding of how risk contributes to the production of *a range* of gendered risk knowledge. Criminalized men and women are not unitary subjects (Hannah-Moffat 2001). Their subjectivities are fractured; they occupy a range of gendered subject positions that are not fixed by biological, psychological or social determinants. In addition to overlooking the importance of gender, risk theory has comparably ignored the racialized aspects of risk governance. As several scholars of race have noted, the fractured nature of female subjectivity necessitates that we examine not only gender, but also the importance of other forms inequality (Razack 1998; Daly and Maher 1998; Monture-Angus 1999; Bosworth 2004; Sudbury 2005). Unfortunately, I only scratch the surface of what ought to be a multifaceted debate about the racialization of risk.

RISK AND THE NEXT GENERATION

History offers ample evidence of how the iconic status of motherhood and womanhood has been used to regulate women, men and families. Gendered understandings of penality clearly show how 'historically, women have been expected to subject themselves, first and perennially to the family – in obedience to the rhetoric that *good mothers make good families make good societies*' (Carlen 1995: 216, emphasis original). At the same time, women are reciprocally regulated by domesticity and families. In risk-informed gender responsive regimes, women's maternal status and idealized families are also used and reinforced in a wide range of interventions designed to broadly target others' risk of recidivism.[11] For example, CSC offers a Family Literacy Program that

---

11 Also see Plummer (2003)

explicitly links literacy to parenting with goal of 'encouraging positive familial attitudes and behaviour' (Fortin 2004: 17). The 'healthy family' includes an ideal mother who reads to her child and fosters in that child, through example, a love of learning and a desire for education. The importance of families to recidivism is stated in Canadian correctional narratives on programming. CSC has a series of legislative and policy commitments related to families.[12]

The risk of the offender's child becoming involved in crime is also of concern. 'Children of women offenders are characterised as vulnerable and as being at greater risk of problems (e.g., out-of-home placements, arrests, or reliance on public assistance) than children of male inmates' (Hardyman and Van Voorhis 2004: xiii). More straightforwardly, Green *et al* (2005: 147) claim that:

> The combination of children's exposures and the parenting deficits they experience put them at extremely high risk for continuing the violence cycle and becoming wards of the state themselves . . . *targeting parenting among women prisoners thus appears critical for reducing the risk to their offspring* thereby also saving considerable resources in the future.
>
> (emphasis added)

Following a similar logic, CSC's 2004 programme strategy states that 'by encouraging women to establish positive attachments to their children, parenting programmes produce considerable benefits: more stable mothers, who after resolving their conflict with the criminal justice system, can then model pro-social values for their children' (Fortin 2004: 10). The emphasis on parents' responsibilities for modelling pro-social attitudes and crime prevention extends a woman's responsibilities as a risk manager beyond herself to her children and her family, and in the case of an aboriginal woman to her community. She unconditionally assumes responsibility for a host of structural impediments to crime-free life, social and economic marginalization and criminalization. She is expected to ward off the influences of 'negative peers', to overcome her vulnerability to dysfunctional relationships and to 'break the cycle of crime'.

---

12 CSC clearly states that it has an obligation to families as part of the overall mandate of assisting the rehabilitation of offenders and their reintegration into the community, and that they have specific obligations, which accompany the management of aboriginal offenders and women offenders (CSC 2006). For detailed elaboration on these commitments see: http://www.csc-scc.gc.ca/text/portals/families/legislation_e.shtml.

CONCLUSION

Punishment is situated within a broader field of gendered social relations. Yet, few scholars sufficiently articulate the gendered nature of punishment (Britton 2005), and still fewer are attentive to how local practices 'gender risk'. There is, in my view, a need to think a lot more about the institutionalization and gendering of dynamic risk, its meaning and the interpretive processes that enable new forms of penal governing.

From this analysis we can see how risk knowledge is gendered. We can see how gendered and racialized critiques of risk are being addressed through the integration of gendered interpretations of 'risk/need' into broader risk-based approaches to offender management. Feminist critiques of gender neutrality have produced new processes for understanding risk.

This type of analysis offers a method for understanding how seemingly progressive penal practices can be theorized differently according to the institutional conditions in which they are realized (cf. Carlen 1995). Institutional risk practices actively produce gendered penal subjects and operate as gendering strategies that create gendered subjectivities (cf. Smart 1998 on law) that guide the responsibilization of criminalized women. In this case, the combined emphasis on gender responsivity and risk-based offender management enables new (and problematic) ways of thinking about women's relationships, agency, dependency, and responsibility. Gendered interpretations of risk and penal programmes are a mechanism for promoting responsible connections between mothers and their children. The category motherhood, while fluid and able to take on many meanings in the broader culture, is defined in penality according to an established web of meanings. The affirmation and solidification of the maternal bond is implicitly linked to the reduction of risk in women and in future generations.

REFERENCES

Bavolek, S. J. and Keene, R. G. (1999) *Adult-Adolescent Parenting Inventory, AAPI–2: Administration and development handbook*, Park City, UT: Family Development Resources.

Bell, A., S. Trevethan and Allegri, N. (2004) *A needs assessment of federal Aboriginal women offenders*, Ottawa: Correctional Service of Canada.

Blanchette, K. (2000) 'Effective Correctional Practice with Women Offenders', in L. Motiuk and R. Serin (eds) *Compendium 2000 on Effective Correctional Programming*, pp. 160–73.

Blanchette, K. and Brown, S. (2006) *The Assessment and Treatment of Women Offenders: An Integrative Perspective*, West Sussex, England: J. Wiley & Sons.

Bloom, B., Owen, B. and Covington, S. (2003) *Gender responsive strategies for female offenders: A summary of research, practice, and guiding principles for women offenders*, Washington: National Institute of Corrections.

Bloom, B., Owen, B. and Covington, S. (2005) 'Gender Responsive strategies: A summary of research, practice and guiding principles for women' Washington DC: US Department of Justice – National Institute for Corrections.

Bosworth, M. (2004) 'Theorizing race and imprisonment towards a new penality' *Critical Criminology* 12: 221–242.

Britton, D. (2005) *Gender and Prison* The International Library of Criminology, Criminal Justice and Penology, UK: Ashgate Publishing Ltd.

Carlen, P. (1995) 'Virginia, Criminology and the anti social control of Women', in T. Blomberg and S. Cohen (eds) *Punishment and Social Control*, New York: Aldine De Gruyter.

Carlen, P. (2002) *Women and Punishment: The Struggle for Justice*, UK: Willan.

Coll, C. and Duff, K. (1995) 'Reframing the Needs of Women in Prison: A relational and Diversity Perspective' Final repost, women in prison Pilot Project, Wellesley: MA: Stone Centre.

Comack, E. (2006) 'The feminist engagement with Criminology' in G. Balfour and E. Comack (eds) *Criminalizing women,* Halifax: Fernwood.

Correctional Service of Canada (1994) *Offender Intake Assessment Manual*, Ottawa: Correctional Service of Canada.

Correctional Service of Canada (2006) 'CSC legislative and policy obligations related to families and visiting' Ottawa: Correctional Service of Canada. Available from: http://www.csc-scc.gc.ca/text/portals/families/legislation_e.shtml.

Covington, S. and Surrey J. (1997) 'The Relational Model of Women's Psychological Development: Implications for Substance Abuse' in S. Wilsnack and R. Wilsnaclk (eds) *Gender and Alcohol: Individual and Social Perspectives*, NJ: Rutgers University Press pp 335–351.

Daly, K. and Maher, L. (1998) *Criminology at the Crossroads: Feminist Readings in Crime and Justice*, Oxford: Oxford University Press.

Dowden, C. and Serin, R. (2000) 'Assessing the Needs of Aboriginal Women Offenders on Conditional Release', *Forum on Corrections Research*, 12(1): 57–60.

Farrington, D. (2003) 'Developmental criminology and risk focused prevention', in M. Maguire, R. Maguire and R. Reiner (eds) *Oxford Handbook of Criminology*, Oxford: Oxford University Press.

Fineman, M. and Karpin, I. (1995) *Mothers in law: Feminist theory and the legal regulation of motherhood*, New York: Columbia University Press.

Fortin, D. (2004) 'A correctional programming strategy for women', *Forum on Corrections Research* 16(1): 38–39. Available from: http://www.csc-scc.gc.ca/text/pblct/forum/Vol16No1/v16n1index_e.shtml.

Garland, D. (1990) *Punishment and Modern Society*, Chicago: University of Chicago Press.

Geiger, B. and Fischer, M. (2003) 'Repeat female offenders negotiating identity' *International Journal of Offender Therapy and Comparative Criminology* 47(5): 490–515.

Green, B., Miranda, J., Daroowalla, A. and Siddique, J. (2005) 'Trauma Exposure, Mental Health Functioning, and Program Needs of Women in Jail', *Crime and Delinquency* 51(1): 133–151.

Halsey, K., Ashworth, M. and Harland, J. (2002) *Made for Prisoners by prisoners: a summary of NFER'S evaluation of the Safe Ground family relationships and parenting programme*, UK: National Foundation For Educational Research.

Hannah-Moffat, K. and Shaw, M. (2001) *Taking Risks: Gender, Diversity, Classification and Assessment in Federal Women's Prisons*, Ottawa: Status of Women Canada.

Hannah-Moffat, K. (2001) *Punishment in Disguise: Penal Governance and Federal Imprisonment of Women in Canada*, Toronto: University Of Toronto Press.

Hannah-Moffat, K. (2004a) 'Criminogenic Need and the Transformative Risk Subject: Hybridizations of Risk/Need in Penality' *Punishment and Society* 7(1): 29–51.

Hannah-Moffat, K. (2004b) 'Losing Ground: Gender, Responsibility and Parole Risk' *Social Politics*, Special issue on gender, welfare and punishment vol. 11(3): 363–385.

Hannah-Moffat, K. (2006) 'Pandora's box: Risk/need and gender-responsive corrections' *Criminology and Public Policy* 5(1):1301–11.

Hardyman, P. and Van Voorhis, P. (2004) *Developing gender specific classification systems for women*, Washington: National Institute of corrections, NIC accession Number 018931.

Kline, M. (1995) 'Complicating the Ideology of Motherhood: Child Welfare Law and First Nation Women', in M. Fineman and I. Karpin (eds) *Mothers in law: feminist theory and the legal regulation of motherhood*, New York: Columbia University Press, pp 118–141.

Maruna, S. and Immarigeon R. (2004) *After Crime and Punishment: Pathways to Offender Reintegration*, UK: Willan.

Monture-Angus, P. (1999) 'Woman and Risk: Aboriginal Woman Colonialism and Correctional Practice' *Canadian Women's Studies* 19(1).

Oddone-Paolucci, E., Violato, C., Schofield, M. A. (2000) *A Review of the Marital Family Variable as they Relate to Adult Criminal Recidivism*, Ottawa: Correctional Service Of Canada (R–92, 2000).

Oddone-Paolucci, E., Violato, E. C. and Schofield, M. (1998) 'Case need domain: Marital and family', *Forum on Corrections Research* 10(3) at http://www.csc-scc.gc.ca/text/pblct/forum/e103/e103ind_e.shtml.

Plummer, C. (2003) 'Maximizing opportunities for mothers to succeed (MOMS) 2002 annual report, Almeda County, CA: Almeda County Sheriff's Office.

Razack, S. (1998) *Looking White People in the Eye*, Toronto: University of Toronto Press.

Roberts, D. (1995) 'Racism and patriarchy in the meaning of motherhood', in M. Fineman and I. Karpin (eds) *Mothers in law: feminist theory and the legal regulation of motherhood*, New York: Columbia University Press, pp. 205–223.

Simourd L. (2002) 'Risk assessment in contemporary corrections' *Criminal Justice and Behaviour* 29(4): 351–354.

Smart, C. (1992) 'Woman of Legal Discourse' *Social and legal studies* 1(1): 29–44.

Smart, C. (1998) *Law, Crime and Sexuality: Essays in Feminism*, California: Sage.

Steffensmeier, D. and Allen, E. (1998) 'The nature of female offending: Patterns and Explanation' in R. T. Zaplin (ed.) *Female Offenders: Critical Perspectives*, MD: Aspen, pp. 5–29.

Sudbury, J. (ed.) (2005) *Global lockdown: Race, gender, and the prison-industrial complex*, New York, NY: Routledge.

Waldman, N. and Hercik, J.M. (2002) 'Uniting Incarcerated Parents and Their Families' Report for Welfare Peer Technical Assistance Network, Office of Family

Assistance, Department of Health and Human Service http://fatherhood.hhs.gov/incarcerated-parents02.htm#10.

Williamson, A. (2000) *Risk Needs Assessment Project*, Ottawa: Department of Justice Canada – Unpublished Paper.

Worrall, A. (1990) *Offending Women*, NY: Routledge.

Zedner, L. (1991) *Women, Crime and Custody in Victorian England*, Oxford: Oxford University Press.

Index

Please note that references to Notes will have the letter 'n' following the page number

institution: impulse distinguished 88
International AIDS Conference,
Vancouver (1996) 106n
investment options, employer selection
152–3

Jefferson, T 136, 169
Joint Forum of Financial Market
Regulators (Canada) 150n, 151;
Guidelines for Capital Accumulation
Plans promulgated by 146n, 149

Kaplan, A N 154, 159n, 160–1
Katz, Jack 24, 83, 86, 219–20, 223
Kaufert, Patricia 58n
Kavanagh, A M 65
Kerry, John 92n

Langer, Ellen 89
Lash, Scott 76–7, 80, 81, 90, 91
LDD (Long-Distance Dads) Program
237n
Lemke, T 46–7
Level of Service Inventory (LSI) 233
Liebling, A 137–8, 139
Lindee, S 43–4
Linneman, T 4
Lippman, Abby 32, 48
Local Government Act 1988 (UK) 99n
'logic of flows' 80
Lois, Jennifer 21–2, 222–3
Long-Distance Dads (LDD) Program
237n
LSI (Level of Service Inventory) 233
Lupton, Deborah 10, 12, 22
Lyng, Stephen: on criminal victimisation
171; on edgework 6, 23, 75–97, 205,
207, 220; on male skydivers 206, 224
Lyons, Tara 3, 183–203

magnetic resonance imaging (MRI) 38
Mansergh, G 119
marginal masculinity 93
marital/family domain, assessment 232–7
Marx, Karl 14
masculinity: and barebacking 101;
constructing 86–9; and crime 85; 'crisis
of masculinity' thesis 134; definitions
85; edgework model, and
universalizing male experience 82–4;
and femininity 83; gender projects and
social configuration of 84–6;

hegemonic 90, 91, 92, 102, 171–2, 174;
late modernity, social configuration in
90–4; making of, and edgework 86–94;
male activities 83; marginal 93; risky
masculinities, and criminal justice
127–44; social configuration of 90–4;
see also risky masculinities
'masculinity turn', in criminology 130
maternity passport 60n, 63
Matthews, Rick 23, 75–97
Matza, D 213
Maxfield, M 173
Mead, G H 81–2
medical profession: on homosexual
practices 103; see also doctor-
attributed risks, pathogenic effects;
doctors
Mendel, Gregor 62, 66
mental health problems, ethnographic
analysis 131
Messerschmidt, James 86, 89
Miller, Eleanor 82–3, 220
miscarriage, risk of 55, 63
Mitchell, O S 157, 158
'mode of subjectivation' 36n
modernity, late: and agency 91; social
configuration of masculinity in 90–4
modernity process, and risk society
theory 80
Moore, Dawn 3, 183–203, 187
morality: normative 100
motherhood 230, 239–41; aboriginal
mothers 8, 241–2
MRI (magnetic resonance imaging) 38
Mubarek, Zahid 140
Mugford, S 207
Mullins, C 85
mutations, genetic 31–2

Naffine, Nagaire 185
National Institute of Corrections (US)
236–7
needle exchanges 100
needs: criminogenic and
non-criminogenic 2–3n, 232; defined 2;
women's 2–3
neo-liberalism 77, 120, 121
next generation, and risk 242–3
non-directiveness principle 67
non-linear reflexivity 80, 91, 94
normative morality: and ethics 100
North America: AIDS epidemic in 102

suicide and self-harm: in prisons 129,
137, 139, 140, 219
Sutton, R 175
Sydney Morning Herald 122
Sykes, G 213
syringe exchanges 100

TANF (Temporary Assistance for Needy
Families) 237n
Taylor, I 169
TDTC (Toronto DTC) 189, 200
teenage fighter, and risk pathways 209
Temporary Assistance for Needy
Families (TANF) 237n
Tomso, Gregory 115, 116n, 120
transvestite groups 83
Tulloch, J 12
Turner, Ralph 88

uncertainty techniques 9–10
unemployment patterns: and risky
masculinities 134
United Kingdom: breast cancer
screening 40–1; British Crime Survey
data 173; Criminal Justice Act 1991
129n; imprisonment statistics 127, 129;
Local Government Act 1988 99n;
probation service, North West
England 127
United States: DC plans 160; Helms
Amendment 99n; and HIV
transmission 100, 122n; impoverished
males, underclass of 134; National
Institute of Corrections 236–7
unprotected sex 101, 111; intent to
engage in 114–21; *see also* barebacking
Utkus, S P 157, 158

Valverde, Mariana 19
VDTC (Vancouver DTC) 189, 196, 200
violence: adolescents 86; among
criminals 85; controlled 221;
excitement of 214, 219; women,
towards 170, 185–6
voluntary risk taking 77, 205; as

edgework 78–82; feelings and
emotions 79; *see also* edgework;
risk-taking behaviour

Waldby, Catherine 4
Waldman, N 237n
Walklate, S 2, 6, 24, 165–81, 167, 168,
170, 175
Warr, M 20
Weber, Max 81
Weir, Lorna 10, 14, 15–16, 59n
women 241–2; breast cancer risk *see*
breast cancer risk, and genetic testing;
in childbirth 87; delinquents, female
86; experiential knowledge of 33;
female identity 88, 209–10, 215;
genetic counselling, predominance in
55n, 61; 'good woman', and Drug
Treatment Courts 198, 199; labour of,
enlisting in 'genetic risk' knowledge
production 38–41; motherhood *see*
motherhood; needs 2–3; as passive
recipients of genetic information, seen
as 33; stereotypes 185; *see also* female
prisoners, identities; femininity;
feminism; young women, risk seeking
by
Wootton, B 178

Yao, R 159
young women, risk seeking by 205–27;
adrenaline rush 206, 213–15, 224;
drug use 209, 210, 223; illusion of
control 220–3; managing feelings
216–18, 218–20; men distinguished
206, 215; 'pathways through violence'
research 207–8; and peer group
influence 209–13; respect of others
215–16; risk pathways 208–20, 224;
sexual abuse 216, 218; sociology
of risk seeking 206–7; *see also*
feminism

*Zen and the Art of Motorcycle
Maintenance* (Pirsig) 176–7

CPSIA information can be obtained at www.ICGtesting.com
Printed in the USA
270436BV00002B/7/P